THE CATS OF SHAMBALA

Tippi Hedren

THE CATS OF

CENTURY PUBLISHING LONDON

SHAMBALA

Tippi Hedren

with Theodore Taylor
Photographs by Bill Dow

Copyright © 1985 by Tippi Hedren and Theodore Taylor

First published in Great Britain 1986 by
Century Hutchinson Ltd
Brookmount House, 62–65 Chandos Place, London WC2N 4NW

Century Hutchinson Group (Australia) Pty Ltd
16–22 Church Street, Hawthorn, Melbourne, Victoria 3122

Century Hutchinson Group (NZ) Ltd
PO Box 40–086, 32–34 View Road, Glenfield, Auckland 10

Century Hutchinson Group (SA) Pty Ltd
PO Box 337, Bergvlei 2012, South Africa

Set in Palatino

Printed and bound in Great Britain by
R. J. Acford Ltd, Chichester, Sussex

ISBN 0 7126 10812

*To my mother and father,
Dorothea and Bernard Hedren,
who always supported me in
my every endeavor*

Contents

PHOTO SECTION FOLLOWS PAGE 64.

Preface

Lions often roar at dawn here in quiet, remote Soledad Canyon, and since some of them are less than ten feet away from my bed, I wake up every morning to the sound of their deep-bellied choruses, ten or twenty big cats rumbling in sequence, some overlapping, bellowing to each other as faint traces of pink begin to color the desert sky. Sometimes the unison roaring is so loud that the house walls seem to quiver and floors vibrate as the decibels mount, until that final strange bark to say that the conversation is over.

Day has begun on the shady, sandy ground I call Shambala, Sanskrit for a "meeting place of peace and harmony for all beings, animal and human." Tucked into the Santa Clarita Valley only forty miles north of Los Angeles, with the Angeles Forest and the gentle San Gabriel Range nearby, Shambala spreads along the narrow Santa Clara River bottom for about a quarter mile and resembles parts of the African riverine woodland, though the trees are mainly tall cottonwoods instead of the savanna's thorny types and acacias. But the big brown rock outcroppings here and there do resemble the kopjes of the Serengeti and Manyara. In fact, the permanent "African" sets of *Daktari*, a TV series of the distant past, were located only a few miles away.

My small two-bedroom home is perched on the riverbank. Surrounded on three sides by wild-animal residences, its exterior walls anchor several of the compounds. Lions and tigers often sleep with their backs comfortably against my kitchen or living-room or bedroom walls. I can hear them thumping or padding around out there at night. And as the early morning progresses, sun penetrating down into the cool ravine, I can step out on the patio and look across the shallow stream, through the trees, to see four or five lions sleeping peacefully on the roof of an old red open-air bus that would be perfectly at home on any dusty country road in Kenya. In another direction I might see six or seven more of the big cats doing what they all do best—slumbering in the shade against the high perimeter fence.

It all seems so peaceful now. But among the animals on top of the bus is the lioness who once took my head into her jaws. There, too, is Billy, a lion who will let no other human or animal approach me. Here lived Singh Singh, a seven-hundred-pound Siberian tiger

A morning walk with eighteen-month-old Nathaniel outside my home in Shambala

Ladies on the bus

Penny Bishonden

and the most frightening big cat I've ever known. One awful night the gentle, meandering Santa Clara River turned into a raging torrent that did its best to destroy buildings, cats and humans alike. And then fire swept down the low, chapparal-covered mountains, sending the animals into panic. Yet for every moment of stark terror at Shambala, there have been hours, days and months of pleasure and wonderment.

Though its original purpose was to serve as a vast and authentic set for a motion picture, produced by my former husband, Noel Marshall, and me, Shambala is now a rather unique private preserve for the semiretired four-footed "actors" who starred in that film. Almost a hundred of them while away mostly tranquil days in the luxurious manner of former Preakness winners. It is also my home, a long way from the small town in Minnesota where I grew up, a world apart from the film studios of Hollywood where I pursued my career as an actress.

How did I come to a place like this? Where did it all begin?

Shambala
Acton, California

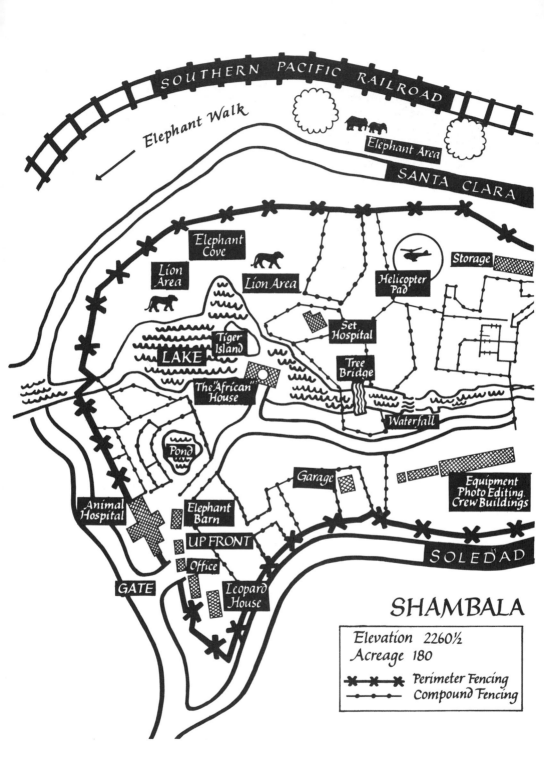

SOUTHERN PACIFIC RAILROAD

Elephant Walk

Elephant Area

SANTA CLARA

Elephant Cove

Lion Area

Lion Area

Helicopter Pad

Storage

Set Hospital

Tiger Island

LAKE

Tree Bridge

The "African" House

Waterfall

Pond

Garage

Equipment Photo Editing Crew Buildings

Animal Hospital

Elephant Barn

UP FRONT

SOLEDAD

Office

GATE

Leopard House

SHAMBALA

Elevation 2260½
Acreage 180

✕—✕—✕ Perimeter Fencing
•—•—• Compound Fencing

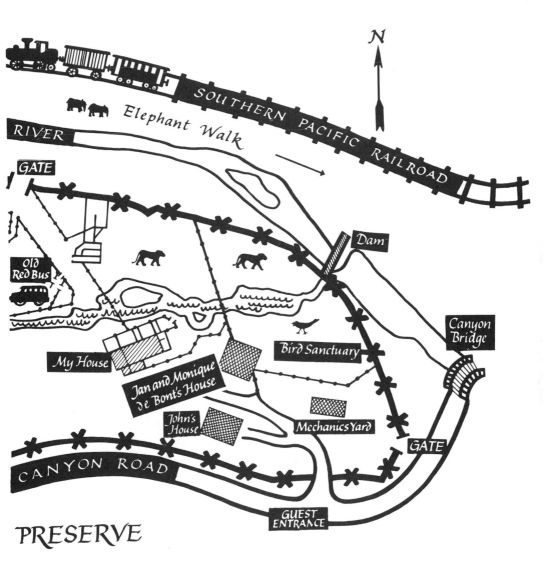

Shambala Preserve, Acton, California

—1—

BEITSBRIDGE

Matter-of-factly, the assistant director, a lean tanned young Afrikander with a stained bandana on his head, said, "Everyone please stand. The lion is coming through!" Startled, I quickly got up from my canvas chair, almost knocking over the umbrella that was shading me from the fierce African sun.

The year was 1969, the place Zimbabwe, and it was as if the Queen of England herself, instead of Ozzie Bristow and his golden-coated companion, were moving across the veldt toward us, thirty-odd perspiring movie-makers in the usual clutter of cameras, lights, reflectors and sound booms.

Named Dandylion, he was a magnificent animal with an amber, deep-brown full mane framing his bewhiskered face. Master of all he surveyed, the huge head held high. Bona-fide royalty, I recall, and everyone on that set of *Satan's Harvest*, a rather forgettable film in which I starred, willingly stood up, including my husband, Noel, who probably felt a bit foolish. But I didn't feel foolish at all. On the contrary, I was overwhelmed.

There is a tribal saying in East Africa that when the lion roars he is shouting, *"N'chi ya nani? Yangu! Yangu! YANGU!* Whose land is this? This land is my land. Mine! Mine! MINE!"

Dandylion

As this furry monarch passed close to a camera, a big paw reached out playfully to tap the cinematographer's ankle. For this friendly gesture Dandylion received a chuck under the chin, and he proceeded on across the set, retaining majesty with every fluid, measured step, paying scant attention to his human audience.

I couldn't believe what I was seeing. Nothing restrained that lion. No chain. No rope. He was free to run in any direction. I asked one of the film crew, "Isn't this dangerous?"

"Not so long as Ozzie is around," he replied.

We were filming near a grove of baobab trees on the South African border, and Bristow, Dandylion's tall, soft-spoken Rhodesian trainer, later explained why everyone was asked to stand: "It's best for humans to always be above the height of the lion." Below it, you present a tempting target for play which sometimes includes impromptu wrestling in the dust, lion most likely on top. The sly paw around the ankle was a very common greeting from a friendly lion or tiger, I soon discovered. I also learned that if the animal is moving fast enough, you can be unceremoniously dumped.

"What happens if he charges me?" I asked, knowing Dandylion would be working in the film for several weeks.

Ozzie laughed. "Well, don't run or he might tackle you. He weighs more'n forty stone."

That would be more than five hundred pounds.

Until that day at Beitsbridge, near Messina, I had never been closer to a lion than circus seats, a zoo cage or across a moat. Like most people I was awed and fascinated by them—and also deathly afraid of them. During my childhood in Minnesota, and my teens in California, there had always been a dog or a kitten around, and I'd ridden horses, both for fun and in film work, so I was an animal person. But it seemed to me that these huge beasts, with gaping mouths, fangs larger than my thumb, and killer reputations, belonged safely behind steel bars or in game preserves. That opinion was soon to change. *To a degree.*

In myth, legend and reality, the king of beasts is usually pictured as a beautiful but brutal scavenger. "The lion's den" and "being thrown to the lions" have long been everyday expressions, and there

George Montgomery

With Karma, on the set of *Satan's Harvest*

17

are deep-seated psychological big-cat "blocks" within most people. All for the good! I think those reservations will remain until the last *Felis leo* is exterminated by one means or another. But nudging my own block was the feeling that there was much to discover about the big cats.

I knew that circus lions had entertainment routines forced upon them and were taught to do things that weren't natural, such as jumping through fiery hoops. I had watched the big cats snarl, pawing air, while the trainer did his whip-and-macho thing, sticking out his chest, posturing. And I had come away with the idea that the cats were magnificent but usually vicious and the trainer was always brave, if perhaps stupid, especially when he put his head between jaws.

Now, with Ozzie and Dandylion, I was seeing a vastly different relationship between man and beast.

Later that day Ozzie brought in Karma, eighteen months old, about two hundred pounds, a lion that thought it was still a cub. Full of high spirits and energy, Karma loved to play, his antics reminding me of the silliness of a pup I once owned. Dandylion and Karma were not the horrific creatures of fiction, man-eaters, or the snarling cats on circus stools waiting to slaughter us all if they got free of the chutes.

The next week Ozzie injured his back, and the doctor ordered him to rest for a few days. I was standing nearby when he returned to the compound where the cats were kept. Entranced, I watched as Dandylion and Karma began jumping into the air excitedly when they spotted him. They called to him in a happy "aa-oow, aa-oow" sound, literally dancing in excitement as he went in to embrace them. Standing on back paws, they returned the embrace, almost smothering him, making affectionate sounds. I could hardly believe that they were capable of love and true friendship.

Yet even in a love relationship they could sometimes be unpredictable, Ozzie admitted, possible explosions always lurking up in the big skulls. "Under certain circumstances, Dandylion could easily kill me tomorrow and never show guilt," Ozzie said. "He loves me, but he could also kill me. He might even wonder why I wasn't coming back to see him the next day."

While they are usually predictable, Ozzie told me, the psyche of the big cat is different from all other animals'. Basic instincts can overpower long training and conditioning at any given time. Instant, deadly action, sustained for only a few minutes, can be triggered by

Noel with cheetah in Zimbabwe

any number of things—something as simple as possessiveness over a pile of leaves. But then the animal may revert back to being a nice, gentle cat, as if not a drop of blood had been shed.

"Dogs often show guilt," Ozzie told me. "Big cats never." They maim without remorse or conscience.

Then I met Ozzie's five cheetahs, animals with personalities totally different from lions'. So lithe, so quick, so beautiful, they were no less friendly. When they purred, their sleek throats vibrated visibly. Of all felines, only cheetahs, lynx, cougars and domestic cats can purr, Ozzie explained. Each species has a bony structure called the hyoid, located at the base of the tongue, making possible that unique sound on either exhalation or inhalation. In addition to being capable of deep, unbroken purring, the cheetah can also chirp like a bird.

"Do watch them for karate chops, though," Ozzie advised.

—2—

GORONGOSA

On most films, members of the cast have occasional days off while the director concentrates on other matters. Noel and I took advantage of my off days to travel to game preserves, the usual tourist occupation in East Africa, and one day we found ourselves in Gorongosa, just below the storied Zambesi River in Mozambique, inland from Biera. Noel had been my agent when we married five years previously. Now he was packaging film projects. It was our first trip to Africa, and we didn't want to miss a thing.

Gorongosa is Mozambique's largest preserve, with an estimated population of 4,000 elephants and 2,500 lions, along with thousands of other exotic creatures. Noel and I rented a car and followed one of the open-air tour buses through the park, finally drawing up in front of an abandoned flat-roof Portuguese-style house. Eavesdropping, we heard the bus guide say that the largest pride of lions in all Africa lived in the old house, a game warden's residence until it was flooded out. Lions were all over the place. Some were on the roof, gazing down at us; others were deep asleep in window frames. Two more were seated on a dilapidated porch swing. One big and comical lion was plunked down in a broken rocking chair. He needed only a plantation hat and a long cigar to be lord of the manor. Altogether there were thirty male and female lions and their cubs in that bizarre family scene.

The guide's lecture was more or less like the recorded ones I've heard in zoos and wild-animal parks all over the world: "Cats have been around for forty million years, and the big cats of today are descendants of the saber-tooth smilodon. . . . Lions are the only family-oriented big cats. . . . Pride members hunt together, eat together, sleep together. . . . Pride members display open affection, more so than in the human family, often rubbing cheeks and making loving noises. . . ."

Unable to take our eyes off that house and all those lions, I'm not sure how much Noel and I heard of the native guide's lecture. Finally we turned away. And as we were climbing back into the car Noel said, "You know, we ought to make a picture about this."

Movie people are always making idle, inane statements like that. But not one in a thousand "ought-to-be-made" pictures is ever produced. What's more, animal films have always been difficult; the late Walt Disney was supposedly the only producer who had the skill, patience and money to pull them off. Some of his documentaries—*The Living Desert*, *The Vanishing Prairie* and *The African Lion*—are classics, but humans, aside from cameramen and editors, weren't involved. There was no interaction between animal and man. Some of the Disney films with interacting humans and dogs, mules, apes or whatever are considerably less than classics.

The first film I made, playing a spoiled San Francisco heiress, was *The Birds*, directed by Alfred Hitchcock, and it left a lasting impression. Gulls, ravens and sparrows inherit the world in that picture, turning savagely on mankind in repayment for years of indifference and cruelty. Seventeen live pecking gulls and ravens were tied to me in an attic scene, and afterward I went to bed for four days, on doctor's orders, there to fight off nightmares filled with flapping wings and bloody beaks. So I well knew, firsthand, about nonhuman actors and actresses. I hardly took Noel's remark seriously, although I did think that working with live lions might be preferable to live ravens.

Noel's first and only experience with wild animals had been as a young man working at the St. Louis Zoo during summer vacations. As far as I knew, he had never paid any particular attention to animals, wild or otherwise. He was solely a businessman. Hollywood was his jungle. Producers and studio heads were his prey.

I was an actress, and if you talk about a story or film idea with an actor or an actress, it is automatically assumed there'll be a nicely tailored part for the always searching performer. Starring part, of course. And it is very true that films have occasionally originated from such flimsy beginnings as a tour in a game preserve. But did I really want to star in a film about a house occupied by thirty lions? What would the film be *about*? And how in the world would we make it?

Easy. Lions become actors and actresses. They act and react. They just do what comes naturally. They roar. They fight. They scare hell out of you. They are also loving and gentle. All the way back to Zimbabwe, Noel and I talked excitedly about the idea. A chance encounter, an impromptu remark, had taken root in our imaginations.

Ozzie Bristow laughed loud and long over an iceless gin and tonic when we told him the bones of the idea. "One lion, yes. Thirty, no."

Ozzie told me that the reason professional trainers usually "double," with wigs and correct costumes, for film actors and actresses who are required to work with wild animals is not only to safeguard the cast. They are there to "handle" the animals so that the scene can be made. Even tame, gentle animals require professional handling for the same reason.

Noel and I realized, of course, that we were ridiculously ill-equipped to "handle" even one lion, much less thirty. And wild-animal handling aside, we really knew very little about producing a film, no matter what the subject. I had concentrated on learning how to act in the half-dozen films I'd made, and Noel's experience as a television director didn't exactly qualify him as a feature-film director. But we brushed those practical considerations aside as if they didn't matter at all. That was unlike me, the real me. It was very much like Noel.

Born in New Ulm, Minnesota, because the nearby town of Lafayette, population two hundred, in which my parents lived, didn't have a hospital, I was a very shy and sheltered little girl. My Swedish father, a country-store owner, and my German-Norwegian mother were always loving but rather strict, and I have memories of hiding behind my mother's skirts, afraid to be introduced to anyone. At seven, eight and nine, my life was reading, listening to music, ice-skating and the Lutheran church. Not much there to prepare me to enter a lion's cage. My older sister, Patty, was far braver and more adventuresome than I would ever be.

Then one day, when I was about ten, I seemed to overcome my abiding fright, of almost everything, while walking up a hill, coming home from school. I had the terrible habit of biting my fingernails, and I said to myself, "I'm not going to do that anymore." And I didn't. I'm not sure how I suddenly understood that self-discipline could conquer all my fears, but I do know that it happened on that hill.

Three years later, when I was a freshman at West High School in Minneapolis, a department store sponsored a teenage fashion show and I was chosen to be a model, one of those chance occurrences that sometimes chart a life course. Soon I was modeling regularly as well as selling teenage clothing on Saturdays. The money, always in short supply in our house, was needed.

My father's health was never good and Minnesota winters were taking a toll, so the family moved to California, where I continued modeling, mostly photos for slick magazines. I did appear, briefly, in one film, *Petty Girl*, starring Joan Caulfield, and received a screen credit as "Miss Icebox." But I didn't aspire to be an actress. My mind was on New York and the fashion whirl. I saved enough money for one-way fare, and after sitting up for three days on the train I arrived in Manhattan on a Friday morning, checked into the Barbizon, the famous residence hotel for women only at Lexington and Sixty-third, and slept all weekend.

Monday morning, with a stack of photos under my arm, I kept an appointment at the Eileen Ford Agency, and Eileen sent me out on a job that afternoon. By week's end, I had made an unbelievable $350. No one told me I was too short—at five feet four—to be a model. It was the beginning of a ten-year career. Soon after, in 1951, while doing a walk-on part in a TV show, I met actor Peter Griffith. We fell in love and married. Daughter Melanie arrived six years later and I don't think I was ever happier than during her babyhood. But Peter and I realized we were heading in different directions. We divorced, and Melanie and I returned to Los Angeles.

Television had swooped up a number of models for commercials. One of twelve commercials that I made during the early 1950s was for Pet Milk's Sego diet drink. One morning, after it appeared on NBC's *Today* show, I received a rather mysterious call from an executive at Universal Pictures, who told me "a producer" had seen the Sego commercial. "Are you that girl?" he asked. If so, would I please come to the studio?

For several days there was a cat-and-mouse game while I went

With Alfred Hitchcock, during filming of *The Birds*

to higher and higher echelons, until finally Herman Citron at MCA, the talent agency, said, "Alfred Hitchcock wants to sign you to a personal contract and if you'll agree to these terms we'll go over and meet him."

I didn't know whether to jump up and down or cry. These small, or large, miracles always seemed to happen to me. My modeling career was waning. Money was running low. I had a four-year-old daughter to support. Now, Alfred Hitchcock! I took one quick look at the terms and agreed.

Not too long before that startling day, I had met Noel Marshall. At the time he was one of the few "commercial" agents in Hollywood, someone dealing in talent specifically for TV commercials. A dynamic, impulsive, sleepless, flamboyant, charming man, he attracted me with his strength and directness, and the million crazy things he'd think of. The oldest of twelve children, he had grown up on the tough South Side of Chicago and had begun in the entertainment field as a page at NBC's flagship station. Before he left Chicago he had directed everything from segments of *Kukla, Fran and Ollie,* the children's show, to coverage of a national political convention. Yet he couldn't find a job in Hollywood TV, and he went to work for Hughes Aircraft, then Sears, before setting up his commercial agency. Noel became my sounding board during the often troublesome Hitchcock days, someone I could always talk to. I needed that.

Hitchcock never intimidated me. Rather, he manipulated me. Sometimes he was brutal. Going into a scene, he might say something absolutely vulgar, totally obscene, to get an underlying current of anger or frustration. It always worked. But during the filming of *The Birds* I enjoyed the times with him when he was charming and kind and witty. He was a master film-maker, of course, a genius. But there were other times when he was so brutal that I'd say to myself, "Do I have to lose everything I stand for to be your friend?"

Noel and I were married after *Marnie,* my second Hitchcock film, was completed, and Noel gave his agency to his ex-wife in the settlement and turned to construction, in which he had no prior experience. Yet he took it on with a mental shrug, as if changing train tracks. I've always thought that he should have been a designer. Long before this, he had designed and then hand-built a car that resembled the later Corvette.

Noel's impulsiveness continually amazed me. One Sunday afternoon, we were trying to decide where to get married, knowing we'd have a guest list of about 250 people. Hotel? Church? "Why don't we get married right here?" Noel said.

We were in the backyard of a unique little house I'd bought on Knobhill Drive in Sherman Oaks, a pleasant residential section out in the San Fernando Valley, another of those bedroom hinterlands of Los Angeles, full of the ghosts of orange groves. "There isn't enough space," I said.

"Well," he replied, "we can add two baths and two bedrooms and extend the living room, then put a concrete pad down here and . . ." Before I could really envision all that, he had run to the garage and returned with a sledgehammer. He then began hacking off the wooden stairway that led from the yard twenty feet up to the street level, and we were pouring concrete with our own pumps the night before the wedding. It set scarcely an hour before the guests arrived.

That was the way life was with Noel.

As Mrs. Marshall, I became stepmother to Noel's three young sons by his previous marriage, the three J's—Jerry, John and Joel. Bright and cheerful, they were a joy. And Noel became Melanie's stepfather. We needed all that extra space on Knobhill Drive.

Hitchcock had me in mind for another film, *Mary Rose*, but I told him, "I can't work with you. I must get out of this contract and I will get out of it."

"I'll ruin your career," he said, and he tried very hard to do just that. Hitch could abandon a dozen actors and actresses, but one did not abandon Hitch. Not easily.

I went on to make pictures with other directors, while Noel added real-estate development to his many other interests. But that wasn't really what he wanted to do. As always, he was looking for a new challenge, another mountain to climb. And he found it that day we saw a pride of lions in serene possession of an abandoned house in Gorongosa.

—3—

LIONS, LIONS
AND MORE LIONS

Satan's Harvest completed, Noel and I went off to Nairobi, then on to the late William Holden's Mount Kenya Safari Club for a few days, and finally on to the Serengeti, in northern Tanzania. After life in Manhattan and California, after high-rises and freeways, business partying and the usually meaningless chatter, there was a definite siren's song playing there in the game preserves, all so new to me— Kruger and Ngorongoro and the 5,700-square-mile Serengeti. As far as we could see, the land undulated gently, colored a greenish gray, with the granite and gneiss kopje boulders poking up suddenly and randomly on the sea of grass. Umbrella acacia trees were dotted around, and there was another kind of tree with yellowish bark that seemed to be mainly along the streams. Above this serene landscape were the birds, sometimes clouds of them. I felt so truly small, so insignificant, there on the grasslands, silently watching thousands upon thousands of giraffes and impalas and fleeing gazelles. Together, Noel and I watched sunsets and heard the zebras bray and the lions roar. Others had made documentaries about the big cats. But that was not the idea we had in mind. We wanted to tell a human story. And our short stay in the Serengeti led to many "what if" conversations: What if the game warden came back to that abandoned house? . . .

Lions in the wild

Back home, we told our family—eleven-year-old Melanie and the three J's—about the abandoned house on the Mozambique flood plain with all those lions living in it. Now clearly talking ourselves into making a picture, we spoke endlessly to friends and business contacts about the funny Gorongosa pride. The lion in the rocking chair. The two in the swing. About putting that whole pride up on sixty-foot international screens. Quite sensibly, most people said we were brain-sick.

Of course, our kids were excited about the idea. They were movie oriented, anyway. They had all acted in TV commercials. Johnny, Noel's middle son, had been acting since the age of five. He'd been a regular on *The Andy Griffith Show,* and his other credits included *Wagon Train, Lassie, Laramie,* and Bob Hope and Frank Sinatra specials. He had appeared in more than fifty TV commercials. Both Jerry and Melanie, with their own share of moppet commercials, had thoughts of acting careers. Melanie had started to model at the age of one. Joel, the oldest, was headed for UCLA to study art and fit that into a motion picture future behind the cameras. All four of them announced that they were "available" for a family project.

Early the next year, Noel and I were back in Africa for another film, *Kingstreet's War,* which co-starred Rossano Brazzi and John Saxon, and the proximity of the game preserves again stirred up that quirky idea of a cast of thirty lions and a story that was yet to jell. We returned to the preserves at every opportunity, talking to every lion person we could find.

The year before, we had met gentle, fun-loving Dandylion and Karma and had seen the eccentric pride at Gorongosa. Now at Wankie, not too far from Victoria Falls, we saw the other side of the big cats: lions in the raw. From a camp on a high bluff we watched elephants and gazelles below us. Then we heard there was a dead male elephant down there. Preserve officials didn't know why it had died, but a pride was feeding on it. Tusks were still on the animal, so officials knew it had not been poached. We drove down, and a quarter mile away the carcass could be smelled. Closer, we saw eight or nine lions. They had eaten away about half of the elephant, and one lion was so gorged he was asleep on the remains. All of them were bloody. It was a hideous, violent scene, and the smell was gagging. A full-grown male can eat fifty or sixty pounds of meat at the first feeding, thirty at the next. I was both revolted and fascinated.

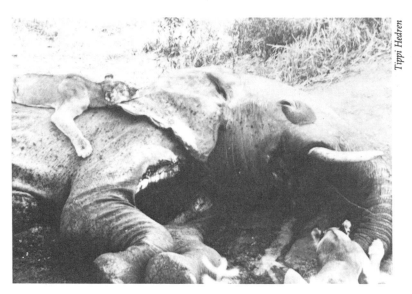

A pride feeding on a dead elephant

Noel and I already knew that our film couldn't be made in Africa, because few domesticated lions existed anywhere between the Tropic of Cancer and Capetown. For instance, that pride at Gorongosa might have fled if we had stepped from the car. Or one or more might have attacked us for intruding, especially if cubs were around. Vehicles represent absolutely no threat to them, but humans on foot are the deadly predators, the lions wrongly surmise. So the cats for our film would necessarily have to be amiable Dandylion and Karma types, wherever they might be found.

We had decided, too, that the film *Lions* was to be both entertainment and a plea for protection of wildlife throughout the world. In Kenya we had heard horror stories about poachers, including those who used helicopter gunships to kill elephants. Whole subspecies were being eliminated. Leopards and tigers, in the wild, were almost extinct. The "skin" business was, and is, one of the most grisly, obscene enterprises on earth. So there would be a subtle message: Please don't kill these magnificent thinking, feeling beings.

We also hoped to show the possibilities of human–big-cat relationships in an entertaining way, the Ozzie Bristow way. And, of course, we hoped to make a motion picture that would make money. Lots of it.

Noel began writing the script later that spring. Titled *Lions, Lions and More Lions,* the bare-bones story was about an American scientist who goes to Africa to study a pride of lions by living with them night and day in a house much like the one we'd seen in Gorongosa. His family arrives to discover that he is away for a few days, but very much at home are the lions and they quickly form a scary welcoming committee. We still weren't sure what was going to happen after that, but there was always agreement that I'd play the scientist's wife, and our children, less Joel, would play their children. Joel had said a flat no to acting but volunteered his services for art direction and set decoration. A suitable actor would be hired to play Hank, the scientist; Noel would direct, and he and I would co-produce.

Truthfully, I never really yearned to be a movie star, though I joined Madeleine Carroll, Joan Fontaine, Grace Kelly and Ingrid Bergman in a select club of players who had lasted through more than one Hitchcock film. I made movies because I had learned to love acting, and Hitchcock taught me more in two pictures than I could have learned from many other directors in fifteen. I was a good technician, I believed, but I had no pretensions about winning Oscars. On occasion I even took roles for the foreign travel involved. How could I pass up the opportunity to emote with big cats and my own family?

Usually, casting is not done until after the script has been completed, and the director has been hired. But in this case, our starring cast, multiple lions, was more important than the human cast or the story. Without the cooperating big cats, *we had no story.* So it was evident that Noel and I would have to round up all the privately owned lions in California, or elsewhere, put them under contract and attempt to teach them just a few basic moves in the fine art of acting, non-Hitchcockian. No whips and chains. We'd use pure affection in the Ozzie Bristow method. Hugs and kisses and soft words. Obviously we did not yet understand that certain lions do not wish to be hugged.

In late November, we went to Africa, U.S.A., in the San Fernando Valley, on the first of these unique casting sessions. Ralph Helfer, veteran animal trainer for films, owned and operated the wildlife park and was accustomed to hearing foolish ideas and the foolish needs of prospective film producers: Was it possible to seat an elephant in a jeep? Could a chimp be trained to touch-type? Did Ralph have an aria-singing parrot for rent? Over the years Hollywood had continually asked Helfer more for the impossible than for the possible.

31

When we told him what our mission was—while we were at it increasing the number of lions we needed from thirty to fifty, for an even grander film—Ralph just hooted, echoing Ozzie Bristow. "Look," he said, "you can't simply force a bunch of adult lions, strangers to each other, to live together. They're individuals. They have to be introduced gradually or they may kill each other. Or you. We're not talking about an African pride now. We're talking about lions that are total strangers to each other. With adults lions, you have to let them see one another through a fence for a long time before you put them together. Even then, there may be fights you wouldn't believe. You ever seen a lion fight?"

No, we hadn't. Noel and I looked at each other, our totally brilliant project beginning to unravel.

I did meet Major that day, a wonderful, gentle lion that had acted in a number of movies. Sitting close beside him, I rubbed my

Kindly "octogenarian" Major with Melanie, Jerry and me

fingers into his thick mane as he yawned. "You know," I said to Ralph, "I really don't understand. This one is so gentle. Why do we have to worry so much?"

"Major is twenty-five years old," Ralph said professorially, and that, in lion years, made him a kindly octogenarian.

Most animal trainers still believe that in order for a big cat to work for you, even nominally, he or she must live entirely alone and have no daily contact with other cats, not even eye contact. If Noel and I were successful in assembling our big-cat cast, we would disprove that theory. But in fact we honestly didn't realize we were trying to disprove anything. That's how ignorant we were.

On New Year's Eve, as 1970 passed into 1971, we met a writer, William Peter Blatty, at a party. We struck up a drink-in-hand conversation with him, and soon he was telling us about his new novel-in-progress, *The Exorcist*, a story of priests and demons. I remember thinking, Demons! Priests! That all sounds as if it might make a fascinating movie. And, of course, we told him about the movie we were planning to make. The next day as we watched the bowl games at Bill Blatty's home, he talked a little more about *The Exorcist* and we talked a little more about our picture. Oddly enough, that New Year's Day was the beginning of a business relationship that would have a large bearing on the filming of the big-cat story—and a profound effect on our lives.

—4—

NEIL

Just by asking, "Who else owns a lion?" Noel and I were suddenly involved in a whole network of big-cat people. There are oddballs who collect only Gladding McBean purple pottery or 1912 Akra marbles or Soul beer cans. They know one another, buy, sell and trade. It is much the same, we discovered, with tiger, lion, leopard, cougar and jaguar people. They acquire and keep the animals for one reason or another, mainly noncommercial. Some even think that having a lion or a tiger for a pet is the ultimate in being trendy. Fortunately, federal and state laws no longer allow such nonsense.

We began searching for feline collectors in early February, driving all over southern California. A little off-the-road mom-and-pop private zoo in Riverside County had a couple of lions and a tiger, a few tropical birds. Someone had just killed their newly acquired baby elephant by feeding it a handful of uppers, dope pep pills, and the owners were grieving for their loss, not much interested in talking about leasing their cats. *Uppers*! I was horrified at such a senseless act, and we quickly drove away. It was my first encounter with private zoos, one that left me disturbed and uneasy about what we were doing.

The following week we were back in the same rugged country at a small ranch where a man had a fine-looking young lioness. While we were talking I was holding her neck chain, and she suddenly took off across the field, dragging me, first on my feet, then on my belly. No match for her strength, I finally let go, learning the first lesson in big-cat handling: never compete with lion muscle. My knees and elbows were scratched, my blouse torn. Dignity shattered. After retrieving his impulsive cat, the rancher said he was interested in renting her out, swearing she could perform in a movie, but he would make no commitment.

The next weekend I learned another lesson. The owner of a two-month-old female cub asked if I would like to feed her from a bottle. Oh, yes, I'd like that very much, I said, and soon nestled her in my arms. But obviously I didn't have the right angle, because when the cub finished she turned around and nipped me in the left breast. The first of many cubs I bottle-fed, I learned from her, the excruciatingly painful way, exactly how to hold them—in the position in which they feed from their mothers' teats: belly down.

After a half-dozen other forays for the purpose of assembling a cast, it was clear that very few owners or trainers were willing to risk their lions in the kind of happy Gorongosa pride that Noel and I envisioned. The alternative, of course, was to create our own pride of fifty *home-grown* lions. We really didn't do much thinking or talking about where or how we would keep or finance that many big cats. Our single-minded purpose was to acquire them, one way or another, then worry about space and money. Noel usually operated like that, leaping over crevasses, walking through fire. And I was with him, every step of the way.

Our fortunes took a turn for the better when we were directed to a man named Ron Oxley and made a date to rendezvous with him in a place called Soledad Canyon, some distance from town. Until that Saturday, I'd never even heard of Soledad Canyon, reached from a country turnoff eight or nine miles from the freeway to the Mojave Desert, on past such places as Saugus and on the way to Palmdale, where the space shuttle lands. Horse and cattle country. Rattlesnake-and-redneck land. On the phone, Oxley told us we could drive out to meet Neil, a lion we could safely hug and get to know.

Melanie, by now an already beautiful long-legged thirteen, spurting up, along on all our cat hunts, was with us again that day. Leaving freeways behind, turning southeast, we were soon driving through the harsh, lonely canyon land, finally arriving at a cottonwooded

Ron Oxley and Neil—a perfect friendship

oasis by a narrow stream, down a steep embankment. A rusty mailbox read "Steve Martin." No, not the comedian. This Steve Martin, an animal trainer, was building a business to supply films and TV. Down there were some big cages, Martin's little house trailer, lots of sand and a small pond. Little else.

Ron Oxley, a six-foot, two-hundred-pound blond, greeted us. A nonchalant thirtyish man with a warm, friendly smile, he was in the process of building up his own animal-rental business, and his acting menagerie thus far included a cougar, a pair of bobcats, a huge black bear and the black-maned lion, Neil. They were all boarding at Martin's. Neil was Oxley's star, having played some villain parts in *Daktari*. But he was seldom villainous any longer, Ron declared. Neil's biggest part so far had been an assignment with Rod Steiger in *The Illustrated Man*. Credits counted at animal casting calls. Important, too, are the credentials of the trainer. Men like Martin and Oxley put the welfare of the animals above their own.

Ron led us to a picnic area down by the little river. "First of all," he said, "don't rush up to the lion."

No fear of that, I thought. Not a muscle will move.

"He doesn't know you. Wait and maybe he'll come up to you. He might brush against you and maybe he'll stop and take your arm or shoulder into his mouth. Don't resist it. Just let it happen. But don't turn your back to him. He has a sense of humor and likes to come up from behind and trip people. If you run or make fast movements he'll think you want to play, and he plays very rough. If you want to pet him, use strong, firm scratching. Otherwise it's like a fly getting at him. Scratch under his chin or deep into his mane, but not on his face."

Nodding, we hung on every word.

A few minutes later, Ron brought Neil down to the picnic area—without a leash or a rope. He was huge, with a massive head. Walking slowly, with the same royalty and dignity as Dandylion, he paid little attention to any of us. First he went over to a cottonwood and did a lovely stretch up the trunk, showing us his full length of nine feet, tip of tail to nose. Then finally he came over to hold court, sprawling out on his belly, paws forward. He still had not looked at any of us. Neil knew how to upstage.

"Kneel down beside him," Ron told me.

I did, scratching Neil firmly under the chin.

Melanie then approached, and Ron said, "Kneel down on the other side."

It was my first intimate contact with an adult lion, and I felt a mixture of awe and excitement and absolute fear. What if that big head swung around, jaws wide open? With Melanie on one side of him and me on the other, I'm quite sure I held my breath for half a minute.

Suddenly, Neil's head did swing around and he took Melanie's entire right shoulder into his mouth. The whole shoulder. It just disappeared into that red, white-toothed cavern.

Melanie began to laugh, and, terrified, I said, "For God's sake, hold still!"

But Neil was just playing a little game. He released Melanie's shoulder and gazed off into the distance with regal unconcern.

I got to my feet, still somewhat shaken. Ron reassured me. "To get to know anything about lions," he said, "you've just got to live with them for a while. Why don't I bring Neil over to your place for a visit?"

Noel and Melanie and I looked at each other, and almost without thinking I heard myself say that would be fine with us. So four or five days a week, Neil became our first live-in lion.

The house on secluded Knobhill was a spacious two-story shake-roof, built into the hillside, with living room, dining room and kitchen upstairs and three bedrooms downstairs on two different levels. A swimming pool and a lanai were within the redwood-fenced yard. Lots of lush subtropical plants were around, banana trees and such. Located on a sharp elbow curve, we were tucked in so that few neighbors had any view of our comings and goings. Directly across the street and uphill was the home of actress Karen Valentine, but even Karen did not have a clear view of our house.

Though such busy streets as Beverly Glen and Valley Vista were nearby, and heavily trafficked Ventura Boulevard was less than a quarter mile away, we had a perfect hideaway for the study of lions. Or so we thought. Although cheetahs were legal, with necessary permits, other big cats were definitely not welcome within city limits. We knew that, but we did not own or plan to keep Neil. He would be just a visitor.

Ron had an unobtrusive green van in which to transport Neil and his other animals, and the van began making regular runs up Knobhill, like the ice-cream truck, usually in the afternoon or evening. After parking at our curve and looking up and down the street, Ron would spirit Neil out of the van, then quickly down the short flight of steps and into the front door. Maybe five seconds for the whole clandestine operation.

Melanie was usually at home, and Noel's sons were in and out, dividing their time between Knobhill and their mother's house, not far away. The other intermittent human member of our household was Emily Henderson, who came in several times a week to clean and do laundry. Coping with a lion was certainly not one of her jobs. As for two nonhuman members, Partner, my beloved mutt, and Puss, Melanie's Alimese—half-alley, half-Siamese—cat, they, above all, were upset by Neil's visits. When Ron said, "He'd probably try to eat them," we made sure Puss and Partner were safely locked up in a bedroom when the green van was out in front.

My date book proclaims that Neil's first visit was Sunday, May 2, 1971, and I remember that he came into the house, stood for a moment on the landing, looking down into the living room, then

Melanie inspects Neil's cavernous mouth.

began to slowly explore each room, and finally went outside to the lanai and the swimming pool. I had an anxious moment when he went to the back fence, put his paws up and stuck that enormous head over. Though there was a vacant lot between us and the next neighbor downhill, I could imagine the lady out cultivating her petunias, feeling eyes on her, glancing up. I was relieved when all nine feet of Neil dropped back to the ground.

Neil made himself very much at home that first day, finally sprawling out in the living room to sleep. Overwhelmed by the idea of a grown lion in our house, I found it hard to take my eyes off him. I was also intrigued by his relationship with Ron. In Africa, I'd seen the staunch friendship between Ozzie Bristow and Dandylion; now I saw the same thing between Ron and Neil. In both cases, it had taken years to develop. Neil had been born in Africa and was brought to the United States as a young adult. Ron sat outside his

39

cage for months, almost every day, three or four hours at a time, before finally going behind the steel bars. Then he sat quietly, four or five feet from Neil, for more than a month. Finally the lion came over to Ron, indicating he wanted to be friends.

"If you got an adult today, you'd have to make a career of establishing friendship with it," Ron told us. Instead he recommended that we get several cubs as quickly as possible and begin friendship routines as well as basic training.

That sounded like fun. "Where do we keep them?" I remember asking.

"Why, here in the house," Ron said, surprised that I'd ask such a question. "The idea is to have constant contact with them."

In the house? Many nice things were in those rooms, gathered from all over the world. The couches were expensive, as were the drapes. Noel looked at me and said, "Okay?"

Absolutely!

Ron went about procuring us a small lion, and as the days went by I became very excited about the prospect of having our own cub. I had completely succumbed to Neil. He was now a constant visitor to Knobhill, and no room was off limits to him except where Puss and Partner were secured. He took full advantage, indoors or out. If any of us was in the pool, Neil enjoyed going to the water's edge, putting a paw on a wet head and firmly shoving down. Ron said that was typical lion behavior.

Other behaviors were similar to those of domestic animals. If Neil was thirsty, he'd let me know by going up to the sink and placing his paws on it. While I ran the water, he drank slowly, lapping it from the underside of his tongue, the way domestic cats do. Soon he found a favorite sleeping spot in Melanie's bed downstairs, and one night the second or third week I went down to find them both asleep, side by side, Neil's big mouth not two feet from her body. She had pulled the covers up to his head. It was a sight some mothers might not relish.

I remember being slightly unnerved the first time I saw Neil "grimace." There is no other way to describe it. He opened his mouth quite wide, baring his canines and pulling his upper lips back. He looked ferocious, yet there was no sound of anger. Grimacing, Ron said, enabled him to get the clearest possible essence when sniffing. Surprisingly, big cats aren't well equipped in the olfactory department and there are two holes in the roof of the lion's mouth that increase the intake of smell, hence the gaping jaws. If a lion had to hunt by scent alone, it would starve. Neil grimaced, wrinkling his entire face, whenever he smelled something pungent or musky. In the house, it could be food or perfume; outside it could be the smell of another animal wafting on the air. Once we recognized the grimace for what it was, Neil looked more funny than ferocious.

Each visit was a delight. One early evening, just after sundown, Neil decided he needed to roar for a while and did it in the area between the pool and the fence. There was no mistaking what was going on. The "MGM sound" reverberated all over Beverly Glen and Valley Vista.

Jittery about the neighbors, I asked Ron, "Any way to stop that?"

"Not a chance," he said with a grin.

The lady whose house was about two hundred feet away soon called to say, "Mrs. Marshall, I think I hear a lion roaring and it sounds like it's coming right out of your house."

Without hesitation, I said, "Oh, yes, I hear it, too. But it sounds to me like a motorbike revving up."

At times there are advantages to being an actress.

Bedmates Melanie and Neil

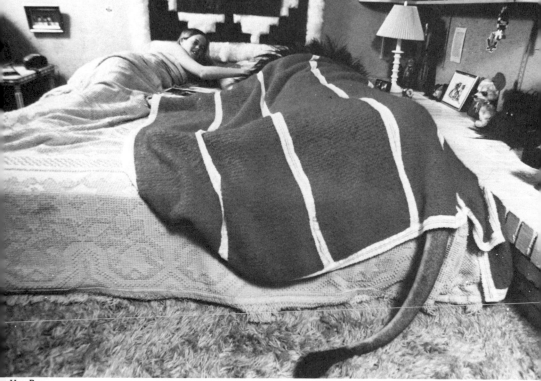

Van Rey

A classic grimace by Neil

For that particular roaring session, Neil was standing, but we soon discovered that lions roar just as readily on their bellies or their sides, sitting, walking or running. Stretched out, half asleep, they sometimes barely bother to raise their heads when letting out a halfhearted roar. A session will last eight to ten good roars per lion. Two lions may start an argument, and others will join in the talk. Or there may be a monologue, with one lion saying, in effect, "It's evening, and here I am." A lion even has a special roaring face, with the muzzle raised slightly and eyes and ears relaxed while the sound comes out of the partially opened mouth, which forms an O. I doubt that Neil was talking to another lion during his roaring sessions. Our house was too far away from any known lion residences. He simply felt like roaring.

With a full-grown lion in the house, I suppose we should have expected friends, even close ones, to react with apprehension to our new acquaintance. Film producer-director Ted Post, one of Noel's clients and a longtime friend, absolutely refused to come to dinner unless we guaranteed that Neil would not drop by. Several other friends made flimsy excuses during this period and consequently missed some novel entertainment. But there were also those who took Neil completely in stride.

I anticipated that Emily Henderson would tighten up a little and show the usual mixture of awe and fear the first time she met Neil. Instead a wide smile crossed her face. I did feel a little strange saying, "Emily, this is Neil." Yet I also felt that a formal introduction to an adult lion was necessary. The human, I've found, needs a bit of a bridge to the big cats.

Despite all the social mixing with our family and his easy at-homeness, Neil soon proved that he remained very much beast. An editor at *Life* magazine heard we were learning about big cats in preparation for a movie and proposed a photo essay. For one shot he wanted the Marshall family at dinner, with the live-in lion seated on the landing, gazing down at the humans as they ate their broiled chicken.

We set the scene carefully with polished silver and cut-glass stemware, flowers and Wedgwood china on the dinner table. And Noel and I, Jerry, Joel and Melanie (John had a special assignment) gussied ourselves up to look like the California family beautiful. With any luck, the picture would be just right for *Life*.

After we were seated, candles glowing, photographer Mike Rougier began snapping away while middle son John, hidden up on the landing, fed bits of meat to keep Neil interested and *in place*. But Neil kept turning his head and didn't have quite the rapt look that *Life* required. After thirty or so clicks, the camera had to be reloaded. That was the way the magazine worked. Zillions of pictures to get one. John stopped issuing the meat tidbits, and everyone relaxed.

Except Neil. He did what his animal dictates told him to do— go get the food. All four hundred pounds of him leaped smoothly over the railing and landed in the middle of Wedgwood and flowers and cashew chicken. The table hung on two legs for a few seconds, balancing as if on a high wire, then tipped over as Neil made another graceful bound into the center of the room.

My first reaction was to yell to Mike, "Did you get the picture?" My second was to bemoan the broken china and stemware and the chicken, rice and salad all over my rug and me. The *Life* people packed up and went home, Rougier thoroughly disgusted because he thought he hadn't got the shot. But a second camera on a tripod had tripped automatically, catching the uninvited diner on the teetering table and the looks of shock on the faces of the humans.

Only Ron was not surprised by Neil's behavior. He told me it was useless to rebuke a big cat or attempt to teach it any manners it did not wish to learn. So, with our dinner table in ruins, Ron just shrugged and took Neil out to the green van. The lesson was for the humans: Don't leave food on the table when a lion is near.

About a week later, on another of the evenings when Neil visited, we had several BOAC public-relations people in for dinner and they were, understandably, quite anxious for a few minutes. We had not warned them that a friendly big cat might come through the door at any minute. Stiffly British about it all when Neil did appear, they forced squeaky little laughs and stood rigidly until they realized that he was not planning to make an evening meal of them.

Yet we soon saw the ultimate unpredictability of the big cats. Later that evening Neil suddenly became *possessive,* one of the most dangerous situations that can develop. It came on without warning, and, so far as could be determined, it was over Ron himself. Neil apparently did not want Ron sharing his attention with others that night. Growling deep in his belly, he began to display aggressiveness, baring his canines, lifting a paw. In a few seconds, he went from friendly lion to terrifying lion right there in the confines of our kitchen.

We had heard about the possessive traits of the big cats, which are predictable. Totally unpredictable are the moments they may choose to display those traits—and the object they choose to possess. Neil wanted Ron, and he was threatening both of us.

"Get out of here," Ron shouted to me, and I ran into the living room, where Noel and all the guests were on their feet, several edging toward the front door.

It was the first time I'd seen a demonstration of possessiveness, and my first lion–human encounter except those staged in circuses with cracking whips and chains. This one wasn't staged. And we were all scared, witnessing the showdown between Ron and Neil from about forty feet away, through the open kitchen door.

Neil's tail was twitching and one huge paw was batting the air. His mouth was open, lips pulled back, and he wasn't grimacing.

Neil attending *Life*'s dinner party

Shining canines were exposed. Snarls came from deep in his throat, choppy and hoarse. I remembered what Ozzie Bristow had said about Dandylion: "He loves me, but he could also kill me." Neil had reverted to raw jungle.

Ron, yelling, "No! No! No! Leave it," was facing him down. Less than three feet separated them. Ron's hands and arms were raised threateningly. They were his only weapons, symbols of some larger threat. *He had to win!* The trainer *must* win the fight, we learned that night. It was a chilling lesson for the future. If the big cat wins, the relationship has to be ended for the sake of the human.

Though it seemed to last for an hour, it was probably no more than two minutes before Neil tossed his head and mane in surrender, then began making subdued muttering noises. The big mouth relaxed finally; the paw went back on the floor. A moment after that, an embarrassed Ron Oxley was escorting Neil out to the van.

As I closed the door behind him, I heard Ron talking to the lion as one would admonish a brat: "They're nice people. Why did you act like that?" It was useless admonishment and Ron knew it.

We quickly poured some potent drinks for our guests, but it was a few more minutes before confident laughter could be heard in the house. Stiff upper lips had been tested all around.

About a week later, we were treated to another display of possessiveness. We were out in Soledad Canyon, at Steve Martin's place, with the same group of BOAC public-relations people, working with Boomer, a two-year-old lion belonging to Martin. In very late afternoon Boomer was being photographed carrying a BOAC flight bag in his mouth. Trouble began when he decided he wanted the bag. Belly on the ground, prize between his teeth, Boomer was ready for an all-night stand until Ron hooked a rope to the bumper of his van and literally towed the lion, bag still in his mouth, back to his quarters.

More than anything else, I think it was that stunning combination of lovable lion and raging beast all in the same beautiful body that became a fatal attraction for me. The lovable lion always melts the heart; the raging beast terrifies the head.

—5—

CASEY

Almost every book about lions that we could find was concerned with behavior in the wild. There was nothing written about affection training. We read what was available, nonetheless, and soon acquired our first lion, a three-month-old cub, property of a physician who lived in woodsy Mandeville Canyon, not far from Beverly Hills. Mandeville is an upper-income lane with a reputation for housing movie people, doctors, lawyers and eccentrics. This doctor was one of those misguided people who think it would be fun to have a big cat around the house. So he'd gotten Casey, an excess cub from an animal park, and was soon amazed to find out how rapidly the tiny *Felis leo* can grow, and just how strong and rambunctious it can be at ninety days. Casey had begun to tear up the doctor's splendid house and was now living alone in the guest house, from which all furniture had been removed. He was a prisoner and resented it mightily.

The grateful physician gave us some cans of Zu/Preem, a perfect nutritional food for cubs or any exotic feline which is extensively used by zoos and similar keepers of wild animals, and wished us good luck. He couldn't wait to see us drive off, and I swear there was a gleam in Casey's eyes when we rolled toward Knobhill. He sat in the back seat with Melanie, gnawing on her hands and wrists, wanting to play, something I doubt he'd done much of in the doctor's house.

At the age of four weeks cubs' eyes are blue-gray, but they gradually change to amber by the time the cubs are three months old. Casey's were already deep amber. At birth the coat is soft, woolly and gray-yellow. Usually there are some dark spots around the face and head. The sides and the legs are also faintly spotted. Although some cats retain baby spots on the lower legs into adulthood, this postnatal pelage begins to turn slowly when the cubs are about nine months to a year, leaving them their tawny, golden adult coat. At the same time the tail tuft begins to appear. Casey still had his baby spots the first day we saw him.

At home, of course, were the cat and the dog, having survived Neil but about to undergo another invasion. Casey was not a physical threat to either Puss or Partner as yet, but they had long ruled the pet territory of the Marshall domain. A lion cub about a foot tall and two feet long was more competition than they wanted or needed. Poor Puss and Partner put up with an awful lot over the next few years.

It was forty-five-pound Casey who began to teach us about the instinctual behaviors of lions. Thank goodness the behaviors are in their genes and there is no way that humans can totally, or even greatly, modify them. Casey first began teaching us some very important lessons about lion language and body postures—what the vocalizing and the different stances meant, and when the lion is mellow and when it is dangerous. Whatever he did, whatever mood he was in, Casey made it evident from the beginning that someday that little cub would be a king.

Casey's baby spots

Tippi Hedren

Casey snuggles up
to Melanie.

Tippi Hedren

We also learned from Casey that the sometimes violent reactions are always for a reason—a big-cat reason. Possessiveness, one of the strongest of the instinctual behaviors, whether in the Serengeti or in Soledad Canyon, is usually the main reason for violence. And it can be over any object, animate or inanimate—a bottle, a can, a handbag, a shoe, a camera case, a jacket, a rock, even a clump of grass or a pile of leaves, a person (Ron Oxley "possessed" by Neil), another lion, another animal. No object can be excluded. Food and sex, not surprisingly, create the most violent reactions. I think it is safe to say that the male lion is the most jealous creature on earth.

I later discovered that possessiveness can be displayed as early as a few weeks. Little paws go around the nursing bottle, and the cub begins vocalizing an "uh-*huh*, uh-*huh*" sound. An attempt to take the bottle away often brings a violent reaction. The human baby, of course, can duplicate this reaction, but not its intensity. Making the same sound, now loud and threatening, the older lion, such as Neil or Boomer, can be extremely dangerous. When Neil was vocalizing the "uh-*huh*, uh-*huh*" sound in my kitchen, it was guttural, deep inside his body, and Ron immediately recognized the potential for violence.

Even at three months, cubs have an incredible repertoire of sound, though the roar isn't perfected until a year and a half to two years. But Casey was vocalizing in moans, grunts, growls and snarls as well as in the happy "aows" and hums. All had a meaning. His grunt, for instance, was a direct complaint. Taking any object away would often bring vocal disagreement.

49

For his nighttime accommodations, Casey chose to sleep with Melanie—in her bed. He was already the size of Partner, but stockier, his teeth were fully formed, and his jaws had the strength of beaver traps. One night we heard Melanie scream and ran into her bedroom. She was clutching her thigh. Casey was sitting up, looking innocent and angelic.

"He bit me," she said, wide-eyed and openmouthed. "He just bit me!"

"Why?" I asked.

"I don't know why," she replied. "We weren't playing. He was just sitting there and suddenly bit me." Her skin had been punctured and blood had been drawn.

That episode taught us about the unpredictability of the young animal, biting without apparent cause. It also taught us something about the medical aspects of raising cubs. Surprisingly enough, the gleaming teeth of exotic cubs carry a dangerous collection of bacteria. That would be expected in the wild, where prey is left out in the sun for days, but not in the environs of Los Angeles. An antibiotic is always necessary if the skin is punctured, and the wound is rarely bandaged. Air must get to it. We also realized that if you simply exist with big-cat cubs, let alone play with them, there's no way to avoid being bitten. The surprise is usually worse than the bite.

In spite of the surprise attack, Melanie and Casey remained good friends. And when we took him out to Soledad Canyon several times that summer, Melanie pulled him into the lake or rowed him around in a boat. Though he swam easily, Casey apparently hated every stroke of it. Some lions love to swim; others avoid water except to drink it. The only way Ron Oxley could ever get Neil to take a bath was literally to drag him into the pond at the end of a nylon rope.

It was in this year of raising Casey, I remember, that Melanie too was growing up. She'd had a mind of her own almost since birth and now she was maturing physically and mentally at a speed that startled me. Like Casey, she seemed to be completely unpredictable. One day she could be childlike, the next a metamorphosis had taken place and she would be a different person. The terrible early teens, of course, which can be a difficult time for both mother and daughter. I had always encouraged Melanie to be independent, but now I began to regret it. Her legs were long; she was as tall as I was, and I knew she was going to be beautiful. That she was going to become an actress as well was inevitable. The girl playing with Casey, the cub, was no longer a child.

—6—

THE HOUSE
OF CUBS

One day as I was driving up Knobhill, Ron Oxley was just leaving. He leaned out of his van, smiling. "There's something down there in your bathroom. Better go take a look at it."

Hurrying on into the house, I ran downstairs, to discover a tiny cub asleep in my bathtub, curled up on one of my sweaters. Six weeks old, Needra, named by Melanie, was another excess cub from Lion Country Safari, Casey's place of birth, down in Orange County. Zoos and animal parks reach a point, for both financial reasons and lack of space, where they simple cannot afford another big cat.

As I was examining our new acquisition, Casey came padding into the bathroom, took one look at the tiny lioness, and I thought he might do back flips. Cubs so desperately need companionship, and here, suddenly, was a sister. Within minutes they became good friends, and the rest of the day they played together throughout the house until dropping off to sleep, in the same space.

Much more active than a male like Casey, as is usual with most female cats, Needra was also much more cunning, always plotting and planning. I could almost see her brain working feverishly: Now, if I jump up on that table, . . . then jump up on the bookcase, I can hit the lampshade. Her eyes would track that exact pattern. Then, *pow*, she would follow it, landing on the shade and toppling the lamp, to her astonishment. Casey was never that cunning.

It was August, 1971, and word was out within the mysterious California big-cat network that those crazy Marshalls over in Sherman Oaks would take almost any healthy little lion. Within three weeks of Needra's arrival, we had three more additions to our growing pride: Ike and Mike, both four months old, and Trans, also male, six weeks old. All castoffs. There were now playmates aplenty. And when they weren't roughhousing with one another, they were playing with rubber dog toys provided expressly to prevent other mischief. Cub Mike preferred tennis shoes and we thought that was cute, never dreaming that one day something would click in his head and he would go after feet encased in, guess what? Tennies!

We well knew they would all be eight or nine feet long, nose to tip of tail, and four or five hundred pounds a few years hence, but we didn't deal with that fact other than by ignoring it. Our vision of the future was confined to that day when we could begin shooting our film—with the willing cooperation of the full-grown cats we had raised from tiny cubs.

Alex Van Rey

John romping with Ike and Mike

Still, over the next months and years, it seemed at times as if we were running an unruly orphanage, an illegal home zoo. Until the Federal Endangered Species Act was passed in 1973, along with many state and local ordinances specifically governing the possession, transportation and sale of these animals, anyone could order a lion or tiger cub from a pet store. One mail-order house in the Midwest sold lions and tigers by catalog. And soon the new owner, someone like the besieged Mandeville Canyon doctor, would discover that the darling little cub was gaining two or three pounds weekly and had teeth like nut picks, and paws that could already deliver a stunning right to the jaw. Big-cat cubs cannot be treated like domestic cats or dogs. Then that someone would call us, saying, "We've got this lovely little lion and don't know what to do with it. It's so big and strong. Would you please take it?"

We almost always said yes, but I was often shocked by some of the pathetic "pet" specimens we were offered. Declawed cats, cats in chains, cats that were terrified of any human being, cats that were even terrified of other cats. A circus gave Cindi to us. She'd broken her leg, but no effort had been made to set it. Grossly crippled, she was no longer wanted in the circus ring. Another cat had been de-clawed, castrated and had his eye teeth pulled.

Despite wanting to help, to rescue all these unwanted animals, I was not at all certain we could handle more than four crouching, jumping demolition teams on Knobhill at the same time. So I put word out to friends that we would be very happy to share the many joys of raising lion cubs.

One taker was Louanne Wells, wife of Frank Wells, then president of Warner Brothers Studios. Frank drove over to relieve us of Trans, an irresistible five pounds of spotted blue-eyed cub. It seemed to be a clever move, for several reasons. Somewhere down the line, we would be looking around for a studio to finance and release our film. If Frank and Louanne Wells just happened to fall in love with Trans, so much the better.

With the help of Melanie, John and Jerry, feeding and taking care of the four cubs still on Knobhill were mostly fun. Melanie couldn't wait to get home from junior high school every afternoon. The kids refused to believe her when she said, "Hey, I've got to take care of my lions." The solution to that problem, of course, was to take eighty-pound Casey to school.

The cubs were often in trouble and often destructive, forcing us to remove such objects as pillows from their reach. We had already cleared away any art object not made of concrete. Bedspreads were prime targets for tugs of war. During daylight we kept the cubs outside as much as possible, hoping the neighbors wouldn't discover what kind of house we were keeping. At night, the four of them usually slept at the bottom of our bed or Melanie's. We wanted them to have that constant human relationship. Later, our lives would depend on it.

The months we spent raising the cubs at Knobhill were marvelous, unique learning experience for us all. The time between five or six weeks and six months, when the lion is becoming quite large and quite strong, is a time of wonder, rooted deep in the past. To observe a cub's daily growth is to have a course in the genetic dictates of the animal. For instance, in order for lion cubs to live in the wild their survival equipment has to be available very quickly, so nature makes sure that their teeth break through the skin of the gums in a few weeks. And their claws are needle sharp even though their eyes, coated with a bluish film, are not yet open. One thing that always disappointed me in raising cubs was not being able to find their baby teeth when they shed them. Of the several dozen cubs I raised, there is only one dental souvenir, belonging to Casey. The teeth are obviously lost in food or in chewing some object like a $3,000 couch.

Bedroom tug of war

Alex Van Rey

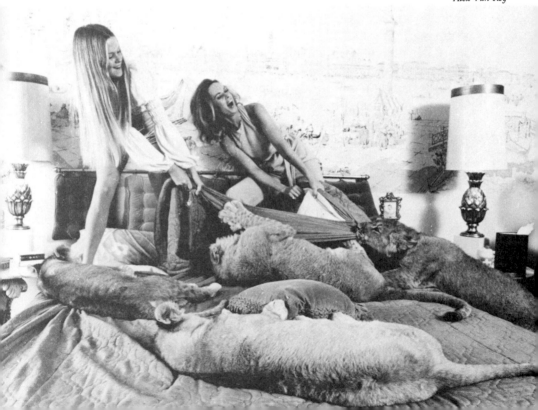

Casey in a destructive mood

From Needra, who had to be bottle-fed for another month after her arrival, we learned that the basic cub language, which carries through to adulthood, undergoing the natural changes of deepening and enrichment, is already well developed at six weeks. The bottle-possessive sound of "uh-*huh*, uh-*huh*," which translates to "It's mine, it's mine," becomes the guttural, frightening possessive sound of the adult lion when it has decided to appropriate something. In the ultimate, that sound has a machine-gunning effect that is positively chilling.

Then there is the cub's plaintive "as-aow, as-aow," which, accompanied by visual searching, means "Where are you? Where are you?" That sound eventually becomes the roar. Cubs practice it without knowing what they're doing, and then develop it to a grander scale as they grow up. The ossified hyoid structure of the smaller cat, which permits purring, is repeated in the big cats except that it contains an elastic ligament which produces the roar. When the sound finally becomes baritone, or even basso profundo, at about two, it seems to frighten the young lions at first. I've heard two-year-olds roar and then appear bewildered by what came out of their throats. Many people seem to associate the roar with an indication of combat or a demand for food. From listening to and observing thousands of roaring sessions, I believe that roaring is mostly loud conversation.

Melanie bottle-feeding
baby Needra

And it should be of no surprise that many lionesses can outtalk males, though the roars of the latter are usually deeper in tone. In volume, they can be equal.

After they have learned to walk without losing balance, the cubs immediately begin to display assurance. It is first noticeable in the tail when it begins to flick back and forth, their little heads raised, determination displayed in every step. Even in cubhood, the tail is an almost foolproof indicator of the lion's mood. Adult or cub, the relaxed position is curved down, with the end (black tufted in the adult) turned up a bit. When the tail is flicked up into the air or when it is switched back and forth very fast, it is an early warning sign. If the lion is an adult, beware! If the tail is horizontal, the lion is probably already charging and it behooves the human to clamber over the nearest fence, hurriedly.

With Needra it was easy to observe the first signs of the dictates of the wild. According to my date book, she was "crouching," part of the hunting instinct buried deep inside her, at seven weeks. It is pretty much the same with all cubs, especially females. By ten weeks, they're crouching and peering around corners, waiting to jump out

56

at other cubs, *or humans*. The warning is written all over their faces, and they can be hysterically funny when they begin a charge and other cubs happen to catch them at it. The charging cub will stop and walk away as if he or she hadn't intended to charge in the first place. Later on, however, the human is wise to be wary if a lion assumes the crouched stance. Great, good fun may be on the lion's agenda, or great harm may be the intention.

Also, the perseverance of the little lion can be observed at eight weeks. If it wants to enter a room, it will start to dig in front of the door until admitted or stopped, which has to be done with a shouted *"No!"* or *"Leave it!"*—words that may be lifesavers for anyone faced with bared canines and a poised paw that can kill a zebra with a single swat. Repeated again and again during childhood, they stay in the memory banks of most, but not all, adult lions.

Lions and tigers—in fact, all big cats—must be taught at the earliest possible age that they have to be careful with humans, that human skin is like tissue paper and that because of their size alone, even in play, the cats can inflict great injury. So they must '"wrestle," for instance, humans with care. And they must clearly understand the meaning of a shouted "No, that hurts!" or similar words, when they're six months old. Of course, some one-hundred-pounders and some five-hundred-pounders never listen.

The cat must learn that human skin is like tissue paper.

Barbara Parkins

Little lions are impressed with loud noises and almost jump out of their skins at the shouted "No!" Adult lions certainly talk to their young with loud sounds if the cubs are doing something obnoxious, and the human should follow suit. Big-cat mothers and fathers don't hesitate to yell at their offspring to keep them in line. But like its more docile cousin the domestic cat, the lion can always tell the difference between a harsh tone and a friendly one. Big cats definitely relate to humans as well as to other cats on a language level.

Next in importance after understanding the firm "No!" or other negative, the cub must be taught to walk beside the trainer or handler on a leash or lead—the same routine as dog walking. Looking ahead, the lion or tiger, weighing three or four times as much as the trainer, will have to be moved from time to time for any number of reasons—perhaps a routine change of space, a trip to the vet's, evacuation in an emergency, or just an exercise walk. Teaching a cub to walk, to stop and to sit down should begin at about two months, and no self-respecting cub will behave during these early sessions. It will resent restraint. Big-cat leads are not the choke-chain type used on dogs. Choke chains would be dangerous for both animal and handler because of the possibly volatile movements of the cat. Cat leads of 2.0 chain involve a loop for the neck and then eight feet of lead chain with a five-inch ring for the human to grasp. It is a coaxing restraint, not one for pulling, but it does offer some control. Steady pressure reminds the cat that the handler is on the other end.

My first pupil on the walking lead was Casey, and he reacted like a rodeo bull for the first few times. Instead of the dog's "Sit" command, Ron Oxley taught me to say, "Put it down!" With lions and tigers it seems to work better than just "Sit." Sometimes they respond right away; sometimes not. I attempt to make them sit down in order to remove the lead quickly and smoothly.

Another milestone in the life of any cub is weaning from the bottle. As with human babies, the process is easy with some cubs; others long for the nipple and make a big fuss. Just prior to weaning, I gradually introduce solid food by putting blendered Zu/Preem into the bottles. Even so, some animals refuse the change at first.

Louanne Wells called me one day to say that Trans flatly refused to go to solids. So Melanie, having weaned two cubs, went over to the Wells home prepared to wean a third one. She put on a bathing suit and went into a shower with Trans. She spread Zu/Preem all over her hands and wrists and let the cub lick it off. Then she smeared cat food all over his lips and paws. Trans decided to convert.

Casey, determined to go his own way

After the young ones are weaned from the bottle, they should be fed as much as they want, at any time they want. Mine first eat Zu/Preem, then Western Plateau, a scientifically designed diet for exotic cats, which comes in a large sausagelike roll resembling hamburger in appearance. Western Plateau gives the cubs a taste of raw meat, and they eat about two pounds of it daily. This is increased as size and appetite demand.

Although big-cat parents can be exceptionally good and attentive to their cubs, or mean and neglectful, the same as in the human race, there are many tender moments between cubs and adult lions. In fact, tenderness and affection are the rule rather than the exception.

The cubs relate to one another by "mouthing," and that form of communication follows through to adulthood. They chew on one another's ears or head or neck, making sounds that are plainly affectionate. The good mother frequently grooms her cubs with her rough tongue, and, of course, adult lions and tigers groom each other. And, similar to domestic cats, the cubs begin "rubbing" at an early age, sliding their heads along each other as well as along human legs. The rubbing continues all their lives, even into the geriatric stages. It is basically a sign of affection and well-being, but it is also used in "marking," staking out territory.

Showing most of the usual domestic-kitten characteristics, the cubs often exasperated Emily Henderson. They thought her mop was an object to be attacked, and they happily went after her dust cloth when it was being swiped back and forth. In determined pursuit of play, they would gnaw at her ankles, sharp teeth sometimes breaking skin. A quartet of cute spoilers, growing at an alarming rate, they meant to be mischievous and usually succeeded.

Yet they had a whole range of almost human characteristics that were equally strong. One morning I was in bed when a sonic boom shook Knobhill, and little Needra, cozily against my feet, was awakened out of her sound sleep. She raced up my body, ending at my shoulder, her head against my neck. Badly frightened, she was shivering.

Holding her closely, I responded as I would with a child, "It's okay, Neenie. Everything's going to be all right."

It was difficult to think that any of these warm, funny, playful little beings, so much in need of human assurance and of love, could ever be a deadly threat to anyone. Yet I knew that within two years they would have the physical capability of inflicting serious injury or worse. That's why the human contact with them was so important.

—7—

CAT FEVER

It just never occurred to me that sturdy, rowdy lion cubs were, in many ways, much more fragile than the ordinary house cat. Tending to become ill very quickly, they have a low tolerance to drugs, and the casualty rate in infancy, even in zoos, is comparatively high. The survival rate of those born in the African preserves is estimated to be not more than one out of four.

Despite the similarities, big cats are different physiologically from the incredibly tough alley cat. For one thing, their genetic dictates tell them always to look well in the wild. Otherwise they'll be killed by their own kind. Death is the swift, sure way that big cats take care of their own kind in the Serengeti or Gorongosa. Sick animals are seldom seen in the game preserves; not for long, anyway. The trait of striving to look well also carries over to domestic-born exotic cats. They hide illness as long as they can, and their threshold for pain is extremely high.

I knew Needra was sick early that first Monday of August. Very weak, she refused to eat. Her little nose was hot and dry. And taking her temperature rectally I panicked a bit when I saw it was 104. A lion's normal temperature is in the range of 100.5 to 102.5 degrees.

In case of emergency, Ron Oxley had given me the name of Dr. Martin Dinnes, a veterinarian who practiced in West Los Angeles, and he soon came over. He made house calls because a number of his patients, from baboons to elephants, were better left in their own environment. It is very difficult to find a vet who will treat wild animals, and young Dr. Dinnes was then in the process of establishing that as his specialty. Now he is known worldwide for administering to a variety of untamed creatures, from newborn cubs to killer whales.

After examining Needra, Dr. Dinnes, a tall red-haired, freckled man, exuding confidence, said, "She has cat fever and that's always dangerous. Do you know anything about it?"

I confessed I didn't.

Feline infectious peritonitis is a devilish sickness, he told me, striking and spreading swiftly through the cat's system, sometimes causing death within a day or two. In this case, Puss might have been the germ carrier.

Dr. Martin Dinnes and a cougar patient

After giving Needra a shot, Dr. Dinnes said, "She'll need one every six hours. Around the clock."

I gave him a blank look.

"I'm sorry, but I can't run over here four times a day."

"But I don't know how to give shots," I said. "I can't give shots. I'll faint." I was squeamish and didn't mind admitting it.

"Get me an orange," he said, "And I'll show you how."

I had to learn to give both intramuscular and subcutaneous shots. Though I'd break out in a cold sweat fifteen minutes before it was time to insert the needle into Needra's little hip, I had no choice. Weak as she was, I could hold her in one hand and administer the shot with the other. Her temperature climbed to 106 before it began to drop back to normal.

Never had I intended to take on any medical duties when I agreed to raise cubs, but I soon discovered that being a vet-technician is part of the job. Conquering squeamishness was good for me.

Then it was Casey's turn. Ike and Mike were temporarily boarding out at Steve Martin's, giving us a breather from demolition. So they were spared. Puss seemed immune. But Casey developed the same symptoms as Needra, his fever mounting quickly. Coping with him presented a problem, since he was now the size of a fat setter, stocky and very powerful. Dr. Dinnes had warned me to use great care with the syringe in giving the intramuscular shots of kanamycin, an antibiotic. There was danger of hitting a vein or breaking off the needle if the animal squirmed at the wrong time. I abandoned the idea of trying to sneak up on Casey and called for Noel or John or Jerry to hold him while I administered the shot. Even though the cub was weakened by fever, they had to struggle to keep him still enough for the injection. Fortunately, nothing went wrong. Needra was now recovering, and in four or five days lovable Casey was back to his old destructions.

That summer Noel continued his work as an agent, and one of his new clients was William Peter Blatty. Bill had given me the completed manuscript of *The Exorcist* and I had stayed awake until 4 A.M. reading it, finally arousing Noel to say, "This is one of the most engrossing stories I've ever read. You're crazy if you don't represent him." I was convinced that the demon book would be a best-seller and then a blockbuster movie.

The Exorcist would soon become intertwined with our hopes and plans to make the lion film. In addition to representing Bill Blatty and the novel, Noel became executive producer of the film that was to be made by Warner Brothers. By agreement, he would share 15 percent of any profits. With luck at the box office, those priests and demons would pay for a lot of big-cat cavorting.

Meanwhile, we went about the job of raising cubs, through demolition, sickness and health, and soon acquired another little lioness, Bridget, a quivering orphan. One of those unfortunate lions originally bought from a pet store, Bridget had been mistreated by her owners and was a very frightened, fidgety cub when we got her. She was transported to us locked up in the back of a panel truck, bouncing around in total darkness. I went wild when I saw her cowering back there. "Why didn't you put her up in the seat beside you?" I asked the driver.

He just shrugged. I can't comprehend people with so little sensitivity and understanding.

Bridget would run every time we came close to her. Fear and alarm in her eyes, she tensed whenever she saw a human. I quickly decided to have her around me as much as possible, indoors and out. So we now had a quintet in the shake-roof house, and one more was soon to be added.

One day Louanne Wells called to say that Trans, now little more than three months old, was absolutely incorrigible and would we please take him back. There went the cat love affair with Warner

Gene Trindle

Angry Trans
and Noel

Melanie and I with Neil, our first live-in lion

Neil ducking Melanie in
our Knobhill pool

The "African house" at Shambala

Tiger cubs

Noel and Casey

Time for dinner

Gregory and Natasha

Only one way out for Jerry

Lillian and Robbie, Jr., nose to nose

Kura and Timbo with a passenger

John observed

A friendly greeting

Tippi, canoe and Buster, too

Water sports

Tigon cub Noelle with tiger father, Nikki, and lioness mother, Debbie.

Noelle

Ike and Mike eyeing their next target

Brothers' president. Louanne cited wreckage and disaster in Trans's wake, and with an inward sigh I said, "Oh, sure, we'd love to have him back." We had never really had him, but I suspected that his performance in the Wellses' house hadn't been exaggerated. Little Trans had an I-dare-you look in face and posture. He could have taken a jailhouse apart. So that day he joined Casey, Needra, Bridget, Ike and Mike on Knobhill Drive.

About that same time, two of the lions, very likely Ike and Mike, stuck their heads simultaneously over the fence when our neighbor to the west was out in her backyard. Terrible timing. Disastrous timing. From what I could learn from the semihysterical woman, neither cub had threatened her in any way, nor did they attempt to jump over into her yard. They were, however, about the size of fully grown German shepherds. And there were these two big-eared tawny heads, with their curious amber eyes, peering over at her that October day. Unfortunately, it was the same woman who had called me when Neil serenaded the neighborhood with his roaring. Already suspicious, now she had actually seen lions.

Early the next morning the doorbell rang and Noel answered it, edging his head around to see who was there before ungodly 7 A.M.

It was a polite uniformed Animal Control officer from Los Angeles County.

"Sir, I heard you have some lions living here," he said.

Trying to figure a way out, Noel replied, "I don't have any clothes on. Excuse me, I'll get a robe."

He closed the door and ran downstairs to whisper to me, "Get Melanie up and get those cubs over the back fence, but leave Bridget." Noel had a nimble mind when faced with predicaments.

So I awakened Melanie and we pushed the quintet of cubs, boosting their rear ends, over the fence into the vacant lot next door for a morning walk. Still in our nightgowns, coats thrown on, we followed them over the fence. Any neighbors awake and looking in our direction would have been treated to some odd goings-on as five lions cavorted around the lot while two women stood nearby, shivering in the early-morning autumn chill.

In the meantime, Noel took tiny, jittery Bridget to the front door, holding her in two hands like a sacrificial offering. "Well, here you are," he said.

The young officer took one look at the spotted cub, clucked his tongue, said, "Forget it," and drove away.

But, of course, we were living on borrowed time on that urban hill and knew it. One afternoon about two weeks later I heard Partner barking. Resembling, in some ways, a brindle boxer, he was a strange-looking mutt. People would say, "Good grief, that's an ugly dog," but I adored him and he adored me. In my eyes he was gorgeous, not homely. Whatever his looks, Partner was smart, and that barking was to let me know Casey was out. Someone had left a door open, and there was Casey out in the street. I followed, closing the front door behind me, and I was halfway across the sidewalk when I thought, Oops, I need the lead. By this time, Casey weighed around 130–140 pounds, almost forty pounds more than I weighed. In a contest of strength, he would be the sure winner. I turned to go back into the house, but the front door was locked. I'd done that. When you live with lions, you learn to shut doors. The lead was in the kitchen. So I ran around the side of the house, through the gate, and up the stairs for the lead, wasting precious time.

To complicate matters, out in front was Ron Oxley's van with big Neil inside. Noel and Ron had gone to Van Nuys to have some papers notarized, leaving Neil behind in the van.

Back on the street, looking each way, I couldn't spot Casey. Heading downhill toward Beverly Glen, I hoped I'd made the right decision. It was five o'clock in the afternoon and traffic was picking up every minute. The danger was, always, that some heroic protector of all humanity, some he-man hunter, would see a cat loose and pick up his rifle.

Holding the lead, I ran as fast as I could and finally saw Casey. He was moving slowly but steadily down the center of the street, headed toward the intersection of Knobhill and Beverly Glen. I could also see the cars zipping along and knew that the chances of a real disaster down there mounted every second. Cars colliding! Heart attack for some elderly person! To those he might meet, Casey would not be considered a cub. He was approaching the size of a well-fed cougar.

Then I remembered a conversation with Ron Oxley. He had told me that big cats really pay attention to you if something about you has *changed* physically. *If you appear infirm, the big cat is apt to zero in on you.* His brain tells him: Something is wrong! Investigate! *This may be food.* It was that deep-seated genetic dictate of the Serengeti grass-lands, a message as old as the smilodon.

Yelling at Casey to stop, I immediately began limping to get his attention. He drew up and stared at me as I turned around, starting back to the house with an exaggerated limp. Hobbling my right leg along with a giant step, using my left leg as a scull, I looked ridiculous, I'm sure. Glancing back, I saw that he had started to follow me, creeping along, going almost down to his belly. I hoped that none of our neighbors was watching this scene: me limping up the street, followed by a creeping cat. But the strategy worked.

As soon as Casey closed on me, I started running for the house, then stopped by the van just as he was about to jump me. Throwing the lead around his neck, I tied him to the front bumper of Ron's van. Immediately, the van began lurching around. Neil knew something was going on outside and made ominous noises.

Then I heard the phone ringing in the house and impulsively ran inside. Doesn't everyone answer their phone? "Sorry," I told the caller, "I can't talk to you. My lion is out."

Just as I reached the front door to return to the van and Casey, the phone rang again. It was the same friend. "Tippi, there's nothing wrong with your line. I can hear you perfectly."

On a marvelous, crisp sunny morning two months later, now early January, I was gardening just outside the house, down on my knees, when I looked up and there was Bridget about ten feet from me, standing on the sidewalk. By now, she was five months old and correspondingly large.

"Hi, Bridget," I said nervously.

She came up to me, nuzzled my cheek, then trotted into the street and began loping away.

I had to make a quick decision whether to go back to the house for a lead or chase her. This time, I chose the latter. She ran for about thirty yards, past the driveway to Karen Valentine's property, then up a wooden stairway that led to a house on the hilltop, overlooking our street.

Taking the steps two at a time, I raced upward behind her, wondering what to do. She finally stopped in front of the hilltop house and I grabbed her by the tail. She was too big to pick up and I couldn't see myself dragging her all the way down the steps by the scruff of her neck. But I saw that there was a chain-link fence around part of the yard, and I yelled, "Help!" repeatedly, keeping a firm grip on Bridget's tail. In a moment, a lady came out of the house.

"I hate to bother you," I said, "but could I put my cat into your yard while I make a call?"

The lady looked a little startled but said, "Sure, I heard you had some cubs down there."

I called Emily Henderson from the house, and a few minutes later she brought a lead up the steps and we took Bridget home.

Time *was* running out for us on Knobhill Drive.

But I really didn't realize how much a part of my life the cats had become until one day a few weeks later when a good friend told me she had bought motorbikes for her two teenage sons. I hate motorbikes of any kind. They're noisy and dangerous. "How dare you do that?" I said to her. "You are literally going to kill your own children by giving them such destructive weapons."

My friend looked coolly at me for a moment and then replied, "Let's not even discuss it, Tippi. Here you are playing with lions and letting your kids play with them, and you're telling *me* that motorbikes are too dangerous for my boys."

—8—

SOLEDAD CANYON

One cannot forever keep six lions in a cluster of shake-roof houses, swimming pools, manicured gardens, Porsches and very civilized people. The final edict came January 14, 1972. The young Animal Control officer was again polite, but also firm. "Get them off this property within twenty-four hours."

I wept.

What possible harm were they causing? They were confined to our yard. Mostly. They weren't destroying neighbors' property. They didn't bark. They were only funny, feline babies, not old enough to be dangerous.

"The law says you cannot keep lions, little or big, within the city limits unless they're in a licensed zoo," said the officer, shaking a finger.

We called Steve Martin out in Soledad Canyon. He wasn't at all surprised. Yes, he'd gladly board them for us. Next day we took all six cubs to Martin's, and it was heartbreaking to watch them go into confinement. For the next week I went out to Soledad Canyon every day to take them for walks along the sandy path by the river.

Then I had to leave on a trip. Dr. Larry Ward, of the newly organized Food for the Hungry, Inc., an Evangelical antifamine group, had recruited me to help with fund-raising for Bangladesh. Starvation was rampant in that battle-torn former East Pakistan nation. With Ward and an airlift expert, I went there to help monitor some of the needs. Now based in Arizona, FFH also gives aid around the world after wars, floods, earthquakes and hurricanes.

Three weeks later, while I was in Dacca, Noel called to summon me home for a film, *The Harrad Experiment*, which he had packaged and was going to produce. But a surprise awaited me when I arrived on Knobhill, another of Noel's laid-back announcements of deeds done. "I bought Martin's acres out in the canyon while you were gone," he said, in the same tone of voice in which he might say, "I went down to buy a newspaper."

Though taken aback by the swiftness of the decision, I said something like "Well, that's great."

Noel had reasoned that it didn't make sense to pay boarding fees to Martin when we knew that the population of animals we hoped to collect for our film would double and triple over the coming months. He was correct. At the time, boarding a single lion cost $25 a day. But there was another reason for the purchase. "We'll use it for the movie location," Noel said.

There had always been a question in our minds as to where to film the picture. As far as I could see, Soledad Canyon wasn't it. "Noel, that's desert out there," I said. "That doesn't look like Africa."

"It will," he replied.

I'm sure I shook my head in doubt. That was river bottomland: sand and rocks and, so far as I can remember, no more than three trees on forty acres. It in no way resembled what I'd seen of lion country in Africa.

The jittery neighbor who summoned the polite Animal Control officer had forced us into a far-reaching decision. But we needed more than just land, and Noel said he was going to start work right away building high chain-link compounds for the projected fifty lions of the assembling cast. Our hope was that none would have to live in cages. We wanted them to have ample space to be lions and do their exercising and sleeping, marking and rubbing. Ron Oxley began making a model of the "Gorongosa house" from Noel's sketches. Noel had put on his "designer" hat. Within a matter of weeks construction of the compounds was well under way.

Boomer, who had frightened the BOAC people when he coveted their flight bag, came along with the acquisition of Martin's land. He was our first adult lion, and he was soon joined by others. Even before I returned from overseas, Noel had bought six more adult lions

from an overcrowded animal park: four males and two females—
Monte, Buddy, Scarface, Buggsy, Suzy and Jenny. They were all on
the ferocious side and had not been treated well. They had no reason
to like humans. We christened them the "Wild Bunch" and decided
to give them a cooling-off period by separating them gradually into
different groups, hoping to mellow them out. Daily contact with
humans was a must. Monte and Scarface turned out to be favorites
of mine.

But misfortune continued to track poor Bridget. Cruelty as an
infant, and then in April she had been thrown thirty feet out of a
truck that was involved in an accident on its way to the canyon.
Now, in early June, she faced the jaws of Jenny, the wildest of the
Wild Bunch females.

Bridget had seen the young lioness in a compound by the pond
and apparently swam over just to say hello. Cubs have a natural
fascination with elders, which can sometimes prove fatal. Jenny quickly
dug under the fence, which was not based in concrete at the time,
and attacked Bridget, her teeth piercing the cub's stomach. If a lioness
has not given birth to a cub, she may well try to kill it. If the cub
dies, she's likely to eat it. The world of the cub is fraught with danger.

Noel and I heard Bridget's terrified screams and ran toward the
commotion, arriving a few seconds too late to prevent injury. We
waded into the pond and lifted the cub out of the water, more dead
than alive. I held Bridget on my lap in a towel as we raced to San
Fernando Valley for emergency service and then took her to Marty
Dinnes, in town, for a three-and-a-half-hour operation.

We felt guilty. The near-fatal injury that Bridget had suffered
was not Jenny's fault; it was ours. We'd been careless, letting the
cub prowl around the compound near adults. Baffling as it may sound,
adult cats sometimes see the cubs as threats, encroaching on their
territories. Actually, no cub is safe in wandering away from its mother.
At times the cub isn't even safe with its own mother. She's apt to
kill it if she thinks it isn't healthy, or she may abandon it for any
number of reasons; the only one of them that humans might understand is lack of milk.

A day later, battered Bridget was back on Knobhill, animal reg-
ulations or not, and I found myself nursing a very sick little lioness.
Dr. Dinnes always felt that sick cats, desperately needing affection,
should be at home and not in his hospital. Two drains were in her
sliced-up stomach. Four times daily I drew the infection out, and
Bridget slowly recovered.

Trainer Frank Tom and Gilligan

In addition to building compounds, we had also begun to build a staff to take care of our growing population in the canyon, and one of its first members was stocky, personable Frank Tom, a Chinese-Mexican. Frank had a pet cougar that needed a home and thought he might as well come to work for us to be near his cat. He became an expert trainer and his talents with judo came in handy a number of times in the compounds. Another early staff member was tiny, mini-skirted Sylvia Loboda, who talked baby talk to the animals, even to the Wild Bunch. Sylvie had first come in contact with wild animals when she hired on with a circus down in Mexico. Unable to speak Spanish, she did not understand what was in store for her. She was placed with the elephants, and during her first performance a pachyderm took her head into its mouth and trotted around the ring. Though she screamed all the way, arms and legs flailing, ninety-eight-pound Sylvie nonetheless reported for her second performance and many thereafter. Her kind of courage was needed in the canyon.

Running a home for big cats requires more than handlers, however, and one of the first of the maintenance staff was tall, kindly Liberato Torres, from Guadalajara. The once-daily feeding also fell to

Liberato and his men. Becoming familiar with all the cats and highly sensitive to them, though not handling them, Liberato became expert in predicting, almost to the day and hour, when the lionesses would drop cubs.

There are also fences to be maintained, fourteen feet high, dug down three feet into the sand and footed in concrete after the Bridget incident. As the compounds expanded, eventually with more than a mile of chain link to be watched, Ben Sanchez became boss of a crew of five. For the sake of both cat and human types, no job is of greater importance than minding the fences.

Lion acquisition continued. We were adding to the pride in the canyon flats almost weekly. Togar and Alice arrived from the San Francisco Zoo, young adults in their prime, about five years apart in age. Big Togar, with a dark mane, was an outcast, too belligerent for the Bay City zookeepers to handle, though they didn't tell us that; they just wanted to get rid of him. He had originally been owned by someone involved in black magic, but for whatever reason he arrived rough, tough and defiant. His low, guttural rumble had enough power to quiver the cottonwood leaves, *and us.* I was afraid of Togar the moment I saw him, yet he turned out to be one of the best fathers

Jesus Torres and Liberato Torres with Siberians Nikki and Leika at feeding time

Will Oliver

Tough Togar in a moment of rage

in the compounds, gentle and playful with the thirty-odd cubs he
sired. Jenny, of the Wild Bunch, was his mate for eighteen of them.
Though she had almost killed Bridget, she was an excellent mother
to her own cubs.

Then Noel surprised me again. "We're getting a pair of tiger
cubs," he announced one night.

Once again I expressed some doubts. "You know as well as I do
there aren't any tigers in Africa," I said. "How do you plan to handle
that in the story?"

"I'm not sure," Noel replied.

The only place in the world where tigers and lions are found
naturally is the Gir Forest in India. The Asiatic lion is very rare, and
contact between the Bengal tiger, a loner like all of the species, and

the Gir Forest lion is probably just as rare. Nonetheless, Natasha and Ivan, six-week-old Siberians, soon arrived from the Okanagan Game Preserve in British Columbia.

For a period of several months after that, while the preserve was thinning its population, an annual event, we received fascinating calls from Canada: "Hey, we've got a couple of nice cubs to give away. You interested?"

I seldom recall Noel ever saying, "Well, we'll think about it," or just plain "No, thanks." We did, however, turn down a hippo.

Neither do I recall his hesitating ten seconds when the Okanagan people called to say, "We've got an African bull elephant named Timbo for sale."

An elephant in a film about a pride of lions? "What does an elephant have to do with that house in Gorongosa?" I asked Noel. "We didn't see any elephants near the house."

"It'll be good for authenticity," he replied. "I'll write some scenes in."

Of course, there is no end to authenticity in an African movie. We could add zebras, giraffes, wildebeests, antelopes, even warthogs.

I was happy, though, to make way for the little tigers. And to accommodate them in the film, Noel changed the script from the zoologist's study of a pride of lions to a study of all big cats under one roof. Movie scripts, I knew, are among the most flexible objects on earth; dramatic license stretches like pantyhose and is frequently just as transparent. But suddenly we were turning a nice little story about a pride of lions into a mammoth production with elephants and tigers.

Looking back, I can see we were rather offhanded about hoping to mix the giant felines, with cameras rolling, at some later date. Undoubtedly many scientists and trainers would have questioned the idea, especially for males. But we blithely went ahead, believing that the mixing of the breeds would succeed if they were slowly and carefully introduced. We were soon to discover, however, that the tiger and the lion are vastly different animals, both in behavior and especially in relation to humans. Even their heartbeat rates are different. The lazy lion's heart beats at about forty per minute, while the resting tiger's has been clocked at sixty-four per minute. Even sprawled out and half asleep the tiger is more edgy than the lion.

The animal we know today probably originated in present-day Manchuria during the Pliocene era and over millions of years became the huge northern tiger, the Siberian, then branched into the southern jungle tiger, the smaller Bengal. Because of the cold, the Siberians have longer, shaggier fur and their coloration is not as vivid as the tropical Bengal's. Both have been slaughtered for thousands of years, and some branches of the family, like the Caspians and the Balinese, are totally extinct. Rapacious man is the enemy, of course, tiger skins having sold in New York for as much as $4,000. Supposedly the Bengal still numbers several thousand, but the Siberian is rapidly becoming extinct, with an estimated three to four hundred still left in the wild. By the year 2000, it is predicted, the only Siberians alive will be in game preserves and zoos.

I settled Ivan and Natasha into residency on Knobhill, joining Bridget, who had almost recovered, physically, from her ordeal with Jenny. Naïvely, we reasoned that if they grew up together there would be little problem later on in sharing the same compounds. Bridget, at six months, began to endure the pestering of the tiger cubs, not yet two months old.

Beauty and the beholder aside, tiger cubs are more handsome than lion babies, in my opinion. Those stripes, clearly visible at birth, are a plus in the beauty contest. But the stripes only begin the marked differences between the two species. At first I was fooled when Ivan and Natasha followed me everywhere and wanted to be petted constantly, both lion-cub traits. They're exactly alike, I thought. Then I began to discover the dissimilarities. Anyone can pick up a lion cub and cuddle it. Not so with a tiger. Screaming, they let it be known they want all four feet firmly on the ground. If I was sleeping with a lion baby and moved, or rolled over, the little lion would make a warm sound and move closer. Ivan and Natasha protested with complaining cries. The adult tiger is notorious for being annoyed if rudely awakened, and a tiger cub a few weeks old will announce that it does not want to be disturbed.

As the tiger cub begins to grow, there is also a notable difference in the play of the two species. Play with a tiger cub can quickly escalate into combat. By a year old, the tiger cub cannot be controlled in play, and we learned not to spar with them. Their genetic dictate is to finish a fight. Their ears flatten back, the eyes become almost glazed, and they go into a fighting mode. At that point the wise human will end contact and walk away.

Yet, as tiny cubs, they make a heart-melting "ff-fuff, ff-fuff" sound, which is emitted through the nasal passage, and the happy adult tiger or tigress makes the identical sound, using it as an aloha, a hello, how are you, goodbye. It is always stunning to me when an animal which may measure twelve to thirteen feet, nose to tip of tail, and weigh six hundred pounds, gives off that gentle "ff-fuff, ff-fuff" sound while licking the back of your hand. But wisdom again dictates not offering fingers to that mouth. They are much too interesting.

As adults, tigers seem to be much more indifferent to people than are lions. They appear to truly like people but usually seem ready to say goodbye after a few minutes. I have sometimes thought that there are two different animals within the same body, the friendly one and the distant one that might be, on occasion, very unfriendly. I have looked into the eyes of a tiger and wondered which animal is at home that day. "As uncertain as a tiger" is an Asian saying that is very true.

One thing, however, was very certain. Ivan and Natasha quickly proved to be better at demolition than the lion cubs, about twice as rambunctious, and to quiet them down I tried turning on TV. It seemed to work, especially with Natasha. She would walk over to the set and stick her nose up against it, something I had never seen my lion cubs do. Or she might curl up on the couch or the king-size bed to watch the tube. But her attention span was usually short.

Rather than a semipermanent home, the house on Knobhill was now becoming a regular way station for cats en route to Soledad Canyon. For instance, in early August, 1972, we acquired Bacchus, a giveaway lion cub, and he joined us for the usual period of association with humans before transfer to the country. In the long run, we felt, nothing was more important than this day-and-night communication. Aghast, friends said, "You mean you let them sleep with you?"

"I make absolutely sure they do," I replied.

The other question that seemed to concern my friends the most was potty training. "Do you train them not to do it in the house?" they asked.

"No, I don't" was my answer. I didn't want to alter their psyches. "I feed them four times a day and put them outside after each feeding and after sleep time."

Bridget was back in the compounds, and I had sent Ivan and Natasha out to the canyon to continue mingling with the little lions, so Bacchus had the house to himself for a short while. After the January problem with Animal Control, we were circumspect about keeping down the population on Knobhill. However, I didn't hesitate

Driving to town

to scoop up several cubs and bring them back to town for a few days' stay. Still schooling myself, I was commuting daily between Sherman Oaks and the new home of the cats.

Keeping wild animals in Soledad Canyon was—and is—entirely legal with the required permits. The county regulation people inspected every so often, always unannounced, to see that strict sanitation and security rules were being observed and that the animals weren't mistreated. There were minimum-space requirements for each cat. Food was carefully checked, and even the freezers were inspected. The painted, rainproof "dens," or animal houses, were checked to see that the straw bedding was recent. So every aspect of running a private zoo in California was carefully administered, and most human problems were eliminated by the remoteness of the area. No neighbors complained, because none was close. But I drove out early the morning of August 18 to be told that Ivan and Natasha had been stolen the previous night. Steve Martin had painstakingly searched the grounds, finding no trace of the babies.

I immediately began calling the airlines to see if anyone was shipping, or had shipped, a pair of tiger cubs. Then we began questioning all of the help, a crew of six at the time. One young man hadn't come to work that day, so he was immediately suspect. Next day, I got an anonymous call. "There are some cubs over here in a silo," a voice said. And as soon as the caller provided the location, we went over to an abandoned farm and plucked the nervous cats out of the silo. They were okay. We soon learned that the young thief had had too much beer and had put the cubs into his truck to have some fun showing them off. When the night was over, he decided it had been a bad idea, and, afraid to bring the cubs back, he abandoned them.

Until that incident, we had never thought of anyone taking the animals. The idea of someone invading a lion and tiger preserve, climbing fences, risking confrontation with a Togar, was not credible. Yet, later on, a large cub, Nancy, was stolen, obviously an outside job.

Three more cubs arrived at Knobhill before the end of September. Peaches, Cherries and Berries, "the Fruit Salad," were excess from the Texas Animal Preserve, courtesy of Marty Dinnes. Each about four months old, they were robust and full of mischief. Berries was the male of the group and the least rowdy. Had I known Cherries would attempt to maim me in another three years, I would have sent her packing. At the time, she was interested only in wholesome frolic.

One afternoon I came back from the canyon to view the wreckage of a cat tornado. Emily had been running the vacuum on the upper level and hadn't heard what was going on downstairs. I found the Texas trio pulling our king-size mattress out of the sliding door to the patio. The cover had been ripped off and the foam mattress looked like Swiss cheese, holes in it as large as dinner plates. They had also had a tug of war with the bedroom drapes, which were ripped out of the traverse rods and were hanging at half mast. The cats ran pellmell when I screamed at them. Then I stood there, tears of frustration running down my face, swearing I wanted nothing more to do with them, with *Lions, Lions and More Lions*, and especially with my crazy husband.

Emily came down, put her arms around me and said, "Don't cry, those little lions are going to pay you back." Pulling myself back together, I could only hope her remark was true.

Mattress replaced, traverse rod and drapes repaired, in another two weeks I was at Western Airlines picking up two more orphan cubs from the Okanagan Preserve. About seven inches high, they were in a flight cage. Cookie, a lion cub, was at the front of the cage, snarling and striking out at me with her paw. Tiny Igor, a tiger, half brother to Ivan and Natasha, was at the back of the cage, saying "ff-fuff, ff-fuff," the happy contented sound of the Siberian. Whatever the future held in store, it was impossible for me to resist them.

Igor had the funniest personality of any little tiger I've ever met. He loved to attack the water sprinklers in the canyon, which went all day and night during the spring and summer to nourish new greenery around the compounds. First I saw Igor crouching, in attack stance, behind a clump of grass; then I saw him move over behind a rock. I couldn't figure out what he was beading on. It was the profile of the tiger going after prey, yet no other animal was in sight. Then, finally, he jumped over a log and landed on top of the sprinkler. Putting his face into the water, batting it with his paw, getting soaked each time, he attacked the sprinklers for months, meanwhile growing larger and larger and larger.

We had about twenty-five cats, youngsters and adults, residing in the canyon when Timbo, ten thousand pounds of bull elephant, arrived. I took one look at him and decided I wanted to be his close friend. At the same time, simply because of his mass, I was apprehensive. When he came off the trailer-truck rig, walking down a ramp, he seemed to hide the sun. We hadn't acquired a small or even a medium-sized elephant for background in the film. This one was a colossus. Captured in Africa at the age of about six months, he was first taken to the Frankfurt Zoo. From Germany he went to New York, where he was acquired by a Canadian animal park. Though he knew a few tricks, he had never performed in circuses. A barn had been constructed at the west end of the property to serve as Timbo's new home. Beyond it he could walk along the riverbank for several miles and then come back for the all-important daily bath in the pond. Steve Martin took on the trainer's job. Not having handled elephants previously, he wanted the experience. Pachyderms respond to one person and usually ignore the commands of all others.

Work was soon to begin on the construction of the two-story, boxy mock-African scientist's house, a replica of the abandoned house Noel and I had seen in Gorongosa. Noel had designed the house, and Ron Oxley had long ago completed the model. But this house would have to be much more substantial than the usual movie set. It would have to withstand the movement of up to fifty big cats, up and down the steps and throughout a half-dozen rooms that would be used to film interiors. That meant upward of twenty thousand pounds of romping lions and tigers. When Liberato and the others set about building the house, Steve Martin sank fourteen telephone poles into the sand to support it.

As much as the gathering of the animals in the compounds,

Timbo arrives in Soledad Canyon.

construction of that house meant to me that we were really on our way to the making of our film. But the animal park was still a meager place. Aside from the compounds, there were only a few other small buildings for tools and food-handling, Timbo's barn and Martin's house trailer. Even so, I could now easily visualize what would some-day be on these acres: a very special motion picture studio for wild-animal features and TV films, complete with modern sound stages, editing rooms, a commissary, even apartments for the human casts.

A slow transformation had begun, turning the desert land into an oasis. Noel had begun to plant cottonwoods and bushes of the type we'd seen in Mozambique. Certain areas were being sodded. He had plans to further dam the little pond and turn it into a lake. The barren Soledad acres were beginning, just beginning, to look a little bit like Africa.

—9—

BILLY

Romance between lions is noisy and seemingly violent. Hisses, snarls and roars accompany the dust-raising sexual act. To begin the mating, the lioness usually teases the male, often flipping her tail tuft under his nose to make sure he has a whiff of her scent, then noisily ambles away. She may taunt him by rolling on her back or sliding totally beneath him in a snakelike maneuver. As the male begins his court-ship role, following the lioness around, attempting to caress her, he is often spat upon and sometimes cuffed repeatedly in the jaw. No other lovemaking I've ever heard about is comparable in the amount of verbal and physical abuse endured by the male lion. The angry-looking prelude may last five minutes or more until the female signals she is ready by crouching down. Even then she makes low, growling, hostile noises as the male grabs the loose scruff of her neck with his teeth, but never lethally. The act is over in a matter of seconds but will likely be resumed ten or fifteen minutes later. A dozen encounters may occur during the day. With the gestation period usually between 105 and 113 days, anywhere from one to five cubs may result. Big cats can breed at the age of two but don't reach their prime until four or more.

Togar and Alice, those two wayward black-magic lions from the San Francisco Zoo, mated in mid-August with all the necessary verbal

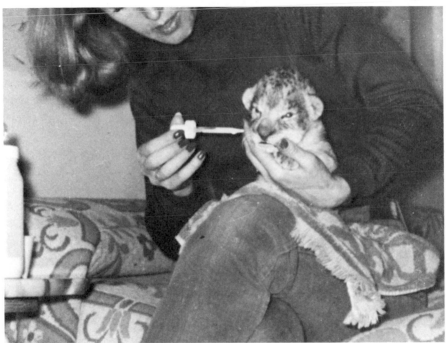

Trying to feed five-day-old Billy

fireworks, and on Thanksgiving Day, 1972, Alice gave birth to a single cub, which we promptly named Billy, after Bill Blatty. There was extra cause for celebration that gray Turkey Day because Billy was the first cub born in the compounds of Soledad Canyon. He appeared to be in fine health. But, inexplicably, five days later Alice abandoned her baby. Jumping up to the top of her den house, she sprawled out and stubbornly ignored little Billy.

A lioness will often reject her cub if she thinks something is wrong with it or if she can't feed it. In the wild she won't hesitate to destroy it. Even in zoos, cubs have been killed by mothers who seem to have an innate sense of abnormalities. Since Billy appeared healthy, we concluded that Alice lacked the milk to feed him. But there was no way to determine that possibility without sedating her. We didn't have the relationship with Alice necessary for a hand check of her belly. I doubt any human could have touched her teats while she was conscious.

Perhaps her problem had nothing to do with milk; perhaps she simply got it into her mind that she wanted nothing to do with her cub. Whatever her reasons, she remained on the roof, staring off into the distance, implacable, unapproachable. Alarmed, I began to wonder about the maternal instincts of the big cats.

The lung capacity of a cub is amazing. Billy could be heard all over the bottomland yelling for his mother, demanding her warm body, her nipples and the caressing of her tongue. They were high-pitched cries that could not be denied. Spotted head moving around jerkily, eyes still tightly closed, he looked pitiful.

Liberato Torres, who had watched as Alice's belly grew large during pregnancy, said, "We have to help that cub."

Hearing all that noise, I readily agreed.

There was a good possibility Alice might harm the cub if he kept up the squawling, so in early afternoon I removed Billy from the compound without the slightest reproving glance from his mother. Alice didn't even look at me. Apparently, she couldn't have cared less as I eased out through the high gate, backing up, keeping my eyes on her, knowing she might change her mind and come roaring down on me.

Within ten minutes I was attempting to bottle-feed Billy, but he refused the nipple and continued to scream. I'd never been near a five-day-old cub. In a panic, I called Dr. Dinnes. Soon, wobbling around on the front seat beside me, still wailing, the little lion went off to the hospital. But Marty Dinnes had no more luck with a bottle than I'd had. Finally he said, "We'll have to tube-feed him."

Marty took a long, flexible rubber tube and measured the length of the cub from his mouth to the arch of his back at the rib cage, then marked the tube with a piece of tape to indicate how far the insertion should penetrate. After he had cut the tube to the appropriate length, he said, "Now we'll have to be very careful, because if we hit the windpipe on insertion and get any fluid whatsoever in there, he'll come down with pneumonia in less than an hour. There's no way to treat it."

As I watched Marty insert the tube into that tiny body, I realized I'd have to repeat this maneuver at home. I stood there, telling myself to be calm. Marty made it look easy. In a moment, he had fed Billy two or three ounces of formula.

I took the handful of spotted-head, petal-eared cub back to Knob-hill and began feeding him every two hours around the clock, setting the alarm during the night. Just as I'd been frightened every time I gave Needra a shot, my hand invariably shook every time I stuck that tube down Billy's throat, scared to death that I'd get fluid into his windpipe. He was so tiny, a little more than a foot long. A human baby seems enormous by comparison. I gave him Esbalic, ordinary puppy formula, adding it to distilled water and increasing it a small amount with each feeding. Then I switched to KMR, or Kitty Milk Replacer. I was in a whole new world having nothing to do with sound stages or cameras or acting. Conquering my fear of that tube, however, was an award-winning performance.

Finally, after three days of anxiety, I managed to put Billy on a plastic bottle fitted with a preemie nipple, and he started nursing contentedly. What a relief when I could lay aside that tube. Still, I had to watch him carefully. He slept on my pillow or snuggled along my side each night, needing constant reassurance. He made that "aa-aow" sound, the "Where are you?" sound, as if I weren't right there. Fortunately, the five days he had nursed from contrary Alice provided the colostrum necessary to protect him from most cub illnesses.

But by now I was an old hand at bottle-feeding cubs. That nip in the breast at Riverside had prompted me to find out the proper way of being a substitute mother. Quite simply you place the cub *belly down* on your lap, head toward your knees, hold the bottle horizontally and find the little mouth with the nipple. Lion cubs like to be snuggled while feeding, even in that odd position, so the other hand is placed along the baby's side.

After two days on the bottle, Billy opened his eyes to see what the world was all about. They were blue and beautiful, though they would not really focus for a week or so. When at last he could focus I was the first person imprinted on him, an event that was to have future consequences. As soon as he began to track with his eyes, he often sought out my thumb as a substitute nipple. His little tongue was already rough. The tongue of an adult lion, used to clean meat off bones as well as accomplish grooming, is like a rasp. Yet great-maned lions the size of Togar unashamedly seek out the thumbs of human friends, licking them raw.

By the time Billy was three weeks old he had gained three pounds and was relatively steady on his paws. He was also becoming very affectionate. He'd stand up and put his paws on my leg while I prepared his bottle, watching me closely as I worked. He was also becoming very playful. Before taking the bottle, he'd refuse it four or five times, batting it away; then he'd grab it with both paws and suck mightily. When he finished nursing on my lap I'd burp him over my shoulder; then he'd soon drop off to sleep. There is no doubt in my mind that the first imprint, on focusing, strengthened steadily in those early weeks. So far as Billy was concerned, *I was his mother.* Alice might as well have been in Mozambique.

For almost two months I took Billy everywhere I went, nestled down in a square picnic basket. Meetings, interviews, visits with friends, even to the supermarket. It was much easier than trying to find a cat-oriented baby-sitter. Melanie was in school or involved in a whole range of teenage activities. Besides, I enjoyed having the cub along.

One day I went to a posh restaurant with Billy hidden under the top of the basket. The tuxedoed maître d' asked, "What do you have in there, Miss Hedren?"

Shrugging, I replied, "A lion."

He gave me a skeptical "Hah-hah-hah-hah" and escorted me to the table. On the way out, I thanked him for a lovely lunch and opened the lid of the basket to expose the sleeping contents.

One of the things I noticed about Billy that was different from Needra and the other cubs I'd raised was his need to be with me all

Billy in his picnic basket

Will Oliver

the time. Quite possibly, this need developed because he was the only cub in residence at the time. He sought me out and followed me from room to room. Whenever I was sitting down he'd jump up and rub his face gently against mine, which is the way lions greet each other. It is certainly a sign of affection between big cats and I also think it is another way of marking and staking out territory. Quite by instinct, I was being marked.

It soon occurred to me that the cub "loved" me, and I loved him, too. But, already thinking of the not-too-distant future when he'd weigh a quarter of a ton, I began to teach him the meaning of a firm "No!" and "Leave it!" He went through the same rambunctious stage that all cubs go through—attacking pillows, bedspreads, Jerry's tennis shoes left under a couch, plants or the fringe on a tablecloth. He was no more nor less a one-cat demolition team than the others had been. But in time I would discover that there was something decidedly different about Billy.

Lynn Gertenbach

Billy at six months

—10—
RAIN

Winter in southern California, something of a joke to those who live in ice-and-snow climates, usually begins in November and lasts through mid-March, with Los Angeles temperatures dipping to the low forties. But as you leave the Los Angeles Basin and go up into the nearby mountains, the thermometer can plunge rapidly. In Soledad Canyon, temperatures often fell to the low thirties or even into the twenties during our "winter." The cottonwoods were bare and the river bottom had a back-East look to it on gray days. But there were always many more shirtsleeve days, and the animals suffered little from the cold. The Siberian tigers loved it; the lions did not. Extra shelter was provided for the adult lions, and the cubs were always taken indoors on chill nights.

Winter is the season of much-needed rain, in gentle portions, but few years are ever the same. It seems we have either deluge or drought. Gentle rains seldom visit off the Pacific. Winter, 1973, was one of those dreaded downpour seasons, and the heavy rain made for uneasiness in Soledad Canyon. Four years previously Ralph Helfer's Little Africa, about a mile west of us, had been destroyed when the Santa Clara turned the valley into a millrace. We'd heard stories from Helfer about some of the animals drowning, some running loose. Down in the canyon, flood is a frightening thing.

During that winter, Noel was working on *The Exorcist* as executive producer, and, because filming was to begin in a short while, he was more occupied with that project than with our lion and tiger population. It was growing at the rate of two or three a month, although we were still short of the goal for our film pride. I remember that the year started off with big, funny Lurch, the largest lion I'd ever seen, moving in. Lions are always topheavy due to the weight of their heads and manes. The heads alone weigh approximately eighty pounds. Occasionally, lions will stand up on their hind paws when they fight, but it is only for seconds simply because they cannot support their massive upper bodies. Lurch's body seemed dwarfed by his head, and I laughed almost every time I looked at him. Gray rather than brown and beige, with wise old eyes, he was a Solomon of lions.

Dark clouds or sparkling sunshine over the San Gabriels, most days I couldn't wait to make the hour's drive from Knobhill to Soledad Canyon. Something was always happening around the compounds, and I was drawn to the animals even when I didn't have a specific errand. Sometimes there would be a roaring session under way when I stepped out of the car, the chorus of basses and baritones rolling along the riverbank. I was content just to be around them, to talk to them, touch them. I would stand for half an hour just watching them.

To many observers big cats look exactly alike—all lions as lions, all tigers as tigers and all leopards as leopards. But each has its own unique characteristics, Lurch in size alone. Their faces are different. One lion might have a long nose, another huge eyes; still others a scar, a torn ear, slightly different mane coloration, or a broken tooth. Some have bowed legs or very short ones. Cindi, the former circus girl, had that badly crippled leg. Each animal was easily recognizable to me, and most knew their own names but didn't always respond. Or the responses might be no more than a tail flick or the twitch of an ear. I learned to read that sort of signal as "Yes, I hear you, but don't bother me just now." Lurch was an ear-twitcher. Others exercised their rights as the kings and queens of beasts and ignored me. I didn't mind. When they did respond, I felt privileged.

One sunny, crisp day in the middle of January, I drove out to the canyon just past dawn and there was nine-foot, five-ton Timbo running with glee, unchained, flapping his ears, trumpeting, thudding along the sand. So that day began with the sight of an African elephant having fun, his trumpeting an obbligato to the roaring of the lions. Before noon Steve Martin's pea-brained peacock Quintes-

Lurch

Brutus

Clockwise: Lurch with his massive head, Brutus of the square face, wide-faced Nero, thin-faced Berries, Frankie with his long nose, and black-tufted Johnny. And some people think all lions look alike.

Johnny

Nero

Berries

Frankie

91

sence was caught by Mike lion, and those gorgeous feathers were in danger of being permanently removed. But we rescued the bird and took it to a trailer camp up the road where it could exist witlessly away from lion and tiger paws. Every day something different happened. Every day was rewarding. I always felt as if the city were a thousand miles away. Most days I had no desire to return to Knobhill.

Of course the cubs were always a special joy, though the first two we'd begun to raise, Casey and Needra, were no longer cubs in terms of size. Casey was approaching his second birthday and weighed almost three hundred pounds. He was, however, a comparative teenager and had only recently begun to grow his mane. Little tufts of black hair were poking up here and there around his neck, like black seedlings on brown earth. There was a funny topknot on his head, his whiskers were beginning to lengthen and hair was beginning to grow out of his spongy chin. He looked completely ridiculous.

Mary Ellen Mark

Casey, approaching two, sprouting whiskers and a mane

I had continued to keep Billy at home, but by early February he was going on three months old, and I began taking him out to Soledad for play sessions with the other cubs. It was time for him to be aware that his own kind existed on earth, along with us humans. Immediately he became great pals with Igor, the tiger cub. They pounced on each other, growled and snarled. They would play awhile and sleep awhile, then I would take Billy or perhaps both of them back to Knobhill. I couldn't help wondering how it would be three years hence when both were fully grown. Would the Siberian turn to the aloof and lonely ways of the wild?

A few days later heavy rains began to fall after three dry weeks. Two frontal systems were out in the ocean, and the weatherman predicted a severe storm. By nightfall of another day, the Santa Clara had risen about a foot and was looking gray and ugly, widening every hour. We stayed out at the canyon.

Next morning the river was threatening to come over its normal banks and we began making calls to have cattle trucks available in case we had to move the animals. By now we were part of the big-cat network, a loose, informal web of aficionados numbering in the twenties, and friends came out from town to help in the event we had to evacuate. Gardner McKay drove out at a moment's notice. The former actor, now a writer, had owned a pair of lions plus two cheetahs and often visited the canyon.

About noon, we shifted some of the animals to higher ground and kept close watch on the churning water. But fortunately the rain stopped in early evening and the forecast was for clearing weather. The flood threat, which occurred almost on the first anniversary of our buying the bottomland, was over. But the sight of that frothing gray-white water and the idea of loading big cats into cattle cars, especially if it had to be done at night, was sobering. Though we knew that Little Africa had been wiped out by this usually timid river, we simply hadn't thought too much about it. What we had seen now made a lasting impression.

Aside from the usual animal vocalization, all that lion and tiger talk, everything was quiet and serene down in our canyon until mid-April, when Timbo decided to knock a wall out of the barn with his trunk. We thought that the walls were sturdy enough in the new barn, but they proved to be little match for his determined swats.

Timbo strikes a playful pose.

Timbo was probably bored, in Steve Martin's opinion. Circus elephants often sway their trunks and bob their heads to keep up circulation and ward off boredom. Timbo did very little bobbing and had enough daily exercise to keep up circulation. The thing to do, Noel said, was to find him a companion.

Life assuredly went on in places other than Soledad. One of Melanie's friends arranged a movie audition at Warner Brothers, and Melanie came home one late afternoon to say that an executive wanted her to read for director Arthur Penn. I knew that Penn did not normally "read" any actor or actress unless he was really interested.

"That's nice," I said, "but don't get your hopes up too high." Mother was being Mother.

The next Thursday I received a call: "Tippi, we want your daughter to start work Monday." The picture was *Night Moves*. Melanie's part was that of a sex kitten, a Lolita role.

"Well, that's great," I said hollowly.

I had very mixed feelings. Melanie was then a precocious fifteen, in both mind and body, and coping with lions and elephants somehow seemed to be easier, in many ways, than coping with the daughter I adored.

—11—

PHARAOH

We had been fascinated by the five cheetahs that belonged to Ozzie Bristow in Africa, so when we learned, via the big-cat network, that a cheetah was available down in San Diego, Noel and I didn't hesitate to make an offer. We had already expanded the film to include tigers. Why not cheetahs?

Fastest land animal on earth, able to accelerate to forty-five miles per hour in just two seconds, with bounds that measure twenty-five feet, the elegant, dignified cheetahs are so different from lions and tigers that I sometimes wonder if they really belong in the same family. Of all the big cats, I think cheetahs are the most uncatlike. Their faces, with the horseshoe black lines, called "tears," running from the eyes to the mouth, also angling back from the eye corners, are so distinctive that they appear to have been made up. The name of the animal comes from the Hindu word *chita*, which means spotted one.

Cheetahs prowled the Pleistocene forests before the lion or the tiger and, led by leash, wearing falcon-type hoods, later served sultans and maharajahs in royal hunts for more than three thousand years. The ability to be tamed and that flashing speed of up to seventy-five miles an hour were what attracted royalty, I'd guess. Never abundant, they are now almost extinct except for game preserves and private owners.

The only big cat with nonretractable claws, except for the dew-claw, the innermost claw a few inches above the base of the paw, hidden in a carpet of fur, the cheetah usually trips gazelles or impalas with its front paws and then swiftly bites into the jugular vein, the dewclaw digging into the prey's hide, holding it. An often solitary animal in the wild, cheetahs never feed on carrion. In domesticity they eat a variety of food, much of it the kind that humans eat.

Five-year-old Pharaoh, at 120 pounds, was large for the breed, the even larger rex, or king, cheetah being extinct. He was virtually a prisoner in San Diego, we learned, seldom seeing his two owners before seven or eight o'clock at night, on their return from work. Although they took him out on weekends for long walks, he spent most of his time in a harness to which a chain was attached. About twenty feet of pacing room was his lot during the average day.

After we picked him up that Easter Sunday, perfectly behaved, sleek-coated Pharaoh rode north with us in the back seat of the station wagon, his head moving from side to side as he watched heavy traffic, seemingly fascinated by it. If we passed a truck, he would turn and look at the rumbling vehicle. Not once did he go to sleep during the almost three-hour drive. I sensed we had a very different animal in Pharaoh.

As soon as we arrived at Knobhill, I said to Noel, "Get the wire cutters." In a moment we had snipped the harness and the small padlock, and, as Casey had reacted the year before on being freed, Pharaoh let out a sound that resembled a big "Ohhhhh." Relief at last. No more shackles. No more pacing on the wire.

I walked him around the house, showing him where the four sliding glass doors were located if he wanted to go out. I took him over by the pool. Peering at it too closely, he slipped over the edge and fell in. Even with all that ancient inbred agility he'd done a stupid thing, and he was obviously embarrassed, shaking himself, not once looking at me. Soaked, he appeared to be incredibly thin. With long, slim legs and a tiny waist, a cheetah tends to look awkward when standing still. The long spine dips, giving a slightly swayback profile. On the chase, however, cheetahs are anything but awkward.

My relationship with Pharaoh began on a jarring note. That night he sprawled out on the king-size bed, and I went over to him, sat down and began to part the fur of his leg to take a peek at that dewclaw hidden in the straw-colored coat. In return, I got a karate chop across my face, the razor-sharp dewclaw etching a bloody fur-row over my right cheek. I still have a hairline scar. Obviously, I'd become too friendly too quickly, a lesson many big cats will teach in a physical way. No cat, big or small, likes to have its claws touched or its tail pulled.

The first thing I began to learn about Pharaoh was his vocabulary, always a good place to start with a new cat. Cheetahs do not roar or make the "ff-fuff" sounds of the tiger, and I'm convinced that each cheetah has certain sounds that are unique to that animal alone—a voice print similar to that of individual humans. I quickly learned to recognize Pharaoh's "happy" sound, which was a distinct chirp, and his "hungry" sound, which was a throaty vibration. And infrequently, but most importantly, his warning sound, a high two-pitched hum. Coupled with body tenseness, it said, "Stay away!" But I never felt threatened by him except at those times when he clearly warned me to feel that way.

Many nights he flopped his 120 pounds down on the bed, demanding space for slumber. We never refused. I often found myself hanging on the edge, wondering why I was letting him take command. His purring sound was so loud that it would occasionally awaken us from deep sleep.

To my surprise, he ate a variety of uncatlike things—cottage cheese, hard-boiled eggs, fish and other food that most big cats would find uninteresting. Of course, he also ate Zu/Preem, chicken and raw meat. In the first few days he would stop eating if I went near him. He would begin that two-pitched warning hum and I would back off. But after a week or so he realized I was not threatening his food supply and would ignore me. Eventually, I could feed him out of my hand—careful to keep my palm flat.

Generally I would close the sliding doors to keep him out of the house when we had dinner, because his head was on the same level as the dining-room table and he made no pretense of not coveting whatever was on the menu. My admonition of "Stay away, Pharaoh," was meaningless to him. The first time robbery took place was when we'd sat down to a fine dinner of linguini and clams. I had no idea cheetahs would be attracted to pasta, but Pharaoh eyed us from the couch for a few minutes, then gracefully walked to the table and cleaned off my plate in one mouthful. Everyone else escaped, food held overhead, to the kitchen, shutting the door behind them.

No cubs were residing on Knobhill at the time and it was soon evident that Pharaoh was no threat to Melanie's white Alimese. In fact, it was the other way around. If Puss was sitting on the washing machine, a favorite perch, and Pharaoh happened to pass close by, he would usually get several taps on the head. I never saw Pharaoh go after the house cat, but he would look at Puss as if to say, "Don't stretch your luck, kid." His relationship with Partner was another matter. The dog thought he should protect me from this supersized cat, and I had to send Partner to Soledad Canyon for a while, simply to prevent bloodshed.

I soon took Pharaoh out there, too, wondering whether or not he might like to live with the other big cats as neighbors. One thing I knew he missed was daily grooming. There was no cheetah around to groom Pharaoh, and I found that he would purr loudly if I tried to substitute. After he washed my hands with his tongue, I would run them over his face and around his eyes. Grooming was not possible for me to solve, but visual companionship could be provided in the canyon, nearness to the other cats.

That, I discovered, was the last thing he wanted. He appeared frightened at the sight of the lions and tigers. His eyes grew wide and he shook visibly when a roaring session began. Pharaoh unquestionably preferred Knobhill. He was not equipped to handle even the sights and sounds of the wild. We decided that if we did use him in the film, it would have to be in a scene in which no other big cats could participate.

So it was back to Knobhill, and, realizing his human orientation, I began to take Pharaoh many places. He loved to ride in cars. If he saw keys in my hand he would automatically stride for the door. He usually sat erect in the back seat of the Cadillac, foreleg on an armrest, a thing of regal, black-spotted beauty, surveying the countryside, checking out the traffic.

Other facets of his personality were also unusual, I thought. Pharaoh endlessly studied objects and bric-a-brac around the house—kitchen appliances, clock in the bedroom, objets d'art in the living room. No other big cat had ever paid attention to such trappings except to destroy them. Curious to know how he would react in another setting, I phoned a friend who owns a dress shop in nearby Sherman Oaks, asking if customers were present. Only a few, she said. Then I asked if I could bring my cheetah over. She gave a hesitant yes. Looking at the dresses and the costume jewelry with the same curiosity he displayed at home, Pharaoh padded slowly around the store, eyes narrowed.

A few days later I called the California Jewelsmith, in Beverly Hills, asking if I might bring Pharaoh along. He would match the shop in elegance, I pointed out. The owners agreed and we stayed in the store for almost an hour, Pharaoh walking slowly by the counters, looking intently at watches and glittering bracelets, at diamonds, emeralds and golden chains. He seemed to enjoy himself immensely, at times appearing to be at the point of purchase. Was this really a jungle beast?

In the wild, cheetahs do spend a lot of time in observance, seeking out high elevations—dirt mounds, rock piles, boulders—there to view the surrounding countryside for prey. Some lions and tigers run for the pure fun of it, but adult cheetahs walk. The only time they run is for the kill. Either they walk slowly and gracefully or they sit. Sometimes they'll lie in that classic cheetah pose, forelegs out, head turned to one side, a pose that delights high-fashion photographers. The behavioral pattern of observing for prey extends to captivity, and Pharaoh soon found a favorite spot on which to perch, the top of a four-foot-high wooden cabinet on our second-story terrace, and look out over the valley. Not requiring the sleep of a lion or a tiger, he would spend as much as an hour in solitude, just gazing out. I sometimes asked him, "What are you thinking about?" As he purred loudly, his eyes would shift, linger on me, then go back to the survey. A cheetah does not have good night vision, yet Pharaoh would watch the lights of San Fernando Valley almost every evening.

Despite being a loner, there were times when he would stay very close to me, touching me with his body. At times he would join us during the cocktail hour when we had guests, throw himself down in the center of the room, stay about fifteen minutes, then disappear, his attitude being pretty close to "I've graced you with my presence. Now I have other things to do." He could usually be found up on his perch, in meditative solitude.

Always when I returned home, the first thing I did was look for whatever animals were in residence—lion, tiger, cheetah—give them a hug, say hello, ask how their day had gone. On one afternoon in late May, on returning home after an absence of three or four hours, I looked for Pharaoh. He was not to be found. None of the kids was home and it wasn't Emily's day to work, so there was no one to tell me of the cheetah's whereabouts. I searched every room and out in the garden and pool area; I went into the street, looking both ways. No Pharaoh.

I called the pound in nearby Van Nuys. No Pharaoh. Then I called several neighbors and one said, "Well, we saw him going down the street about a half hour ago. Just walking along. We tried to call you—"

"Which way?"

My great pal Pharaoh

"Down toward Valley Vista."

Why did these things always seem to happen at rush hour? It was then about four-thirty, and I grabbed a lead and took off down Knobhill in the car, feeling a mixture of exasperation and alarm, a not uncommon reaction when one lives with big cats. Going slowly, calling Pharaoh's name, I looked into every yard. Then I drove around the hairpin curve and on down the hill, going back and forth along Valley Vista, getting more anxious by the minute. Traffic was building rapidly, and so was my desperation. Pharaoh might have been hit by a car—or shot.

Returning home after an hour's searching, I again telephoned the pound. This time there was an affirmative. Animal Control had Pharaoh in custody. There'd been a call to police to report a "wild cat" sitting in a vacant lot at the busy corner of Valley Vista and Van Nuys Boulevard. Two patrol cars had answered the emergency, officers alighting with guns drawn. Then one of them said, "Hey, look at the collar. That's not a wild cat, don't shoot."

Of course, I knew exactly what Pharaoh had been doing—watching all the sights along Valley Vista, having a great time.

He stayed in jail overnight.

—12—

A DAY AT
THE VET'S

Of the big cats, leopards, jaguars and cougars are the expert tree climbers and are as much at home in the limbs and the foliage as they are on the ground. Adult lions and tigers know they are ill-equipped and clumsy in the branches, not good at climbing, so they wisely stay close to the ground. A few bold ones may leap up four or five feet and sprawl out on a huge low limb. They are the exceptions. But the young, frisky lion or tiger, not knowing its limitations, will often try to conquer a tree. Fun-loving tiger Igor did just that, at about the age of fourteen months, and came crashing down, badly breaking his left shoulder.

Middle son John helped me lift Igor, who was larger than a big German shepherd and probably weighed 140 pounds, into the back seat of the car. In great pain, he whimpered all the way to Dr. Dinnes' hospital. More and more I was coming to realize that all of the trials and tribulations of raising children were inherent in the raising of cats. I felt almost as much compassion for that whimpering young tiger as I would have felt for a child with a broken leg. But at least with a child I could have explained the hurt and said we were on the way to the doctor's.

The procedures for dealing with the broken bones of a cat are much the same as those used for humans. The cats have to be anesthetized, and Igor, one of John's favorites, was on the operating table for four hours while Marty repaired the lateral break with a metal plate affixed with screws. After it was over, he walked into the waiting room, a grin on his face. "You'll be proud of me. I matched the stripes when I sutured the incision."

A tiger's black stripes are on the skin surface as well as on the coat. A tiger without its fur would still show its stripes, just as the naked leopard or cheetah would show its spots. Marty was a very conscientious surgeon.

I had learned very early that taking a lion or a tiger to the vet was not the same as transporting your average, friendly Great Dane for the purpose of healing. Riding the freeway at fifty-five miles an hour or pulling up to a stoplight and looking into the rearview mirror to see a Togar or a Siberian tiger three feet behind you added a certain exhilaration to the drive. Penny Bishonden, my trainer-vet-tech, had her van especially fitted for transport of the big cats. Chain link is

Penny Bishonden working three lionesses

Tippi Hedren

Dr. Jon Bernstein at work.

welded over the side windows and there is another chain-link panel directly behind the driver and passenger seats. The rule is that two people always accompany the transport of the cats in case of a breakdown or accident.

Only three or four vets in the Los Angeles area are qualified to treat the big cats and have the needed facilities to handle exotic animals properly. The average vet has had his or her share of canine bites and tabby scratches, but in dealing with a sick or injured big cat the danger factor zooms a hundredfold. To begin with, you do not put one of these animals on a lead and simply walk through the front door. Often, the vet comes out to the van and sedates the cat there, if necessary; then it is rolled, dazed or unconscious, inside on a gurney.

Among the special pieces of equipment needed to handle big cats are "squeeze cages," in which the bars on one side of the cage can be cranked inward to reduce the space and permit the vet, or the vet-tech, to reach in and treat or tranquilize the animal. All specialty veterinarians, zoos and animal parks have them. The term

Timbo has an X ray.

"squeeze cage" sounds awful, but the apparatus is simply a painless and easy method of holding the cat steady while performing treatment. Even the simplest procedures—medication in an inflamed eye, for instance—can become difficult if the animal weighs five hundred pounds. Cats are suspicious of any deviation in their lives, and a trip to an animal hospital is a huge deviation. Vets who treat them often deserve medals of valor.

Unfortunately, cats are pretty much susceptible to the whole range of human ailments and diseases from arthritis to cancer, in addition to a few that are particularly feline. For instance, they appear to have more than their share of respiratory problems. But the ones in captivity by and large enjoy better health than those in the wild, and they have access to the latest medical techniques.

One of the tigers out in the canyon had a human-type eye problem involving his peripheral vision, and we had an eye surgeon, whose practice seldom extended to animals and never to tigers, correct the deficiency. The problem was congenital, as are many of the afflictions that strike big cats. During this same period, lion Ike, of the rambunctious Knobhill duo of Ike and Mike, died of an enlarged heart at about two and a half years old. His longtime playmate and den mate, Mike, soon developed a deep depression as well as kidney trouble. Marty Dinnes began treatment, which included dialysis, and Mike eventually recovered.

If one of the cats died of causes that were not evident to the vets, such as injury or old age, we usually requested an autopsy. We feared, always, any virus that might sweep the compound, and we inoculated yearly as well as wormed when needed. But even these procedures tend to be difficult. In fact, just weighing a six-hundred-pound tiger, and we weighed all the animals annually, is not without complexity.

Then there is the time to be merciful. One lion had injury to the brain stem which led to failing eyesight, then to total blindness. Marty Dinnes recommended euthanasia. We said yes.

In Africa or India, the big cats seldom live beyond ten or twelve years due to the stress of continuous hunting and constant combat readiness. In captivity, human-provided food and the lack of stress, plus good veterinarian care in most zoos and preserves, add years to the life of the animal. They often live past twenty, except those struck, at any time, by disease.

Sadly enough, few zoo-kept big cats would long survive if turned loose in the Serengeti or India. The human relationships many have developed—just the sight of humans every day removes the fear factor—would place them in jeopardy. Though they might learn to hunt for themselves, disease or a poacher's bullet would probably end their lives. Insofar as lions are concerned, most prefer to stay comfortably in one place and do absolutely nothing as long as they are well fed, whether they are wild in Africa, on exhibition in the San Diego Zoo or slumbering on the flats of Soledad Canyon. The romantic notion of freeing all the lions in the world would be quickly voted down by any lion with a full belly. From my own experience, our lions, if not hungry, would walk to the corner, yawn, and come home.

A memorable cat, Hudu, came to us in the summer of 1973, and we were warned that he was not a very good lion; that he should be put off somewhere by himself. Oh, my Lord, another Togar, I thought. Such a warning must always be heeded, just as reassuring statements like "This cat is so nice and gentle" must be taken with a few grains of skepticism. But a change in surroundings can always

107

make a difference in behavior, and from the first day he arrived Hudu did not seem all that bad to us.

He was a big lion, almost as big as Lurch, with a full amber mane. And after he had been in Soledad for a week or so, Noel entered his compound and, closing the gate behind him, just stood there. The lion and the man did not look at each other. Generally, a big cat does not like direct eye contact. It amounts to a challenge. Finally, about thirty minutes later, Hudu walked past Noel, moving slowly over the sand, and then returned to place his paw over Noel's foot, pinning it down. He stood that way, motionless, for three or four minutes, looking off into the distance, and then Noel reached down to touch him, his heart returning to a normal beat. Hudu could have just as easily attacked. Beginning with that afternoon, they became close friends, and Hudu of the terrible reputation turned out to be one of the nicest cats in the canyon.

After a while he lived with a little dog, Timmy. We planned to put a dog into the film, and Timmy was to be that actor. A mixed-breed terrier, an orphan from the Van Nuys pound, Timmy truly enjoyed the company of the huge lion, and vice versa. They could be seen asleep, dog tucked up against Hudu's back. This was, of course, a very rare relationship.

Meanwhile, the experiment with breaking up the Wild Bunch seemed to be working. We had put the four males in with calmer cats. Monte, for example, was already mellowing out. So, big-cat behavior could be changed, to a degree, if the human was patient. But I knew my limitations, and at this point I did not attempt a one-to-one relationship with any of the Wild Bunch.

—13—

UNDERSTANDING BIG CATS

When we first began to gather our animal cast, we hired several professional trainers to help Steve Martin, but we soon ended up parting ways with them. Using fear tactics to control the big cats, they couldn't shake off the professionals' mind-set which dictated that our "actors" should live alone to avoid distractions. That was not what our film was all about, so we decided to create our own staff of handlers.

After hiring young people locally to do maintenance work, we watched for those who spent extra time along the fences observing or talking to the animals. We wanted sensitive, compassionate trainers; ones who had no preconceived notions about relationships with the cats. Those candidates eventually turned out to be the best handlers, although several who thought they wanted to have a life with the lions and tigers changed their minds, saying, "I'm scared to death of Togar." My answer was always the same, "So am I!" But for every Togar we had, there were a half-dozen mellow big cats.

By the hot summer months of 1973, we were all becoming increasingly confident of our ability to read the minds and postures and talk of the lions and tigers, to guess what they might be thinking and intending to do. We were especially confident in dealing with the Knobhill gang, the ones we had raised from cubhood. Some of these cats were now young adults and quite large. Casey and Needra, for example. But I'll always remember the last Sunday in July as a day when our confidence was shattered by a silent streak of gold.

Some people living in a trailer camp down the road asked Noel if they could pay a visit to see the big cats close up and perhaps meet one or two of them. Thinking it would be good for neighborly relations, Noel said, "Sure, come on up," and suggested a time well before the supercharged feeding hour. So that Sunday seven or eight adults and several children passed through the high chain-link gate with that first-time visitor's look of awe clearly in their eyes. Some

Needra charging

were armed with cameras, as usual. We took them to the pond area, where several young adults lived—the human-oriented Knobhill graduates, including Needra. But just as Noel opened the compound gate I turned my head, saw Needra crouching down and thought that the look on her face was not particularly good. I followed her look, and she was obviously getting a bead on a little boy. Before I could even open my mouth, she had streaked out through the gate, leaped on the child and knocked him down.

Fortunately, we were able to pull her off before any physical damage was done. But we were puzzled by Needra's behavior. She had always been such a sweet cat, always so good around humans, that we had never had the slightest hesitation about introducing her to people. *Hadn't I bottle-nursed her at the age of six weeks?* She'd spent hours on my lap or in my arms; she'd slept at my feet. Noel and the kids had played with her to establish that special big-cat–human relationship. She was Noel's favorite lioness. Melanie adored her. Yet we knew that cats are entirely predictable around "little people," animal or human. Any small child or a newborn foal might be a target; an adult or a horse might be excused. Size is a definite factor in a big cat's reaction.

What that Sunday demonstrated was the blinding swiftness of that reaction, the power of the muscles, the single-mindedness—and the necessity for us to read signals in a split second. Say something. Do something. By the time I had read Needra's face, her body posture and the tenseness in every muscle, she'd made up her mind to attack and it was too late to stop her. As far as she was concerned, that child was prey. Before sundown, we made a rule that no one under the age of eighteen would be permitted to enter the grounds. In retrospect, we realized we had handed Needra a child target.

Though it was not a factor in this case, we also knew there is a difference in the brain activity of the male and the female cat. The female has a much more active brain. She's more alert at all times, more clever; more rowdy. Of course, in the wild she does most of the hunting. In the future we would have to keep a much closer eye on the Knobhill gang, especially the females.

Throughout this period and for the next two years, while we were trying to raise money for the film, we had ample opportunity to think about the dangers, possibilities and impossibilities of dealing with this harum-scarum bestial cast. *The Exorcist* had finished filming in May, but it would be two years, if then, before Noel could expect any share of the proceeds. It takes almost a year to edit and prepare a major film for release; sometimes several years before a profit is realized. Even then, the participant may not be able to shake loose any money from the distribution company.

As it turned out, it was to our advantage that no money was available. We could use the additional time to attempt a better understanding of big-cat behavior, especially their postures and language. Berlitz can teach you to speak French in a short while, but learning cat language is not so easy. What we were planning to do—involve a number of humans with free-running lions and tigers in more or less uncontrolled situations—had never been done before.

We knew of, and had already used, some of the proven handling techniques in moving the cats around the canyon in their routine exchange of living spaces. Changing homes every few weeks gives them new vistas and new neighbors. Sometime in the future we would have to make many moves with them for different scenes in different places, routing them all over the "African set," a few at a time or a dozen at a time. So the moves were basic training for us, part of plumbing the big-cat psyche.

What was in those big heads and behind those curious amber, dark-pooled eyes was instinctual thought processes that were so simple that they could be numbered. Yet there were some complexities that popped up now and then, defying patterns.

How could a two-ounce twig held in the hand possibly distract a fully grown lion or tiger, or even a group of them, long enough to establish authority? I don't know how or why. I do know that it works. A scissoring of the arms, extended outward on an angle of about forty-five degrees, along with a shouted "No!"—meaning "Don't even think about it"—is often enough to stop a charge. Why? I don't know. But it does work.

Of the other control factors, a long hog-handler's hickory cane with a crooked handle, available in any good feed store, acts as an extension of the human arm and is very persuasive without even touching the animal. Distraction is the key, I believe, to the successful and safe handling of the big cats. But use of the cane, for instance, is double-edged. If the handler habitually goes into a compound carrying a cane, mingling with six or eight cats, he may well be jumped by one or more of them if he goes in without it.

Another measure is sometimes used. Hand-held fire extinguishers, with their *whoosh* and innocent white vapor, are prime attention-getters, useful in breaking up cat fights or diverting attention when

Lions are among the laziest creatures on earth.

a human is in trouble. A human cannot break up a fight between two five-hundred-pound males by shouting or waving a cane.

The nearest things to a gun permitted in our preserve are the air pistols used, infrequently, for dart tranquilizing. The pellets are issued only by licensed veterinarians.

By now, we knew that there were three basic situations that could generally bring on big-cat attacks: (1) tampering with, or appearing to tamper with, their food; (2) involvement, in any way, with lion–lioness or tiger–tigress romance (*Humans, stay outside the fence!*); (3) becoming involved with the key manifestations of possessiveness.

This last basic is the trickiest of all to understand. Food and romance are clear-cut; human enough to comprehend easily. But big-cat possessiveness is seldom clear-cut until it occurs. Once it does, with roots that may go back to the genes, it is a trait that never goes away. An object of any kind can absorb the cat for hours. And a human becoming the object of possessiveness is the ultimate in a precarious relationship. The cat does not understand the reluctance of the human to be possessed.

Noel having a little talk with Gary

In addition to these basics of safely living with the animals, there are a dozen other situations that appear to come out of whim. They are unexplainable but no less dangerous. *A cat attacks for no apparent reason at all!* I ask myself, Why did he or she do it?, and there is no answer.

There are definite pecking orders within the compounds, involving both food and territory. Some of the cats are dominant over food; others will dominate over their compound mates, protecting particular territories. The territories are clearly established within the compound, and the dominant cat will behave differently on his or her ground from the way it behaves outside the compound. The human is relatively safe when the cat is away from its own territory. If the cat is in its own space, it is sure of itself. Away from home ground, there is much to look at, much to smell. The strong single-mindedness of the cat goes in a different direction.

When cats come into a new compound, in the normal exchange of space throughout the preserve, they immediately spray and "mark." Walking around, smelling everything, they urinate on what seems important. Any self-respecting dog does the same thing. The big cats go one step further. They take delight in spraying humans, and the male tiger has a six-to-eight-foot bull's-eye range. I always warn visitors not to stand too close to the fences, or at least to keep their eyes on posteriors aimed their way, tails raised like flagpoles.

Another fascinating aspect of behavior within the compounds has to do with trees. Big cats often nuzzle trees, licking them to taste the sap. At times, they become possessive of a particular tree and all the king's horses plus an earth-mover will not part a lion from his tree until he is ready to say goodbye.

Within the close and, to me, remarkable society of each of the compounds, some of which are four acres in size, there is a dominant male and a dominant female, and when a new lion or lioness is introduced problems may arise. If the newcomer tries to dominate, a fight is likely. But there are subgroups within the main group, and perhaps the newcomer will dominate a subgroup or even be willing to become dominated without battle.

When we introduced Chelsea lioness, who was born in the canyon, into her new group, aggressive Penny was the dominant female and remained in that position with few challenges. But Lena lioness and Chelsea fought on and off for two days to see who was going to dominate the subgroup. Chelsea won, but the challenge remained. Lena would fight again. We always watch such battling carefully, and if there is a danger of more than a few superficial bites and scratches, we remove one of the combatants. But we prefer to give it several days. *One lion or lioness will take charge, and that is the way this society must be run.* Members vote with their teeth and claws and roars. Lions do not want to live alone, and the fights are the price to be paid for societal living. Quite often, the one who can make the most noise, threaten the most, is the winner—a page from humanity. Adult male tigers want to live separately from other males, the instinct of the wild, but enjoy the company of females, lioness as well as tigress. Lolita lioness ferociously battles other lionesses but lives happily with Bengal tigress Zazu.

Many of the big-cat instinctual behaviors seem to apply to humans as well. They are always more restless when high winds whine down through the canyon, stirring up dust devils. They tend to prowl around their compounds on nights of a full moon, eyes gleaming in the whiteness. In high heat they seek shade and are totally listless. The tigers may get into the lake and lie there for hours, their faces just above the surface of the water. All human traits, so far as I know.

In compounds where there are both lions and tigers, no lions are evident when it snows or rains, but the tigers are out, licking their lips, faces often skyward. Frolicking in the cold air, they love to roll and wallow in snow. The lions, shaking their paws out in disgust, step into the stuff as if it were flypaper.

In a compound of several acres, the cats will invariably collect along the fences, and they do so, I believe, for human contact, seeking friendship and affection. Nosy animals, they also like to watch what is going on nearby. The fence crew at work. A volleyball game. Cats in the compound next door. But then, in a marked departure, there are those times when instinct takes over in split seconds and there is no blurring of the differences between man and lion. Cats, so loving and playful in the morning, can be killers in late afternoon when offal and muscle meat are brought to the compounds. Feeding time is the most important time in their lives. More important than the sex drive; more important than dominance in their living space. It is the time when almost all their instinctual traits can be observed.

At about nine months, when cats go onto red meat, muscle meat, some of their jungle and savanna instincts begin to emerge. They are absolutely certain that everyone on earth wants their dinner. They also seem to be thinking, This is the last meal I'll ever have and I want every morsel—yours too!

By the time they are two years of age, these instincts are fully developed. Several of the largest lions turn into wild men or wild women at about 4 P.M. Canines bared, they charge the fences. Chelsea lioness, for example, is horrific at white-bucket time, seemingly causing the cottonwoods to quiver. If anything, the females are more

Intoxicated by the smell of sap, a big cat takes possession of a tree.

ferocious than the males. For first-time visitors to the compounds, it can be a period of terror.

In the wild, when the predator goes after the hoofed animal, the first thing it eats is the stomach. All kinds of grasses are lodged in there, and the big cats can get their vitamins and nutrients in nature's efficient way. So grass is brought into the compounds to supplement the natural grass that is quickly nibbled off when it rises from the sandy loam. But the big cats will never be vegetarians, and they eagerly await the sight of the white buckets when Liberato and his helpers bring them around. The meat is delivered to us from Los Angeles in frozen blocks of a hundred pounds each, and roughly a thousand pounds is defrosted daily for the next day's feeding. Each adult receives approximately ten pounds daily.

Snow-lover Katrina

Nature has wondrously provided a special dental structure for the big cats, a bit different from that of other animals. Some of their teeth are ideally suited for tearing flesh, others for breaking down the pieces into smaller chunks. In fact, the head of the big cat is a superior eating machine, and most big cats are very particular about what they want. Some, like Boomer, prefer whole defeathered chickens; others like big chunks with bones attached; still others, little pieces. Some don't like spleen; others refuse chicken. Some love turkey necks. Liberato knows their preferences and attempts to please. They're all thoroughly spoiled. Powdered vitamins and brewer's yeast are sprinkled over the meats as the crewmen fill the five-gallon white buckets. Feeding takes six of the crew three hours daily.

Some of the cats can eat together, but the ones that turn into volcanos have a special feeding area in each compound. These spaces are about ten feet square and we can lure the animal into the space, then swing the interior gate shut from the outside, avoiding human contact. These procedures are routine, and once the problem eaters are satiated, having consumed every last morsel, they return to their normal personalities.

Among the surefire behavioral dictates among big cats is the "take-down," that stalking throwback to the wild—survival of the fittest. It was demonstrated in a frightening way when one of Liberato's crewmen was in a serious auto accident. After his recovery we put him back to work, but the animals sensed immediately that something was wrong with his locomotion. They tracked him whenever he walked alongside a compound, pacing slowly and crouching with him along the fences, eyes riveted on him. Without doubt, they wanted to get at him. We told him not to dare enter a compound. The genetic dictate to "take down" an animal that is not quite right, which I first encountered with cub Casey when I lured him up Knobhill by limping, was never more in evidence. After a few nervous weeks, we regretfully discharged the employee.

A far different and less easily explained situation occurred when newspaper publisher Otis Chandler, of the *Los Angeles Times*, visited Soledad Canyon. The reactions of the cats to Mr. Chandler were puzzling. Natasha, the Siberian tigress, normally a gentle cat, tried to jump him, and Buster, my personal leopard, one of our best P.R. cats, always reliable when introduced to a guest, tried to bite him. Noel apologized, but the publisher sensed what might be the problem. "I'm a big-game hunter, you know," he said. Had the cats sensed an enemy, or was it just coincidence? I don't know.

A few of the other cats were also signaling annoyance of some kind that day. Their tails whipped around as the publisher passed by. Similar to the house cat, the tail of the big cat can show serenity, provocation or wild anger. Where big cats are concerned, it is definitely an off-limits appendage. Only in an emergency will I grab a cat by the tail. It is an insult. Even my most gentle lions, Boomer and Scarface, will turn around if their tails are pulled. Their looks say sternly, "Knock it off!"

Facial expressions, body postures and the tail can tell an awful lot about what a big cat is intending to do, if anything. But there are occasions when there is no time to read the animal. His actions may be entirely predictable, but events transpire in split seconds and the average human simply cannot react quickly enough. For instance, we'd been told by Steve Martin, Ron Oxley and others to always avoid tripping when walking near a cat. If you trip and fall, it is an invitation for the cat to spring and do a pin-down. Even the gentlest cat is likely to mount a sprawled-out human. Their advice to me was: *If you do trip, try not to hit the ground. Get back on your feet instantly.*

Zuru and Tongaru had been acquired from a northern California man in late 1971 when they were about five months old. The owner couldn't afford to feed them. Though litter mates, almost mirror twins, these two cubs were night and day in difference of personality. Zuru was a sweetheart; Tongaru was already a little monster. I kept them on Knobhill for several weeks, struggling with Tongaru every single day.

By August of 1973, they each weighed upward of three hundred pounds and resided together in the canyon. Zuru was still a sweetheart, Tongaru still a monster. One afternoon John was walking with Tongaru near the newly completed African house, by the lake, when he tripped over a rock hidden in high grass and landed face down. Before he could even try to push up, Tongaru was on him, his big mouth closing over the back of John's head. The lion did not try to penetrate the skull; rather he seemed content to just hold John's head in his mouth. Another behavioral reaction had occurred: *Once the human is lower than the lion, the human becomes vulnerable.* When John tripped, it was playtime for Tongaru. Occasionally we gave the big cats appropriate toys: secondhand bowling balls and the like. Tongaru now had a human toy beneath him.

Steve Martin had seen John go down and had seen the lion pounce. As he came closer, yelling at Tongaru to "Get off," the lion began to growl, making that distinct sound of annoyance, the machine-gunning guttural "uh-huh." This body beneath him was his "possession" of the moment. He was answering Steve, in effect, "He's mine, he's mine." John had the presence of mind to stay completely still, though the three hundred pounds of growling cat enfolded him, the canines still clamped on his skull. John's face was in the sand, arms outstretched.

Steve and another handler, Jeff Haynes, ran to the mechanical shop for fire extinguishers and returned, hoping that the white cloud of gas and whooshing noise would divert Tongaru's attention. But they only made Tongaru angrier, and the "uh-huhs" grew louder. Next Steve and Jeff tried a sheet of corrugated tin, waving it in front of the lion, hoping that the metallic sound would cause a retreat. Both the extinguishers and the sheet metal had been used effectively on previous occasions when a cat was misbehaving. Tongaru wasn't impressed.

John had now been under that huge body for almost twenty minutes. He was completely helpless. Yet Tongaru, a cat that was shaping up to be every bit as tough as Togar, had not done what he was quite capable of doing—crushing John's skull, biting his neck or any other place. He seemed content to just hold the human firmly, not kill him. Finally, Steve and Jeff tried a third tactic that had also worked in the past. They each got on a side of a four-by-eight-foot plywood panel and rushed the lion, yelling at him. When everything else fails, an annoyed big cat will usually respond to size. Anything that towers over the animal becomes an immediate threat or is at least given respect. The plywood wall was several feet higher than Tongaru when it came hurtling at him. The game was over. He saw it and jumped back, releasing John.

Though he'd been around lions and tigers for two years, John had never experienced being trapped under one. He was visibly shaken from his twenty-five-minute ordeal. He was treated for scalp wounds at the hospital in Saugus, but not much could be done for his mental state. He returned to the canyon about two hours later vowing never again to trip while accompanying a big cat, never again to work with Tongaru.

—14—

CHERRIES

In planning to shoot our film, we soon realized that no scene involving the animal cast could be directed to any extent. After setting up situations, we would just roll three to six cameras and let happen what would happen. Noel's script was really an outline except for the strictly human scenes, of which there were few. In effect, we would be making a semidocumentary within a fiction piece.

Of course, we knew that we could cause certain situations to occur. The use of food as a lure, and a reward, standard animal-trainer techniques, could send a pack of lions and tigers up or down a flight of steps. By our introducing one group of lions to another, we knew, a fight would ensue. We also knew that certain individual lions would fight other individual lions, if that was what we wanted. The tigers would happily spar in the water without enticement.

In staged fights, the saving grace is that the lion doesn't want to get hurt any more than Sylvester Stallone wanted to get hurt in *Rocky*. There is horrendous noise, a lot of posturing, a lot of talking, lots of dust, but the Cowardly Lion of *The Wizard of Oz* is more truth than fiction. Lions say the biggest "ouch" on earth. While they are quite capable of hurting each other in the extreme, they seldom do it.

The only formal animal training we envisioned for the film involved getting a pair of tigers to ride in the back seat of a cut-down 1937 Chevrolet, and a pair of lions to make mock attacks on two humans, to be played by trainers. All the rest would happen as it happened, and we were hoping for a number of "gift" scenes in which the animals would do something totally unexpected.

By now, we had come to realize that no rational actor would play the part of Hank, the Gorongosa scientist, and do scene after unrehearsed scene grappling with the big cats in one way or another. No leading man that I'd ever had, including the very physical Sean Connery, would be likely to take on that role. Neither was it a part for a stuntman. Hollywood's stuntmen can do a variety of things, and superbly, but working with wild animals is not one of them. To come out in one unmutilated piece, a stuntman would have to live with the cats for months or years, as Noel had done, and learn what Noel already knew about their behavior. Of even more importance, the cats would have to get to *know* the stuntman, as they knew Noel. Obviously, the only sensible candidate for the role of Hank was Noel himself.

Noel was, of course, already functioning as producer, art director, landscape architect, casting director and financier, as well as writer and part-time lion tamer. He did not fly planes upside down, leap from high buildings or drive the freeways at a hundred miles an hour. But he was tough, having grown up in the Chicago slums, and he was fearless, or almost fearless, in relations with the big cats. He loved them, played with them, understood them. With the exception of Togar, he believed in intimidating them with his voice and bare hands before they intimidated him. He bluffed them time and time again; he dodged their charges like a matador. I shudder now to think of all the risks he had taken.

As for the rest of the cast, our plans did not change. I was to play Madeline, Hank's wife; and John, Jerry and Melanie would play our teenage children. Once again it was for safety's sake: we all knew the cats better than anyone else. We had lived with them; we recognized the posturing and the danger signals. Risk would be far less with our own family than with any other performers we could hire.

Red-haired, freckle-faced, blue-eyed Joel, aspiring to be an artist, still had little affection for the cats, nor would he act in *any* film. But we hoped to put his talents to work in various ways. He was attending UCLA in his second year, majoring in art, but did many other things well—carpentry, landscaping, electronics, auto body repair. A rather shy, soft-spoken young man, he had a fine eye for design, a talent

Joel with a friend

that undoubtedly came from his mother, a professional artist.

Noel and I predicted that there would be criticism, within and without the Hollywood community, for endangering the lives of our children in the film. We were already hearing it: *You mean you're going to put them in with the wild lions and tigers?* We discussed both the criticisms and the dangers with our children. They did know the risks, particularly John, who had just spent some time pinned down by Tongaru. And they made the mature decision that if the criticism didn't bother us it wouldn't bother them. We gave them percentage points in the vague but possible profits of the film.

So we had assembled most of our cast, both animal and human. But we had not yet collected the money we would need to make the film. Few days went by that Noel wasn't on the phone, or at lunch, trying to raise it. Just the cost of feeding and housing our cats was in the thousands. The film, as we envisioned it, would cost over a million. And we had no idea where to get it.

* * *

In late August, when Billy was nine months old, almost four feet in length and weighing about a hundred pounds, I knew it was time to take him to Soledad Canyon to live; in fact, it was well past time for his transfer from human surroundings on Knobhill. In size alone, Billy was no longer a cub. Beginning to take on the physical characteristics of his father, Togar, he was a powerful young lion with a marvelous intelligent amber face and amber eyes. Soon his black mane would begin to sprout. Over the past nine months we had developed a close relationship. As with Partner or Pharaoh, all I had to do was pick up the car keys and Billy would run to the front door, awaiting me. He loved to ride and it's a wonder he didn't cause wrecks when he perched in the front seat beside me.

I remember that I talked to him on the way to the canyon—

A playful tussle between Noel and Casey

Mommytalk, of course—station wagon zooming along the Antelope Valley Freeway, lion standing up in back. Tears were running down my face when I finally took Billy to the compound to live with tiger Igor, lionesses Cookie and Needra, and six other young cats. I felt as if a child was leaving the family. I'd lived with this four-pawed infant from day five on earth and my maternal instincts spilled out unashamedly.

Over the next weeks and months there was no visit to Soledad that did not include some time spent with Billy. He would usually hear my car drive up and come sprinting to the gate to meet me. I would let him out and we'd go walking through the desert, usually following the riverbank.

There were times as we were walking together that he would stop me by wrapping a paw around my ankle, then take my hand and push it toward his mouth so he could suck my thumb. The spotted baby still dwelled within him, as it does in fully grown lions, but Billy's tongue was no longer the texture of fine sandpaper. It was more like a grater now, fitted by nature to strip meat from wildebeest bones. My skin became raw after a few licks, but I suffered the pain because the relationship with him was so special. After the long walks, lion moving slowly along near my knees, we would sit for an hour or more by the lake, or under the trees, and he often went to sleep for a while. There was no more peaceful or docile lion than young Billy during these mild autumn days in the cottonwood leaves.

On a Sunday morning during one of my visits to the canyon that fall, I went into a compound that housed a group of lions I didn't know very well. Thinking I would probably have to face them soon enough with cameras rolling, I wanted to be around them for a while. Frank Tom went with me. I was always reluctant to enter a compound alone where a group was living; no one can watch seven or eight cats simultaneously. Suddenly, a lioness in the group zeroed in on me. She wasn't a Knobhill graduate. Reading her, I shouted, "No!," scissoring my arms, but she kept on coming and knocked me down. Frank restrained her while I rolled away. My face was slightly scratched from contact with the sand, but more than that I was unnerved. Embarrassed as well. Though the knock-down left me sore for several days, what hurt most was learning my limitations. I had wanted to be in command in *any* compound, except Togar's. I wanted to be able to say, "No, you're not going to jump me" and make it stick. The incident taught me a great deal. From then on, I was much more careful with cats that were not my intimate friends.

In our search for backers, we soon realized that what Noel needed in order to sell the moneylenders on the idea of our film was some spectacular footage—a half reel that he could take to Paramount or the Bank of America or contacts in Tokyo or London. Trying to explain the film to money men was impossible. This was not the normal script and we certainly had no superstars. We had no panting bedroom scenes and no human violence, ingredients that the major film distributors and bankers seem to understand best. However, we thought surely that if they could see some of those magnificent big cats in wild action . . .

A test, for sample filming, was set for Saturday, December 8, 1973, with dual Cinerama cameras to record a pride of lions in a sort of chase by the lake. In one scene I was to "fall" on an old tree bridge over the river, then twenty or so lions and tigers were to either step or jump over me as they crossed the big log. If all went well, it might be a nice sales piece—Madeline as a jumping hazard in a lion and tiger steeplechase.

While the cinematographer loaded the rental cameras, Noel decided to rehearse the scene. When the cats were assembled, including many of my good friends—Casey, Billy, Igor, Boomer, Needra and others—I began running, then did my "fall" on the big log over the water. The cats stepped or gracefully jumped over me, paying little attention to the female body draped over the log. But when Cherries, one of those three unruly Texas "Fruit Salad" cats, about two years old and two hundred-odd pounds, slowly walked across me, she looked down as if to say, "Well, what are you doing in that strange position?" Then she turned back and started batting my head with her paw. She was getting a little strong, and I yelled at her to stop. She went on to the end of the log and then looked back.

Watching her, I saw her eyes seem to narrow and I knew I was in trouble. Not only was I lower than she was, I was obviously helpless. "Hey, you guys stay with me!" I yelled to several of the handlers.

The next thing I knew Cherries was running hard at me again, then she was on me, both paws on my shoulders, pinning me to the log. She took most of my head into her mouth, grasping the back of the skull. I could hear her teeth scraping bone and the sound was truly unforgettable. There was a resonance to it that I still find hard to describe. It was like being in an echo chamber as her teeth raked my skull. John and I would now share the same memory.

Noel ran to me, jumped on the log and grabbed Cherries by the scruff of the neck, pulling back on her. I lifted my head as she released it, and there was her face about a foot from mine, mouth wide open, teeth glistening white. Her skin was being stretched so that there was an Oriental look at the corners of her eyes. It all seemed to be happening in slow motion. There was little pain. There was a lot of terror.

The scalp bleeds profusely, I learned, and a gush of red spread over my face and into my eyes. I was in shock, I'm sure, but I do remember something very feminine that occurred in the next few seconds. I've always taken great pride in having long fingernails, and

The feline parade just before my scalping

I spotted a ripped-off nail end on the log. I reached out, picked it up, and put it into my shirt pocket, thinking I would have the manicurist glue it back on Monday.

Rushed to the emergency room at Sherman Oaks Hospital, holding a bloody towel to the back of my head, I was angry at Cherries for biting me, angry at Noel for placing me in that vulnerable position, angry at myself for not being able to control the aggressive lioness. But I wasn't angry enough to pull out of the film. When the doctor said, "We'll have to shave your head," I answered, "No! I'm filming. No shaving."

The lacerations weren't deep, he admitted. So he cleaned me up, put on butterfly clamps, gave me a tetanus shot and an antibiotic, then sent me home to Knobhill. I remember we stopped after leaving the hospital because I suddenly wanted an ice-cream cone. The hurt child in me came out; the shock had not entirely worn off, I suppose.

That night, in quiet anger, I told Noel, "That was the most frightening thing that has ever happened to me. I never want that to happen again. Do you understand?"

"All right," he said. "We won't film the test."

"Oh yes we will," I said. "You're not going to cancel. I just won't work with Cherries anymore."

So Cherries stayed in her compound the next day while we filmed the log scene, all of the cats behaving nicely. We screened the results the following night. Sensational! Exactly what Noel needed to augment his vocal efforts to raise a million-plus dollars.

To this day, I've never worked with Cherries. Although I admire her beauty, I don't trust her. Once bitten, I put the guilty cat on my quit list and we were never friends again.

—15—

A SHATTERING
AFTERNOON

Twelve inches of snow covered the compounds of Soledad Canyon the night of January 5, 1974, and, of course, the tigers loved every cold centimeter of it. They wallowed in it, ate it, batted it. The lions, meantime, looked mournfully out of their huts, wanting nothing to do with the icy white stuff that ruined their sleeping sands.

Several weeks later Needra mated with Hudu, and I soon realized she was pregnant. She was still "my baby"; I checked her every day. She looked extremely healthy and I anticipated one to four fine cubs. A lioness of three years is going into her prime of cub bearing, and big Hudu had all the qualifications needed to sire. At age six, he was robust and capable of impregnating any number of lionesses.

Because cubs are so tiny at birth it is sometimes difficult to determine if a lioness is actually pregnant. If she carries only one cub, it is almost impossible to make the determination. But Needra did bulge a bit, and 106 days later she went into labor. Melanie, John, Noel and I stayed up with her all night, talking to her, soothing her with our hands, and a little after dawn she gave birth to two cubs. Both appeared healthy.

What was unusual about this wintry natal morning was Needra's willingness to let us pick up her cubs so soon after she'd snipped the umbilical cords. Lionesses most often will not let any human near

The "African house" under a blanket of snow

their newborn. An anxious big-cat mother can be deadly. But Needra allowed us to hold Melanie and Merrie while she cleaned them off with her tongue. She made the allowance, I'm sure, only because we had raised her from six weeks on. Obviously she trusted us. But unfortunately little Merrie died in my arms of an intestinal infection two weeks later. Thus far, nine cubs had been born in the canyon and six had survived. In comparison to the delicate big-cat cubs most human babies of the developed countries are durable specimens.

Cubs must be separated from their mothers at about six weeks. Otherwise, the lioness will often instinctively teach them to be wild. In captivity, wildness is a useless burden, harmful to the animal, dangerous for the human. So the longer mother and cub stay together the more difficult the inevitable separation. Putting her on a bottle, I took cub Melanie back to Knobhill to live with Pharaoh the cheetah and a new cat, Cleopatra, a leopard. Also in residence was a tiger cub yet to be named. Trying to run a very discreet urban preserve, we hadn't had a visit from Animal Control in more than a year. Luck, as well as discretion, was a factor.

Mariah

It was obvious that Pharaoh and Cleo might not get along too well—there were menacing sounds from both on first sight—so we had to keep them separated. The cheetah, now accustomed to ruling Knobhill, resented the leopard's presence. The fact that she was female made little or no difference. What we didn't need was a brawl between these two rather large animals, so Cleo stayed with us only for several weeks while we attempted to indoctrinate her to human-kind. With rare blue eyes, the lovely leopard quickly became attached to Noel, which meant trouble for me later on. I was Noel's "lady," and Cleo didn't care much for that arrangement. She displayed her jealousy by ignoring me completely. Even before she left Knobhill, I realized I wasn't on her friendship list.

Mariah, the first leopard we raised from cubhood, had been everywhere at once. She would be on my shoulders, then grabbing at my knees, then on the top of my head and down to my ankles again. When leopards are hyper, they're hyper all the way, literally bouncing off the walls. Out in the canyon, Mariah, one of the most attractive animals I've ever met, was still hyper. Yet she would sit up like a begging dog, pawing the air.

For years, most people thought that black panthers and leopards were different animals. They are one and the same but clothed differently. Black leopards, more commonly known as panthers, are melanistic (dark-colored) instead of saudic (light-colored) and expose their spots in strong sunlight. They have the identical personalities of the orange, black-rosetted type. I think the pale, hypnotic eyes of the black leopard are the most compelling of all cats' eyes. Several times, experimentally, we tried to mate a black male with a spotted female, hoping for black cubs. No luck.

An animal of high intelligence and dignity, the leopard can be very affectionate. Though much smaller than a grown lion or tiger, usually weighing from seventy to two hundred pounds, the leopard, a cunning stalker, is a creature of sleek grace and high speed when on the attack. Though not very vocal, they speak in hisses, growls and a series of guttural coughs. The guttural bark of the leopard can be heard all over the sand flats of the canyon. The estrus sound of the female is low and moaning.

I especially love to watch a leopard walk. The gait is both stealthy and graceful. Moving on the toes, head held rather low, jaw often relaxed, the animal is a study in supple motion. But like the cheetah, it spends a lot of time in observance, motionless, watching intently, pale eyes fastened on an object, perhaps a human or another animal.

In the wild, the leopard is an expert tree climber, and ours lost little of that ability in the compounds. I always looked into the trees when the leopards were out of their houses. Once, I heard someone shout, "Cat's out of the tree," and turned to see Cleo coming at me hell-bent. I called to her, "Come on, sweetheart, come here," hoping for a peaceful connection. But she lunged into my arms, biting me on the shoulder, her claws grazing my head. There is not much love between us. The leopard, above all other cats, does not like to remain in exposed positions too long, probably because of deep-seated fear of other, larger predators. Leaves and branches provide cover.

Unfortunately, sickeningly, no other big cat is hunted and killed in greater numbers than the leopard. In the 1950s and 1960s, as many as ten thousand skins were imported into the United States annually, but that figure plunged after 1970 when the Mason Act, prohibiting the manufacture or sale of leopard products, was passed in New York State. Three years later the federal ban was imposed and the leopard could breathe a little easier in India, Kenya, Somalia and Ethiopia.

To add to our leopard collection, we acquired Buster, a four-year-old, from animal dealer George Toth. We were told that he was a bad and unpredictable cat. But I gambled that we could change all that, simply with affection, if it was true in the first place. Buster lived up to his reputation by biting elephant handler Jeff Haynes in

Pepper, our black leopard

John with eight-week-old Nikita

the shoulder the moment he passed into his compound. Still I had a hunch about Buster, believing he could be turned around with patience and human contact. I planned to provide much of the latter myself.

At about the same time, John drove north to British Columbia with his girlfriend, Lin Breshears, to pick up a tiger cub we later named Nikita, at the Okanagan Game Preserve. Nikki took up life with John and Lin by biting a hole in their water bed. This young Siberian was to cut quite a swath through the canyon acres. Generally, by the time a Siberian male is three months old, the look in his eyes says plainly that he is not afraid of man or beast. Nikki had that look, but he and John became the closest of friends.

* * *

It was quite obvious that the so-called Knobhill cats, the ones who had stayed with us in the Sherman Oaks house, even for a short while, viewed us differently than did the ones who had come straight from animal parks or zoos to Soledad Canyon. We were family to Casey or Needra; we were not family to Togar or Tongaru or the Wild Bunch. And above all there was Billy, the love of my life—until a shattering midsummer afternoon in 1974.

Billy was then about two and a half years old, physically a grown lion, but our relationship had not changed very much since I'd held him in my arms at the age of five days. I think he would have been happy to live on Knobhill until he died, staying by my side night and day. And I'd always felt totally safe with him. I could even feed him out of my hands, something I'd attempt with very few other lions and tigers. His canines were two inches long, but he still took my thumb into his mouth to suck it.

Billy had a sweet look about him, even when he was slightly angry with me, which sometimes occurred if I'd been away for a while. He might not even look at me at first when I'd go into his compound. But I'd scratch him under the chin for a moment, hug him, talk to him; we would make up and be on our way.

On this particular afternoon we'd gone for our usual walk, heading northwest along the river toward the first trailer camp, and then had returned to the picnic table by the lake and the newly constructed African house. Billy was sitting quietly by me, watching some coots on the lake, when Sylvie Loboda approached me to ask me about something.

Tiny Sylvie, who always made me smile when I heard her baby-talk to the cats, got to within twenty feet of me, and suddenly Billy charged her. I was speechless; dumbfounded. Billy knew Sylvie well. She knew him. She'd worked for us for two years. Yet there he was, up on his hind legs, claws out, canines bared; snarling.

Sylvie shouted, "No!" and I echoed her as Billy returned to me to begin pacing back and forth in front of me, *protecting me*, of all things. I stopped him and put my arms around him, kneeling down. He glared at Sylvie, making deep chest threats, the same terrorizing sound that his father, Togar, made, almost like a machine gun. I could feel the anger in him.

Noel had heard us yelling and came on the double toward the lake, shouting at Billy as soon as he saw him. But once again Billy left my side and charged, meaning to kill Noel, it appeared. He seemed to have gone berserk. Noel backed off, frantically weaving crossed arms, shouting, "No! No! No! Leave it. Leave it!"

Jeff Haynes came running up to help Noel, and he too was charged, with Billy making the unmistakable guttural sounds that meant "Stay away." I'd never heard a lion give such strong warnings. Jeff backed off, as Noel had done.

Every time Billy charged he would come straight back to me, continuing pacing and slowly pushing me away from Noel, Jeff and Sylvie. By now, it was obvious that he saw them as threats to me. Something had clicked in that big head, changing me from mother

The full-grown Billy still sucking my thumb

figure to his lady. Never again would our relationship be the same.

Unable to calm Billy, Noel shouted, "Get out of sight," and I began to work my way slowly toward the African house, moving a foot or so at a time while Billy continued to "protect" me, keeping up that chilling chest rumble. Finally, I reached the house and slipped inside, knowing that Billy would never understand why our relationship had changed in a matter of moments; why his protection wasn't wanted.

With me out of sight, it took Noel and Jeff about twenty minutes to calm Billy down enough to walk him back to his compound. Noel did it with soft words and patience. But the next day we visited Billy and it was immediately evident that he wanted to break down the fence simply because Noel was standing beside me. He was in an attack posture and being noisy about it. We now knew it could be Noel, Sylvie, Jeff Haynes, Frank Tom, Liberato, the kids—anyone. The only time I could ever again be with Billy was when I was completely alone. No more walks with him, for fear we might run into a crew member or someone else. Yet we discovered that same day that Noel or Sylvie could approach Billy alone and he would be as docile and friendly as ever. Out of sight (and hearing), out of mind.

Billy had never been a vicious animal; his only problem was, and still is, a single-minded possessiveness toward me, and nothing will ever change that circumstance. That is the way of the big cat.

Not long after the episode with Billy I paid in pain for another fit of possessiveness when I tried to take a camera away from lioness Barbra. I had put the camera down for a moment while in her compound and then made the thoughtless mistake of trying to jerk it away from her. Though she was a young cat, weighing about 150 pounds, her teeth could bite through a brick. She closed one canine on my left arm, puncturing it. I had a tetanus shot and a sore arm for a couple of weeks, but out of it came a relatively inexpensive lesson. In trying to take something away from a cat I had gone about it the wrong way. From Barbra I learned to do it differently—distract the animal, offer it something else. Or simply surrender and say, "Okay, you want the hat, take the hat." There are times, however, when the object may be harmful to the cat and it is necessary to recover it, one way or another, even with whooshes of the fire extinguisher.

Not many days later I flew to Honduras to help with a Food for the Hungry relief mission after a devastating hurricane struck that

138

country. When I returned, about two weeks later, one of the first things I did was visit Billy. I made certain no other human was around when I entered his compound. He was on the other side of the stream, and though I spoke to him, moving slowly toward him, he wouldn't even look at me. He turned his back and busied himself with all sorts of lion things: he drank from the stream, inspected the fence perimeters, checked out the cats in the next compound. I remained motionless. Then, quite suddenly, he leaped over the stream in one fluid vault, passing in front of me. Then he stopped and took my knee between his teeth, applying the slightest pressure imaginable. He had missed me.

We'd lost cubs, for one reason or another, but thus far death had not touched any of the adult cats in the canyon. Then in November, Pharaoh became ill. I think the cheetah had been ill for a much longer time, but that jungle and savanna dictate instructed him to look well no matter what. By the time I was aware of any sickness he was already far gone, kidneys and other organs deteriorating.

Cheetahs have an average life span of twelve years, and Pharaoh was supposedly eight. Whatever his age, it was heartbreaking to watch that beautiful animal begin to shrink; to see the glint in his eyes fading. When a big cat knows it is terminally ill, it will stop eating and drinking. The situation does not reverse. After efforts by several vets in the Los Angeles area, I drove Pharaoh to the University of California at Davis, home of what I think is the finest veterinary school in the country. Dr. Murray Fowler, head of vet medicine, went to work, but to no avail. Pharaoh died three days later and I returned to Los Angeles grief-stricken. I'd lost a great friend.

The death of a big cat always sends me into depression. To think that the magnificent animal is gone forever is something I do not handle well. The size and looks of the animal are factors, I'm sure, and if a close and friendly relationship has been developed with the cat the loss is devastating. Perhaps it is because one does not expect ever again to have that special bond with an animal so unique.

I have a particular loathing for taxidermists and for those people who display stuffed trophies of the wild. None of our animals will ever receive that final insult. When death occurs, they are buried on the property, usually beneath one of the trees. There is as much dignity about it as we can provide.

—16—

THE PERFECT LOCATION

Since 1971, many drafts of the script had been written, radical changes resulting from a better understanding of the animals and what they were capable of doing or were likely to do. In the first script there'd been relatively few big-cat scenes because we knew so little about them. Now the animals were in almost every scene.

For example, we knew from firsthand experience the happy, not angry, destructive tendencies of the big cat, still a cub at heart. So Noel had written a scene where five or six of the animals invade the living room of the African house and happily demolish all of the furniture. Five cameras would grind from concealed openings in the walls, and the cats would have at it with consuming joy. A writer who had not observed the great fun cats have with such destruction would probably never have thought of that scene.

Although script changes often occur until the last day of shooting, we considered Noel's latest blueprint for the film mostly finished. And what we had, we thought, was a mixture of comedy, drama and genuine big-cat behavior of a totally unique kind, punctuated by moments of stark terror in the encounters between animals, and between the human and the animal cast. Underlying the slim story was the plea for preservation of the grandeur of these and other wild animals. But standing back, this many years later, I realize that mixing

140

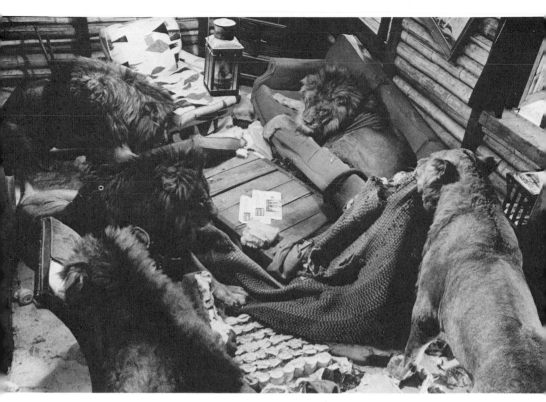
Cats demolish the living room of the "African house."

these elements successfully was not only difficult but perhaps impossible. The animals were the real stars of the film, a circumstance usually reserved for documentaries. Of course, we weren't thinking about all these variables down in the canyon as the year 1975 began. We marked time, still waiting for money.

The year got off to a bad start on the first Saturday in January when Hudu bit Noel on the hand during an impromptu learning session in the African house, where the lions and tigers were mingling together without restraint. Noel went to the Sherman Oaks Hospital, the wound was treated and the doctor on duty declared that it had to be sewn up. Noel protested, saying that in our experience any wound from cat teeth should be left open to drain and heal. The few bites we'd suffered thus far, aside from scalp lacerations, had healed nicely with that procedure.

The doctor insisted and sutured the wound. By midnight, at home, Noel was in agony and red lines extended from his hand to his armpit. Millions of bacteria exist on big-cat canines and do damage with terrifying speed. I immediately drove Noel to St. John's Hospital in Santa Monica, where he was diagnosed as having advanced blood poisoning. The onset had taken less than twenty-four hours, and within another twelve hours Noel was on the critical list, near death.

It was a close call. Though he was released three weeks later, the medication course lasted two more weeks and another lesson had been learned. We now knew to keep puncture wounds open, suffer the antibiotics and let nature do its work, defying suture-happy doctors.

As the year progressed, one problem or another seemed to arise each week. We continually hovered on a financial precipice. The expense of housing and maintaining the animals mounted steadily. But not once did we consider turning back.

On the far horizon there was sunshine. *The Exorcist* had smashed all box-office records when it opened the previous year, Hollywood pundits predicting that it would become the largest money-making film in the history of Warner Brothers. Noel's name was up on the screen as executive producer, and we hoped that we would receive a few million dollars somewhere down the line, perhaps even within six months. One Hollywood columnist, Army Archerd, had called the film's profits "devil's money." We were delighted, of course, devil dollars or not. Now we could proceed with *Roar*, the new title for *Lions, Lions and More Lions*, a name much too long for marquees. Or we thought we could proceed, maybe by year's end. But future *Exorcist* money did not solve immediate problems. The animals *had* to be fed; the maintenance crew and the few handlers *had* to be paid.

Practically every weekend that spring we entertained money men in the canyon. Five or six potential investors would be brought out to tour the compounds, meet the cats, see the African house and listen to a spiel from Noel about *Roar*. I would either make lunches on Knobhill and bring them out or pick up something from the deli. The money men watched and listened, were seemingly awed by the animals while nervously posing with them for photos, but didn't offer any cash.

The financing of an independent production, one that has no studio or distribution company ties, is akin to fishing day after day where few fish swim. It requires endless patience and aggressive tenacity. Unless a superstar is signed, along with a name director and a distribution guarantee, banks tend to keep their coffers tightly closed. An entertainment-related company here and there, now and then, may be persuaded to dole out some money; occasionally, an entrepreneur-type company head, wanting a fling in Hollywood, will invest corporate funds. Mostly, the investors in indie productions are private individuals seeking tax shelters. They are not easy to come by. We kept trying.

As broke as we were, it was foolish to keep bringing animals to the menagerie that spring, but we did anyway. Noel added cougars to Frank Tom's resident puma, Gilligan. A few more mouths to feed. The cougar is, of course, America's native and only "lion." Also called puma, catamount, panther and mountain lion, the sleek animal once ranged from southeast Alaska to Tierra del Fuego. Though most people think of it as a Western feline it was more common in the East long ago. About the size of a leopard, but stockier and with longer legs, the cougar can outjump tigers or leopards, dropping from as high as sixty feet unerringly to the back of a deer. From a standing start, it can leap fifteen feet into the air.

Hated by sheepmen and cattle owners, though it doesn't raid herds that often, the cougar is an endangered species. As an example of the official vendetta against the animal, until 1969 it was classified as a predator in California. Then it was reclassified as a game animal and over five thousand permits were issued at fifty cents each so that brave hunters could track down the six hundred animals estimated to be alive. No one knows how many are alive today. Yet the beleaguered cougar kills only what it needs for sustenance. In captivity, the only safe home cougars will ever have, they're a bunch of Garbos, liking to be alone.

During early summer I was with a group of church women on another Food for the Hungry project, helping settle incoming Vietnamese in the Sacramento area, when John called to say that lioness Samantha had died of unknown causes. The cat had become weak, gone into convulsions and was dead within hours. I rushed back to the canyon.

Two days later another cat died under the same circumstances. Then another. All with the same symptoms. We called in a battery of scientists from UCLA, two vets from the Los Angeles area, and finally Dr. Fowler from the Davis school. All concluded that the killer was a virus, and the task of attempting to identify it began.

There was no pattern to this bug which attacked over a span of weeks. It would strike a four-month-old cub, then a fully grown

143

previously healthy lion like big, funny Lurch. It killed haphazardly. It killed Hudu and Bridget and lovely Needra.

Noel called me in the Sacramento area, where I was again working with Vietnamese, to say, "Needra's dead. You have to come home. You can't save the world." He was weeping openly, the first time I'd ever heard him do that. It didn't help my own heartbreak. I flew home biting my lip.

Barbra died. Igor, the tiger I'd picked up in a carrying case at Los Angeles International so long ago, was suddenly dead. John grieved for Igor for weeks.

But heartbreak was soon a luxury for all of us. We were frantic. Somehow the virus skipped over the leopards and the cougars. They seemed totally immune. But for weeks I almost hated to pick up the phone at Knobhill or drive out to the canyon, certain John would say, "We lost another one last night." He was now managing the compounds.

The virus ran its course in about four months, leaving fourteen lions and tigers dead. Not one of the experts could identify it or be positive about its origin. We thought about the cougars. They were the only new breed introduced recently. But the vets tended to discount any involvement of the mountain lions, guessing that the germ might have been airborne. Not knowing what it was, nor how to protect the animals against it, we could only pray the virus wouldn't visit again.

Toward the end of that siege came a scare from different quarters. We awakened on the morning of August 13 to hear on the radio that a brushfire was threatening to come over the mountain and might head toward Soledad if the wind picked up. August, September and October are fire months in the mountains around us. Southern California usually suffers several devastating brushfires each year. Noel and I looked at each other. What else could happen to us?

Jerry had joined John in the canyon, helping to take care of the animals for the summer. By now, the brothers had been around the big cats for three years and were competent handlers. Though John seemed calm on the phone when we called him, we drove out to mobilize trucks to move all the furry populace if necessary. Fire threat is even scarier than flood threat to an animal handler. The idea of mixing raging flames and big cats is scariest of all. Loading them in smoke and drifting ashes would be a nightmare, we thought.

By early evening the fire had been water-bombed into containment and we canceled the alert. But it added to the unease of that hot summer. Temperatures down on the river flats were over 100 degrees every day. The cats stayed in the shade, lifeless. Vegetation was so dry that we could hear it crackling.

Then, to answer the question of "What else could happen to us?" Noel learned that his share of Bill Blatty's profits from *The Exorcist* would not be forthcoming after all. The agreement between them had been oral. And there, for the time being, went the pot of gold to make *Roar*. A lawsuit was instituted. Noel had earned his share.

The year continued the down pattern and on October 1 we sold our Knobhill home. To feed the cats and maintain a minimum crew was costing about $4,000 a week. We had two rental homes in Beverly Hills and made plans to occupy one of them temporarily. But the move from Knobhill was a wrenching one, though we were moving to a finer home in a more affluent neighborhood. I loved Knobhill. There were so many happy memories lodged there. The wedding. The kids growing up. Fun with the cubs.

What wouldn't sink in, or maybe we wouldn't allow it to sink in, was that *Roar* and all those animals out in the canyon *now owned us.* We were captives of that unmade movie and the eighty-odd cats, plus Timbo, that we had collected to make it. Even if we'd wanted to quit at this point, there was no way to do it. *Sell the cats? Offer them free?* No right-minded person would take all those cats, and I would have been suspicious of the takers anyway. There are too many eccentrics out there who would quickly answer an ad giving away lions and tigers. Zoos are not financially capable of taking care of a large number of big cats.

We were stuck. Not unhappily.

After Christmas we went shopping for two mobile homes to place down by the river in Soledad Canyon. We would eventually live in one of them; the other would be for Dutch cinematographer Jan de Bont. The mobile home in which John was living was up on higher ground.

Prospects looked no brighter in 1976 than they had been in 1975. It was probably inevitable that sooner or later we would have to sell both Beverly Hills homes and the other properties, as well as 650 undeveloped acres we owned in the Newhall area. The animals had to be fed; the maintenance crew and the handlers had to be paid.

I knew something about hard times. Another Christmas long ago, when I was ten, I unwrapped my one present—a can of pineapple, a fruit that I loved. My father had been ill again and there was no money in the house for the usual gifts. There had been other lean times. I knew what it was to be broke.

That spring, I hocked my wedding ring, my pearls, my gold watch, my topaz, and the fur coat Hitch had given me. The animals had to be fed. It didn't really bother me to lose the baubles temporarily. And I had long ago decided not to wear the fur coat again. My consciousness had been raised against the killing of any animal for its coat. But it all would have been much easier had not Noel been such a workaholic. Blinders on, he kept up his twenty-hour days. We had little or no social life, less and less time to spend with each other. I went to family gatherings by myself. We were both so consumed by our concern for the animals and our anxiety about money that, almost without our knowing it, our marriage was beginning to come apart.

We suffered another setback that spring when Jeff Haynes quit us, leaving Timbo without a regular trainer for almost a month. Liberato provided Timbo's five hundred pounds of daily rations—a grown elephant will eat a hundred thousand pounds of hay and twelve thousand pounds of dried alfalfa yearly—but there was no one to walk him on a steady basis. Mostly, he stayed in his barn and I talked to him each day, handing him carrots or some other treat. But I could tell that he was restless and lonely.

Then on a fine Sunday morning there was a knock on the door and a tall redheaded young man named Tim Cooney was standing there. "I hear you need an elephant trainer," he said.

"We certainly do" was my quick reply.

Tim had been with a circus but was tired of all the traveling. He went to work for us that same day, just sitting in the barn with Timbo, talking to him, feeding him. In fact, Tim sat there for three weeks, reading magazines, speaking now and then to the elephant. Then they began their morning exercise walks. The lights came back on in Timbo's eyes.

Despite all the little alarm bells that kept going off, our family of animals was still growing. More tigers this time. Ron Oxley gave us Panda Bear, a female Siberian. He'd wanted to work the tigress, but finally decided it was too dangerous. Only the Bengals are pliable and reliable enough for show business. Then the Okanagan Game Preserve contributed Singh Singh, another Siberian, litter mate of Natasha and Ivan but a totally different animal. We were warned that Singh Singh was an absolute monster, but we still had romantic

146

Elephant trainer Tim Cooney

notions about being able to tame the wildest of beasts. We'd been so successful with a number of the "bad" cats that we thought that with time, love and kisses, conversion of almost any animal was possible. But within a few days Singh Singh gave evidence that his former keepers had been entirely candid. The sounds that came out of him were horrific. Noel gave orders for no one to enter his space. Liberato put his food and water through the fencing, departing immediately. Feces were washed out daily with a hose. The only practical solution was an old one, often workable—provide Singh Singh with a mate. Panda Bear, of course. He was handsome, she was beautiful, and the results had every chance of being pleasing.

Over the next several weeks in the canyon, twelve lion cubs were born and only two died. Birth is always a good and promising sign. And then on Monday, August 16, Noel called with good news.

"I don't believe it," I yelled back into the phone. "I do *not* believe it!"

Singh Singh, beautiful but bad

EMI, a British entertainment company, was going to invest half a million dollars in *Roar*, providing we put up collateral which included one of the homes in Beverly Hills. Another investor, Banjiro Uemura, a Tokyo producer, would put up another half million.

I sat down. Weak. Jubilant but weak. Five years of dreaming, planning, sweating, gambling, praying, hoping—just surviving—had finally paid off. What did some hocked jewels and a house in Sherman Oaks matter? At last we had the money we needed and we could start in a month or so. Gather a crew, rent lights, cameras, sound equipment. Anything and everything to make movies was easily available just by picking up the phone.

* * *

Whatever the plans and grand machinations of the two-footed Hollywood types around the compounds, the sometimes more predictable four-footed ones continued their unique ways during this high-adrenaline time. Thirteen days after EMI and Banjiro Uemura saw the wisdom of investing money in a fantastic film about big cats, lion Luna strolled out of the perimeter fence. Someone had left a section ajar and she was seen on the other side of the fourteen-foot-high steel mesh, moseying toward the railroad tracks and the low chapparal mountains to the north. A handler had her by the tail for a few seconds before she pulled loose and bounded away.

Luna was an adult, about four years old, and while she did not have the reputation of being a bad cat, no one really had a performance line on her. She wasn't one of the Knobhill gang. Frankly, we didn't know what she would do. Insurance covering this sort of thing, an adventuring lion, had been impossible to obtain at a sane price, and it behooved us to bring her home as soon as possible. She might harm an animal or a person, though the former was more likely.

Luna's pugmarks, the paw prints, led upward, so we knew the general direction in which she'd gone. A lion's front paws have five toes; one, corresponding to the human thumb, is set higher than the others. So the tracker sees only four toes in front. In the back, the first toe, or human big toe, is missing completely. The paws are digitigrade, enabling the cats to walk on their tiptoes. The pugmarks of a lion are unmistakable and easy to follow.

As darkness fell, we searched for Luna with flashlights in rattlesnake terrain—not the best of endeavors, but we spent some time that night moving gingerly around under a moonless, black sky. We were hoping to pick up the unmistakable round eyes of the big cat. From the lynx on down, cats, including the tabbies, have vertical slits within almond-shaped eyes. The pupils of the big cats darken after the sun goes down. In moonlight or flashlight glow they glisten nonetheless. But Luna was not to be found.

In the morning we began mobilizing for a twenty-four-hour-a-day search in the canyon country and the low mountains to the north. Though brush-covered in many places, the mountains are mostly treeless and offer few hiding places for an animal as large as an adult lion. By midday, about twenty people were involved, most carrying walkie-talkies. We had not notified the authorities, knowing that the press would be alerted and TV crews sent out, probably in helicopters. What was a possibly dangerous situation might be quickly compounded.

Among the other things that we didn't want to happen was a free-for-all lion shoot. There were some stalwart hunters in that canyon country who would have been all too happy to get out their rifles and go four-wheeling. So it was necessary to work out a code word that would not identify the nature of our search, nor the object of it, to unwanted ears. We chose "Perfect Location," as if a film company were looking for the right camera site; that voice code was to be used when Luna was found or when the search territory was shifted. We had hired a helicopter and it was already spinning around the hills.

A CB station was set up in the filming office, an old portable dressing room that had been bought at an auction when a little studio went out of business. It was located in the area of the preserve we called Up-Front, near the elephant barn. The guarding radio frequency was manned dawn to dark.

The first day's search proved futile, and the long second day passed without sight of the lioness, despite the intensive aerial and ground search, which now involved about forty people, including a number of "friend" volunteers. By nightfall we were becoming desperate. A lion on the loose without food for three days is inviting disaster. We were hoping Luna had found a rabbit or a possum. Not cattle. And though we couldn't prove it, Noel and I kept insisting, "She's not a half mile away." A tiger might have been far-roaming, not a lioness.

The second night was long and tense. We had fully expected a call by this time to report that Luna had been sighted. Logically, people in the area would call either us, Ron Oxley or Steve Martin. We were the only keepers of big cats within miles. But no one called. Luna had simply vanished.

Lookouts, including my sister Patty, down from Portland on a visit, were posted in likely places surrounding the acreage. All were carrying walkie-talkies, but it was midmorning of the third day before Luna was spotted. I was manning the receiver in the office when it suddenly crackled and a handler said, "I've found the Perfect Location . . ." Then the voice died away before he could identify himself or say where he was.

Frantic, I kept hitting all the switches until finally I got the giggles. We'd spent three frustrating, nervous days and thousands of dollars in chopper rental, and one or more fifty-cent batteries had pooped out.

A few minutes later another handler came running into the office to say that Luna was up under the road bridge, where my sister was posted, about the length of three football fields away, still on our property. Noel and I had been right. Luna had not wandered far. She was camouflaged in a lush, cool, green area by the river and seemed perfectly content to stay in that jungle hideaway.

We were readying a truck to go fetch her when Noel came up to say, "No, no, I'll just walk her back."

He went up under the bridge, found the lioness sprawled out and said simply, "Come on, Luna, let's go home."

She got up and gladly followed Noel back to the compound. I was waiting there for her, and as she went in all her four-footed roommates ran up as if to ask, "Where did you go? What did you see? What did you do?"

—17—

THE ACTORS

With *Roar* scheduled to start October 1, the beginning of September was a wonderful period. Our new mobile home was maneuvered down the steep dirt road to a resting place by the river, shaded by cottonwoods. We had vague plans to move from Beverly Hills by Thanksgiving or so, settling temporarily in the canyon. But first I began the quest for a wardrobe—four days of shopping. All actresses look forward to these sprees before a picture begins, hoping that at least one outfit will be a stunner. Alas, my clothes for Madeline were drab and uninteresting. But assuming the role of costumer, I shopped for the rest of the cast as well.

By late in the month, when the summer's brassy bake oven was departing the high desert, to the profound relief of furred inhabitants and sweating humans alike, we were almost ready to roll cameras. Considering what we'd first seen down in the canyon five years previously—a few animal cages, a little trailer, several cottonwoods, rocks, sand and chaparral—there'd been quite a transformation. About twenty acres, with the big, boxy two-story mock-bamboo scientist's house, on the edge of the lake, as the focal point on the set, looked an awful lot like East Africa. I thought Noel had done a superb job in design and landscaping. I doubt that the major studios could have done a better job.

Most of the support buildings for a miniature studio—camera shop, wardrobe, editing rooms, machine shop, electrical shop, kitchen-commissary to feed a hundred—were also complete. Made of ply-wood, they were hardly MGM or Paramount, but they served the purpose adequately. Constructed in a line, they were about thirty feet back from the river. Then there were the various animal support buildings in the Up-Front area, near the elephant barn, most notably the ten-thousand-pound freezer unit for big-cat food. Nearby was the animal hospital, with space for two cats and a refrigerator for the storage of various medicines and antibiotics.

One rather unusual aspect of our movie lot was two yellow-circled paramedic-helicopter pads that Noel had bulldozed out on each end of the property—just in case. There are minor injuries on almost every big action film, occasionally serious ones and, on very rare occasions, death. Most big action films have a trained first-aid person on duty, and in some cases a fully accredited doctor stays with the picture until completion. Our electrician was our licensed paramedic. Due to the equipment, and the high voltages of electricity used, all motion picture sets are potentially dangerous. Wild animals, particularly the way we planned to use them, simply added to the hazards. Anticipating some bites and scratches, we hoped and prayed none would be serious. We didn't care to think about the possibility of death. It was never mentioned.

Young Jan de Bont, award-winning cinematographer of *Keetje Tippel* and *Max Havelar*, foreign hits, and an Oscar nominee for the German film *Turkish Delight*, was on the site and ready to work. Since animals do not keep a regular schedule, aside from mealtimes, Jan was "resident cinematographer," unusual for any film, available for work night or day and weekends. With his beautiful actress wife, Monique Van de Ven, star of *Keetje Tippel* and *Turkish Delight,* he was living in the mobile home up the road from ours, a three-minute walk from his place of work. Director of photography on more than twenty Dutch and German feature films, he had also been behind camera on many music specials for European companies. We knew that his work was excellent and had reason to believe he would look a tiger in the eye without flinching. The flexibility of a European cameraman was needed. *Roar* could not have been made with most American cinematographers, pampered by the industry and unions alike.

Still photography, not only for publicity purposes but for a pho-tographic record of the day's shooting and the sets, is a key job on every film. I did not know any Hollywood stillman who would take

Jan de Bont and his wife, Monique Van de Ven

on the challenge of lions and tigers six feet away, so I chose a quiet, unassuming darkroom employee named Bill Dow. He had printed many of the photos I'd done for Food for the Hungry, and I was very impressed by his work. Bill had never been on a film set in his life, nor had he ever aimed a camera at a charging big cat. But he was the exactly right person to learn on the job and would never think of looking at the time clock.

Our animal cast now numbered 132 lions, tigers, leopards, cougars and jaguars, plus the elephant, three aoudad sheep, and the exotic savanna birds that Joel had begun to gather for background in some of the scenes. He still did not care to be around the big cats but was thoroughly enamored with his ostriches, flamingos, marabou storks, black swans and other feathered creatures to be found in

Africa. They were his exclusive wards. Joel was also serving as set dresser, the person who "dresses" the sets, indoors or out, to make them authentic for the period.

The three tawny aoudad sheep, from the mountains of North Africa, lived up the slope behind the crew kitchen and sometimes came down to visit the cook, wisely staying away from the cat compounds. We planned to acquire some Grévy zebras and rent a few chimpanzees later on for added authenticity.

Of the human cast, for the first week of scheduled work, on hand were Melanie, John, Jerry and myself. We would go before the cameras as needed and even do our own stunt work, saving that cost. Noel, of course, as director and as Hank, would be involved in every day's shooting whether or not he personally appeared before camera.

The other principal player, Kyalo Mativo, would not be needed for a while. Tall, thin, agile, the thirty-five-year-old black actor had been born in Kitui Province, Kenya, in the Nairobi area, of a Kamba tribal family. His mother had been carrying a bundle of thatching grass on her head and Kyalo, pronounced "Chaalo," in her womb when she gave birth to him on a dirt road at high noon. No midwife was present and she took baby and thatching grass on home. We wanted an authentic African, who spoke with that particular lilt, for the role of Hank's assistant zoologist. Mativo filled it, in all ways.

Two other candidates for the part, one a Senegalese, the other a Nigerian, had failed the first test—introduction to the big cats. We took the man from Senegal to meet gentle Boomer lion and he literally had to be carried out of the compound. His body was rigid with fright. The Nigerian candidate was not as afraid, but his wife and children, who came out for the test, were petrified. They were ready to run the first time the lions roared. They vetoed Daddy working in the film.

Mativo, on a four-year scholarship to study film at UCLA, had written and directed for the Voice of Kenya TV station and had acted in two short German films. A funny, charming man with a wry sense of humor, very political, he declared to us, "I will only be with those animals while we're filming." He kept his promise, vanishing from the set the moment a scene was over. He cheerfully admitted that he was deathly afraid of the big cats.

As for the rest of Roar's "starring" human cast, by now we had a great knowledge of big-cat behavior, plus tremendous respect for them. John's roughing-up by Tongaru had not made him afraid of all cats. My bloody experience on the log with Cherries had not made me afraid of all cats, either, but it certainly made me cautious. Hudu's gnawing on Noel was the result of excitement rather than his being a target, but Noel too had learned caution. All of us who would come face to face with the lions and tigers on many occasions felt much the same way—fully aware of the danger, respectful, careful.

Noel made no pretense of being an actor. Yet, on the eve of filming, there was still no actor that we knew of who also had the ability to handle groups of lions. Noel thought he could do that as well as or better than any of the Hollywood cat trainers, some of whom also claimed to be actors.

I thought so, too. Over several years I'd seen Noel enter the compounds and watched the lions and tigers inundate him. He would yell, "Come on, lions," and they would come running, hugging and kissing him, pressing him to the earth and rolling on him. They gave open affection to him, and the caliber of his acting was of secondary importance. He'd grown a scraggly beard and I sincerely believe that a lot of those lions thought he was a lion. What many people find difficult to understand is that the big cats *do love to play*, and in Noel they'd found a human playmate.

By now, we also knew that lions and tigers responded to confidence. Noel sometimes laughed at a charging lion and literally embarrassed the animal into stopping. His best defense, usually, was in dodging out of the way, like a rodeo clown. A lion's anger, or annoyance, dissolves quickly.

All things considered, only Noel Marshall could act in and direct *Roar* and probably survive it.

As final preparations for filming began, Jerry Marshall, to be son Jerry in the picture, and Melanie Griffith, to be daughter Melanie, were both nineteen years old—born on the same day, but very different people, not unexpectedly.

Brown-haired, brown-eyed Jerry was a practical joker whose favorite pastimes were girls, body surfing and tennis, not necessarily in that order. Even though he'd done those half-dozen TV commercials, I could never determine how serious he was about an acting career. Easygoing Jerry would have been perfectly happy to play tennis seven days a week and see a different girl every night.

Sensitive Melanie was as headstrong and outspoken as ever, and very talented. She made plain her desire to be a fine actress. I loved her dearly, cherished her, but, as an old-fashioned mother, I sometimes found it difficult to understand her. After making her debut

Kyalo Mativo,
of Kenya

with Gene Hackman in *Night Moves*, she had gone on to co-star with Paul Newman and Joanne Woodward in *The Drowning Pool*, and in *Smile* with Bruce Dern. She had a bright career ahead of her, I thought, whatever she chose to do.

Thickly bearded John Marshall, at twenty-one an outgoing young man, always laughing and eager to please, was in many ways like his father. His parts in *Wagon Train, Laramie, Lassie* and other TV series, plus all those commercials as a moppet, qualified him as a seasoned actor.

So the three children knew quite a lot about this frustrating, tiring, boring, glamorous, heartbreaking, miserable, murderous but exhilarating and occasionally rewarding business of making movies. Of the three, John knew the most about big-cat behavior.

Had anyone said we were going to make a home movie, I would have questioned his sanity. But in a way, that's exactly what we were

157

A family affair: Jerry, John and Melanie

doing—shooting it in our backyard, the whole family involved. If so, *Roar* would eventually qualify for *The Guinness Book of World Records* as the most expensive home movie ever made.

Of the lion and tiger cast, Robbie was the star. A huge and handsome Rhodesian lion, though born in America, Robbie had the finest black mane I'd ever seen on any big cat. We first met him when he was eight or nine months old, being raised on dog kibble, of all things. Never had I heard of anyone feeding a big cat dry canine rations, but Robbie apparently hadn't suffered. When he was about two, his owner could no longer take care of him and called us.

On taking up residence in the compounds, Robbie quickly and easily converted from dry meal to muscle meat. The first time I renewed acquaintance with him, he promptly knocked me down and rolled over me. Pressed to the sand, I was embarrassed, not hurt. I realized he was just greeting me in a physical way and had no ill intents. But I did set about teaching him not to knock me down again.

Robbie soon became good friends with the tigers, and very protective of them, especially Gregory. In fact, he became possessive of Gregory and was always very vocal about it. Casey, Berries and the other cats he lived with learned to stay away from Robbie whenever he had one of his streaks over Gregory. But his relations with humans, generally, were affectionate and nonthreatening, though he was probably the most powerful lion in the compounds, even stronger than Togar. He was certainly the most photogenic.

As for the production of the film, we projected completing *Roar* in six months and within a budget of three million, including outlays for animal upkeep and maintenance of the compounds. The idea of making it for a million had long ago vanished. There were a number of contingencies built into the schedule. Most films are made by working a five-day week, six on location, but this, undeniably, was not most films, and there might be times when we would work on Sundays without paying the union's "golden time." We knew, too, that there would be interruptions from the winter's gray skies and rain and from unknowns in handling the animal cast.

Obviously, we could neither afford nor obtain a regular Hollywood crew for the production. The unions would have required two handlers for each animal used, and on some days that would amount to sixty people over and above the usual grips and electricians and camera operators. Also, by doing a union shoot, we would have exposed that many more bodies to danger, perhaps upward of two hundred people. And a great many film technicians, we realized, would decline to work with a bunch of free-roaming lions. Money was easier and safer made at Paramount or Warners or in TV production.

Our filming would probably be sporadic, using employees on a daily or weekly basis. And we would probably break almost every union rule in the sacred books, so our crew or crews would have to be nonunion, many of them eager young people who would do almost anything to work on a film, at nonscale prices. But at the same time we would be offering these young people a chance to enter the unions. After a person has worked one film, union or nonunion, the prized card becomes available. Then there were older technicians—electricians, grips, camera assistants—who did not have a card for one reason or another. They too would be hired if qualified. Of all the entertainment films produced in the United States, less than half are made with union crews.

Despite the fact that we were doing a nonunion shoot, we managed to gather a crew that had more experience than anticipated. The camera people and the sound men were all highly experienced, as were our electricians. Our production manager, Charles "Chuck" Sloan, a soft-spoken man in his forties, was second in command to Noel, boss of the daily operations. Chuck had a television background as well as an affinity for big cats. He had helped raise some of them, and knew the compounds. Among the other crew members, only a few, like pigtailed judo man Frank Tom, had had experience with the cats.

A local girl, Alexandra Newman, had no experience when she began doing routine chores with the animals, but she finally became especially good with the tigers and leopards. She also became qualified as a vet-tech.

A striking, dark-haired girl, Alex eventually became involved with jaguars. So far as I'm concerned those cats are the most dangerous animals in existence. Given a choice of being trapped in a room with a jaguar or a tiger, I'll take the tiger any day. Jags are the only cats with enough spunk to go after an eight-foot adult crocodile and are probably the best swimmers of all.

Patricia and Henry jaguar were the offspring of a pair that had been boarded in the canyon. The arrangement was that we would receive the cubs in exchange for the board bill. As infants, they were cute and cuddly, much like little lions and tigers in play patterns, and Alex hand-raised them, adoring them. She bottle-fed them and made them part of her life, determined, against the odds, to foster

Alex Newman with Mariah

a pair of good, friendly citizens. Grown-up, they were not much larger than a leopard but were stockier, with broader faces.

Certainly one of the most beautiful of all cats, the jaguar, native of Central and South America, once roaming north as far as Arizona and California, can grow to seven feet, nose to tail tip, and to weigh up to 250 pounds. There's a black variety in which the coat appears to be pure velvet, faintly imprinted with the family rosettes. In the jungle, the jaguar lies on boughs covered with orchids, which provide camouflage, while awaiting prey.

One day, while Alex was changing straw in his den house, Henry, then fully grown and weighing about 175 pounds, suddenly decided to end what had been a warm and easy human relationship. Without warning, and almost silently, he went after Alex, perhaps with mayhem in mind. A helper with a cattle prod, or Hot-Shot, was in the next space over but couldn't get to the raging jag. Alex managed

Mike Vollman with Natasha

to prevent serious injury by holding a small chain-link screen in front of her upper body, and then escaped. Like me with Cherries, she could never go near Henry again. He reacted with rage each time he saw her. And wondering whether or not Patricia was another time bomb, we later gave both of them to a zoo. I sighed with relief when they went up the canyon road.

The route to handler, for men, was generally through the maintenance gang or the fence crew. Darryl Sides, of Palmdale, one of the most agile, quick-minded people I've ever known, started in maintenance and eventually became foreman of the handlers. I once saw him scale a fourteen-foot-high chain-link fence in two upward surges, going like a monkey, to save a maintenance man who had strayed into the lake compound.

Young Mike Vollman had come home to California after working as a pitchman, running the balloon-bust concession, at a Midwest carnival. He signed up at State Unemployment and found himself working on our fence crew a few days later. Within two weeks, he was apprenticing as a handler. "Trainer" is a designation usually applied to those who persuade the animals to perform. Vollman became a fine handler and trainer.

Big-cat handling, we had discovered, has to be learned on the job by living daily with the animals, following in the footsteps of a highly experienced handler, listening carefully to him, observing his actions in the compounds and watching his relationships with each of the animals. There are no schools; no shortcuts. The one prerequisite for a cat handler is a deep desire to be around the unique animal. It can never be just a job.

Noel recruited Rick Glassey and Steve Miller from Marineworld, U.S.A., in Redwood City, California, to work specifically with tigers in several scenes. They'd been working in Marineworld's Tiger Moat as trainers. Put under contract, Glassey and Miller would be bit players in water and attack scenes. Tigers in the lake can start out having fun with sparring matches which can quickly turn into deadly fights. Lions attacking a human, in mock, can easily forget they are supposed to be playacting. It would have been too dangerous to cast these minor parts with otherwise qualified actors and actresses, even if they agreed to work.

The handlers would be involved off camera, frequently camouflaged in green to match vegetation, in every scene that involved the animals. First, the cats had to be walked to the area where the scene was taking place; then, while the cameras were running, they had to be "handled"—controlled, sent in a specific direction or enticed to do something of one kind or another. Getting ten lions to run up the steps of the African house was simple, we already knew. The handlers would show them a white bucket of meat and up the steps the animals would come. All trainers use food, whether handling a poodle or an elephant, for reward. But we had yet to discover how—or if—the animals could be enticed to perform some of the other actions called for in the script.

163

The fencing crew to be utilized during filming was composed of some of the regular maintenance people plus young, strong hourly employees. Up to twenty people would be used to quickly erect portable cyclone fencing and isolate an area into which the cats could be safely introduced. When large groups of cats were in a scene, we knew that we'd have to fence off areas up to two thousand square feet to prevent one lion or another from taking an afternoon stroll.

Big-cat experts were still telling Noel he was stark daft to try to make this movie. They predicted disaster. Multiple big cats, of mixed breeds, would be put into totally unnatural situations—cameras and lights and sound booms and the strange faces of the filming crew—and expected to behave naturally. The mixing of the breeds alone in one small area was potentially explosive—excited cats running loose and attacking one another, possibly attacking us. Okay, no film had ever undertaken these exact risks. Wasn't it time to try?

Then there was the uneasy matter of insurance and the usual completion bond, a necessity in financing most films. The investor wants some kind of guarantee that his money won't be in total jeopardy. But no insurance company would even consider the risks we planned to take, though we disagreed over the amount of risk. The lack of a completion bond didn't worry me as much as the lack of cast and crew insurance. If someone was maimed for life or fatally injured, Noel and I would be solely responsible. But I suppose we were so excited about having the start-up money that we refused to believe that serious injury would occur. No one in Las Vegas has ever gambled with such abandon.

Sensibly, we should have delayed the beginning of the film until the following spring so that the cottonwood leaves would be green for five months. Soon we'd face winter freezes in the canyon and brown leaves, which meant that we couldn't film wide exteriors from November until March. But then again we had the money—or some of it—the big cats and the family cast. We were not about to be put off by the calendar or the problem of tree leaves not matching.

Noel briefed most of the crew members on the next-to-the-last day in September, telling them what to expect from the big cats, especially warning them about possessiveness. Stressing that clothing and other personal objects should not be left on the set within reach of the animals, he pointed to a jacket a crew member had dropped across a log. It was now within the paws of a lioness. "Let me show you what will happen," Noel said and started toward the lioness.

As he approached, she closed her eyes and started the familiar guttural "uh-huh, uh-huh" deep down in her throat. When he was about twenty feet away, she raised her head and began snarling, baring her canines, determined to protect the jacket. Noel took a few more steps and she charged him, making a ferocious noise, stopping about ten feet from him when he stopped. They stayed frozen for a moment and then she returned to her prize, muttering and snarling every few seconds.

"Okay," Noel said. "Watch what happens now."

He picked up a half sheet of plywood and then charged the lioness. She scrambled away from the jacket, and Noel grabbed it, tossing it over the fence, where a handler picked it up and quickly hid it.

Noel "mixing" the big cats

"Possessing" a jacket, a lioness dares man or beast to take it away. Possession is the single most dangerous situation when working with big cats.

Twenty or thirty feet from Noel, the lioness looked a little confused for a moment or so, then began to relax. The jacket was out of sight, out of mind.

A few minutes later, Noel walked up to her, scratched under her chin and laughed at her. But her snarls and the image of her bared fangs hung over the set, and two members of the filming crew decided they would seek work elsewhere.

The last thing Noel did that afternoon was to tell the remaining workers to always wear jeans or similar pants. They were welcome to go topless, but the big cats were attracted to bare, shiny legs. One does not sensibly bait lions and tigers with fingers or legs and barefoot toes.

I took a long walk that peaceful evening, going by all the compounds and the elephant barn to say hello, finally visiting the birds, my mind really on other things. Joel had his full population in place on this eve of shooting. If the camera was aimed toward the lake and the African house, the flamingos could be placed unobtrusively in the background, lending realism to the set. But I worried from time to time about their survival. The cats watched them as one would eye whipped cream on chocolate pie.

Had I been readying to act in the morning, I would have been running over my scenes in the script, worrying about getting enough sleep, how my face and hair would look. But Noel was starting with staged lion fights, and I was mentally wearing my co-producer's hat that evening. We were going to be dealing with live lions and tigers, not props, for months. We had a new and inexperienced filming crew, and the potential for serious injury was great. Melanie, Jerry and John would be at arm's length from the cats in many scenes. They were the ones I worried most about. Not Noel, not myself. But I knew that I must not show my fear, never reveal the doubts that I had that night. Perhaps this film *was* too dangerous to make.

-18-

ROLL FILM

Filming began, with staged lion fights, on Friday, October 1, 1976, a day still vivid in my memory. In midmorning, after the big cats were walked into the set on leads, Noel said to Jan de Bont, "Roll film." Six long, frustrating years were summed up in those two words. All the preparation time since Gorongosa, all the money we'd spent, came whirring up on the camera sprockets. Almost a million of our own funds, plus the investments of EMI, Banjiro Uemura and others, was on the line.

Robert Gottschalk, then president of Panavision, was investing by lending us needed, and costly, camera equipment. Other term and credit arrangements had been made. An investor from San Diego, Jack Rattner, a financier by trade, had been drawn in because his wife, Eve, began raising lion cubs. The funding structures of indie productions can be works of art and often just as nebulous.

Less than a week later *Roar* was shut down when Casey, of all good lions, bit Noel in the hand, sending him off to Palmdale Hospital. It was a serious puncture, though miraculously the right canine missed tendons and bones as it went through flesh, piercing the palm. Noel's hand was literally impaled.

Having raised Casey from cubhood, we knew him better than any other lion in the compounds; that snap of his jaw came out of

A reluctant actor

frustration rather than any rage at Noel. As predicted, the situations in which we placed the cats caused the accidents; and the accidents caused costly delays. Seven days this first time, seven days without the usual production insurance to meet the cost of close-down and crew layoff. Placing the blame on Casey would have been not only futile but wrong.

Characteristically, Noel left the hospital for a few hours and tried to work, but, with the infection still spreading, the pain was too great. I think the first hard signs of our fatalistic obsession became evident that week. Noel would work, by God, from a wheelchair, if necessary. I was equally determined. But the obsession was not limited to Noel and me. Others in the family had it as well, in varying degrees. We were going to do this homegrown movie until death did us part.

We were already encountering the unknowns. For fifty years or more, sandbags—ordinary small canvas bags stuffed with sand—have been used to anchor bottoms of big lights and sometimes cameras or any other equipment that had to be made stationary. Who was to know that lions would take a liking to sandbags? Become wildly possessive over them? Drag them into scenes that were under way and defend them? One morning I watched as a lion backed the whole crew into a corner because he thought they were going to take his sandbag away.

One problem that surfaced in the early days of filming was the safe movement of lions and tigers from camera setup to camera setup, or the movement of them within the area where we were filming. We did have the portable sections of cyclone fencing to make temporary corridors for the passage of two, ten, twenty or thirty cats, but time was lost in rejuggling these sections. Finally, we discovered that for most circumstances we could use human fences, with our cast and crew and handlers lined up at arm's length to make corridors for big-cat passage. The animals apparently viewed the bodies as barriers and acted accordingly. We would place a handler at strategic spots between the crew people, so if anyone suddenly lost his nerve there would be an experienced hand to fill the gap and turn the cat back into line. Once we found out how to to do it, we moved lions and tigers speedily and without great difficulty. In fact, we discovered that by extending the arms with the hickory hog-handler's canes we could use fewer people on the human fences.

Yet we always knew that some of the cats in front of the dual or triple camera setups and moving along the human fences were potentially dangerous. One of the possible troublemakers was Tongaru and everyone watched him as if his dynamite fuse was always lit and burning. That fall of 1976 I think he wanted to dominate all things on earth, fellow lions as well as paper-skinned humans.

About a week after Noel's accident, Casey and Tongaru got into a fight—not one staged for the camera. It was a real slam-bang, no-holds-barred lion battle for dominance and terrifying for all bystanders, including the handlers. A fight between two grown lions, both having made up their minds to win, forgetting their usual inclination to avoid pain, is just about the scariest, loudest piece of animal conflict that can be witnessed by man. The guttural roars alone send ice up the spine. To attempt to separate them is to ask for a ride to the surgeon's table. You watch. You listen. You hold your breath and hope that neither will be seriously injured. They seldom are. But the sight and the sound are nonetheless electrifying. The lion's head is usually cocked a little bit to one side and his open mouth is framed by the mane, which seems to be standing on end. Within the big red

170

Tippi Hedren

Noel risking his life to break up a lion fight

oval his white canines hang down like spikes and you can see the row of smaller grinding teeth lining each side by the tongue. Up close, it all looks like a terrible dragon's castle. Very close, too close, you can smell the hot, foul raw-meat breath.

Tongaru won this battle for dominance. As for poor Casey, of Mandeville Canyon and Knobhill, his feelings were hurt more than his strong body.

I don't know how much this thundering donnybrook had to do with Melanie's decision to quit the cast, but soon after she said, "Mother, I don't want to come out of this with half a face."

"I understand," I said, and I did. She was young and lovely. A promising screen career was ahead. A lion like Tongaru could destroy everything in seconds.

Frank Tom roughhousing with Nikki

We hadn't yet done any scenes with Melanie, so she could be replaced if we could find someone to take her role. There were always young actresses around Hollywood who would do almost anything for a part in a film. Dozens of them. But how many had the guts to do scenes with lions and tigers? Melanie knew the cats; perhaps she knew them too well.

I decided not to dissuade her, as if we could. Noel agreed. So did John and Jerry. If she was suddenly afraid for her life she should quit. We replaced her with actress Patsy Nedd, a little-theater product and a friend of Melanie's since childhood. She had played with the cubs on Knobhill, but she knew nothing about big-cat behavior. Patsy had a lot of courage.

Indeed, Melanie's decision seemed quite sensible two weeks later when we were doing a sequence in which the family tries to escape from the cats in a rowboat. For one angle, Jan de Bont wanted a pit dug so that he could have his main camera lens on the level of the lake's surface. Then he would pull the camera back and let the cats jump over him as they went on to "attack" us.

"Okay," Noel said, "but I want you and your assistant to wear football helmets. I want something on your heads when they jump that close."

Jan agreed, and the property man was sent to town to buy a pair of football helmets.

The pit was dug and a green tarpaulin placed over it, with some shrubbery at the edges, so that the other cameras would not reveal the hidden one, a standard procedure. Each camera was camouflaged. Jan climbed under the tarpaulin. But just before Noel said, "Roll film," Jan removed his helmet because he couldn't get to the eyepiece of the camera. So his head, not the helmet, was now pushing up against the tarp, an inviting oval projection.

Along came Cherries, my old nemesis, and she saw this nice ball, which was the top of Jan's head, moving around under the tarp.

Casey "rising" to fight Tongaru

It was the same as playing with toes under blankets, which she'd done on Knobhill; the same as playing with bowling balls, which she'd done in the compounds. How could she possibly resist? She grabbed Jan's head through the tarp and ripped off his scalp from the back in one piece. His head was literally peeled.

I saw it happen and yelled, but everyone thought I was acting. No one paid any attention to me until I screamed over and over, "Jan is hurt! Jan is hurt!"

The Palmdale Hospital was becoming known as the "Noel Marshall Lion and Tiger Wing" and Jan was rushed there, an assistant director holding a towel to his head. I knew the feeling. One hundred and twenty stitches were needed to replace his scalp.

Meanwhile, Jan's assistant, a man who'd been in the pit alongside him, hired just that day, came up to me and said, "Tippi, look, I'm going to quit. You take my day's pay and buy that poor son of a bitch some flowers."

But the tough, determined Hollander was back on the job three weeks later. His wife, Monique, was not at all sure he should stay on, though she said little about it in public. Jan had obviously caught the strange obsession of *Roar* and had no intention of giving up. Big cats had never been filmed in such a manner and he knew it.

The crew was not similarly obsessed. They had seen Noel injured the first week of filming; they'd seen the battle between Casey and Tongaru; they'd seen Jan de Bont rushed away to Palmdale. They held a meeting and resigned en masse. One of them said to me, "Am I scared? You're damn right I'm scared."

Having filmed for twenty-six days thus far, we celebrated Christmas, 1976, in our new Levitt mobile home by the edge of the sparkling river, the cats caroling us at dawn. Cameras did not roll again until March, winter weather having turned our lush "East Africa" set brown and leafless, and then one day Noel said to me, very quietly, "Melanie's coming back to work." He'd called her about it and she agreed. In the interim, Melanie had made three films—*Starmaker* with Rock Hudson, *She's in the Army Now*, where she met her future husband, actor Steve Bauer, and *The Garden*, a low-budget Israeli picture. During that time we'd talked often, but her decision to return caught me completely by surprise.

I was elated but asked her, "Are you sure? Are you absolutely sure?"

Nothing had changed since she'd departed the cast in October. The risk of being mauled or bitten was still there. We knew more about handling the cats in scenes, but the dangers still existed.

"I'm sure," she said.

Noel knew, of course, that I had hoped she would return. Yet I couldn't bring myself to ask her, couldn't overcome the fear that she might be injured. Noel shrugged that off.

Now she was back and so much fun to have around. She had a marvelous sense of humor and did impressions, including a hilarious one of Marlon Brando. She also got along well with the crew. The family was all together again. But Melanie did not live in the canyon. She had a little house in Malibu Beach and commuted daily, a long drive.

Though they were excellent, the scenes with Patsy Nedd, the actress who replaced Melanie, had to be reshot. And as she went back to work, now and then I would look at my daughter while she was in a scene with the cats and pray to God that she wouldn't be hurt.

—19—

TO TRAIN
BIG CATS

Every day on the set brought some new insight into the behavior of
the big cats. Despite its age-old reputation of being a man-eater, the
tiger in the wild usually flees from man, and the killing of a human
usually occurs only when the tiger is surprised or placed in a position
of defense of self or cubs. There are dozens of accounts of tame tigers
in India, also the source of most of the "man-eater" stories.

In fact, the tiger is the original scaredy-cat, although the most
ferocious, under certain circumstances, of all cats. The adult is frightened silly of small animals as well as by a number of other odd
things. There was a remarkable scene in *Roar* in which big Ivan backs
down from a tiny lion cub. And certain natural conditions—lightning,
for instance—that a lion takes in stride will panic a tiger. Our tigers
were scared to death of silver light reflectors. If you want to walk
into a room of tigers and take command, wear a silver suit.

Though the tiger can be as noisy as the lion, and the sounds of
a tiger fight are chilling, the mortally wounded animal has been
known to die without a sound, an icy defiance in its eyes. I've seen
only one fight involving tigers and hope I'll never see another. It
occurred on the veranda of the African house when Nikki decided
to challenge Ivan for dominance. Nikki, three years younger than
Ivan, both from the same parents at the Okanagan Game Preserve,

Gregory makes a dramatic entrance.

had been hand-raised by John, and we'd had Ivan since he was six weeks old. So both animals had had constant human contact for years, but that factor didn't make the slightest difference on this particular occasion.

The fight began with sound from Nikki that surely started in his bowels. His body was like a bellows. Then, in slow motion, he began to skirt Ivan, and at that point we saw them make direct eye contact, something tigers seldom do unless they intend to battle. Six or seven lions were also on that balcony, and they wisely fled as Nikki and Ivan pyramided, rising to twelve or thirteen feet, their paws briefly joined, almost boxing. Then they dropped to the floor again and skirted each other before pyramiding once more. The sounds that came from both tigers were unlike any others I've ever heard, metallic and from the belly. On all fours again, Ivan moved savagely to get his brother by the throat, and there is little doubt he would have

177

killed him if Noel and the handlers, who had to wait until the pyramiding was over, hadn't jumped in.

All of us were speechless for a few minutes as the brothers were taken back to their separate compounds, never to be put into the same space again. In fact, we had to build a plywood barrier so that they couldn't even see each other.

The older the tiger, the less social it is, but one of the Soledad adults, Gregory, who lives with Debbie and Wendy, is generally as trustworthy and friendly as any mellow lion. The 650-pound Siberian eats chunks of steak out of my hand as delicately as a house cat, yet I'd never dream of challenging him. To do so would risk looking up at an animal whose head would be higher than a standard ceiling. I tell visitors to retreat quickly when a tiger pulls its ears back.

Almost all big cats like to enter human domiciles, being every bit as curious as little cats, and Gregory likes to come into my house by slipping his huge body through the open kitchen window, then bounding across the sink to go on a room-by-room exploration. Gregory has, and has had for a long time, one particularly annoying habit. He maneuvers his rear end into position and sprays a large glassed Japanese silkscreen of a tiger, usually his first target. He has hit it bull's-eye on a half-dozen occasions even though I watch him closely when he's in the living room. It isn't a big spray and I quickly wash the glass with soap and water. I've never decided whether or not he sees the picture as a tiger's big head or simply wets it down because he did it the first time he entered the house.

I am constantly reminded that the tiger is a different animal from the lion despite some similarities, and the differences broaden as the tiger ages, most of them reverting to the old ways of the jungle. We were totally wrong about being able to mellow Singh Singh and Panda Bear. Of Singh Singh, Mike Vollman said, "He has that 'I don't care' look in his eyes." If anything had to be done in his space, at least three handlers would enter, all armed with Hot-Shots. He was far more dangerous than either Togar or Tongaru, and for some strange reason he would literally go berserk if production manager Chuck Sloan happened to pass close by. We even checked to see if his former owner resembled Sloan in any way. The answer was no.

Yet there was Natasha, a Knobhill graduate, who watched TV as a cub and now enjoyed it as an adult, with Westerns and ice-skating still her favorites. I confess there is something outlandish about a tiger sitting in your front room with a rapt look on her face as horses prance across the screen.

Of the two sequences in *Roar* that required training tigers, a scene involving a pair of Siberians, Nikki and Gregory, riding in the back of a cut-down 1937 Chevrolet took most of the time. On paper, it was a simple, funny, benign scene—these two huge animals sitting as passengers in the back of the old car as it scooted along an African road, Noel and Mativo in front. Yet no scene involving tiger performance is simple.

After the top was cut from the Chevy, making it into a convertible, we put the old car into the compound where Nikki and Gregory lived. Taking away the seats, because they would have been torn up within hours, we left the doors open so that the tigers could sit in it whenever they wanted to, or sleep in it, if they chose. They are much like the lion, tending to occupy human spaces if they can.

The car sat out there for about two weeks; then Rick Glassey and Steve Miller began feeding Nikki and Gregory little pieces of meat, tossing a piece into the back seat so that they would jump back there, then into the front seat, so that they would jump up there.

Natasha watching the tube

Day after day this went on. Finally, Rick and Steve asked them to stay put in the back seat, enticing them to remain still by rewarding them now and then with a chunk of beef. But the Siberian has a short attention span, another reason why the Bengal, a more patient cat, is used in circus and nightclub work. Nikki and Gregory did not live together during this period of training, and we feared that Gregory, the younger tiger, might challenge Nikki for dominance.

During the fourth week, Rick started the engine of the car while the tigers were perched in the back. Frightened, they jumped out and ran. Next day, Rick and Steve were back in the compound and started the engine again. They ran it a few minutes, turned it off, and started it again. After the fifth or sixth day of hearing the engine

Training Nikki to ride in the back seat

periodically, the tigers became accustomed to the sound and finally stayed in position in the back seat.

Then Nikki and Gregory had to be trained to stay put with the car in motion. At first they leaped out simultaneously whenever Rick shifted the gears. But a week later they were sitting placidly in the Chevy as Rick and Steve made slow circles in the compound. In fact, the tigers seemed to enjoy the ride. Finally, the car was driven out of the compound. Up and down the dirt road they went, in sessions lasting an hour or more. We had our scene. But it had taken seven weeks of daily work and great patience to convince the Siberians to do such a simple thing as sitting in the back seat of that moving car.

Making motion pictures involves a certain amount of trickery, anyway, and there were some knowns in dealing with our animal cast. We could always trick them into doing certain things. If we wanted a lion to appear as though he was dismantling a room, all we had to do was leave him alone for a comparatively short while. Destruction would begin and the animal would have fun while carrying it out.

There were times, however, when our best-laid plans backfired. One of the key scenes of *Roar* involved Togar chasing the family around the second-story balcony that extended on all four sides of the African house. Because Togar was going to be on the loose for a while, Noel took special precautions, ordering the fencing crew to wrap chain link all the way around the balconies of the house, and to put the wire mesh across the upper stairwell to block that exit. None of us was allowed in the house.

Because Togar had a reputation for ferocity, I said to Noel, "Why don't we use a double?"—thinking one of the nicer cats could do that chase, of which the objects would be John, Jerry, Melanie and myself.

"That scene needs Togar," Noel replied.

The night before it was to be filmed, a squeeze cage, which is about nine feet long, five high and five wide, was rolled up to Togar's space. In the morning, the door was opened and a piece of meat was placed on the forward end. Togar came in and the door was closed behind him. He was then wheeled to the African house, and the squeeze cage was placed on an elevator that had been rigged the day before.

Up went Togar to the second floor, and Noel yelled to the handlers who were spotted around to get ready for the lion. We were certain he would charge out bellowing, searching for someone to

Tongaru pulling the boat back to shore

chew on. But when the cage door was pulled open, Togar stepped out, looked around without a peep, much less a bellow, yawned, then went over to a corner and sprawled out in the midmorning sun. Big, bad Togar, father of almost twenty cubs, had obviously changed over the years. We had provided so many females for him and had treated him so well that he wasn't inclined to fight or chase anyone. Noel put a lead around his neck and walked him back to his quarters.

Tongaru, fresh from his victory over Casey, was substituted for Togar thereafter, and there was no question of his ferocity. John would forever remember being pinned under that hot, snarling body for twenty-five minutes. Only Frank Tom, our most experienced handler, could reliably cope with Tongaru, who was truly a Jekyll and Hyde. Even so, whenever Frank went into the compound of Tongaru and Zuru, he made absolutely certain which of the identical twins he was facing.

There were some uncertainties with the cats, but one certainty was the love of a chase. Whenever a human runs, the cat is sure to follow, and they are expert at open-field tackling. For one scene, Noel had them chasing us around the lake and the only possible escape route was via the old rowboat. It was the same scene in which Jan de Bont had been injured, only one sentence in the final *Roar* script— "And the family rows around the lake"—but it took months, off and on, to shoot.

It also provided one of the best gifts of the film, one of those unwritten, unrehearsed contributions of big cats to cinema art. Melanie, John and I were in the boat, and no matter where we pointed the bow, they followed us along the shore, obviously waiting for us to disembark and continue the fun of the chase. As we came paddling around one point, John was sitting with his back to the bow, and Melanie and I were facing forward. The idea of the scene was that we were paddling so furiously that no one looked up to see that we were indeed running aground, not escaping. The moment the boat touched shore, we—the actors, seeing the welcoming party of big cats—attempted to shove off. One lion had other ideas. The second the boat started to reverse, he put a paw on the bow and dragged it back to the waiting cats. While the cameras ran, he did it fourteen times. That lion was John's old nemesis, none other than Tongaru.

—20—

TIMBO

Even though we were filming, caring for the big cats remained our first concern. Cookie, five years old, one of the lions that had transited Knobhill as a cub, had developed cancer, and it was heartbreaking to see her being ravaged. I was not prepared for the similarities between a big-cat cancer victim and a human victim.

My logbook notes:

April 10. Cookie in bad condition.
April 19. Cookie walked length of compounds to tree bridge, walked across that and stayed there all afternoon, just staring off into space.
April 23. Cookie in hospital. Diagnosed as liposarcoma. Begins chemotherapy.
May 7. Cookie back home, drinking water but not eating. A bad sign. She wants to die.
May 14. Cookie losing her coat.

Alex Newman, functioning as vet-tech, gave her massive doses of Vitamin C, but it was a losing battle and I knew it.

Cubs kept arriving that spring of 1977, and I didn't have time to raise them all, help produce, and also act in a motion picture. Alice, mate of the reformed Togar, had five babies, one of which died

184

of pneumonia within a day. Then within another day Alice rejected the others, all healthy, and suddenly I had a quartet of new bottle feeders on my hands. There were already seven parceled out to various human surrogates, both female and male.

To raise cubs properly one must have a lot of love for animals in general, and it helps to have been around rambunctious puppies and kittens. It is almost a full-time job, and for that reason I always chose nonworking people or placed our cubs in homes where someone would be around most of the time. The need for tactile love and close proximity of the human is constant. Danger signs in a very young cub must also be watched for constantly: listlessness, dullness of the eyes, lack of appetite, fever. Death comes on with breathtaking speed.

Despite the time involved and the vet bills, we tried so hard to keep all our new cubs alive. It often took hours just to get food into them; many sleepless nights were spent just watching over them. When defeat came—a half-dozen died in my arms over a period of several years, most often with feline infectious peritonitis—it was always crushing. Yet the pleasure of seeing those that survived grow up made it all worthwhile.

Somehow I always found the human surrogates I needed if I was too overwhelmed to do the job myself. Leo Lobsenz, director of Elsa Wild Animal Appeal (Elsa, of *Born Free*), found time to be the substitute father of a number of cubs, often taking them to schools in the Los Angeles area or to Elsa fund-raising events. The tiny animals were always welcomed at the Braille Institute because the blind children could touch and play with them. Gardner McKay raised several cubs. Pat Breshears, mother of John's girlfriend Lin, became an expert in cub care and was overseer of a half-dozen human "mothers." One of them, artist Penny Bishonden, later became an expert trainer and vet-tech at Shambala. The cubs that she had raised now weigh in at upward of five hundred pounds. Penny is a good example of the depth that can be developed in a human–big-cat relationship. She had been in close contact with those animals for almost ten years. Visibly, she is their best friend if not their "mother."

Close, tactile contact is a must with cubs, but beyond that is the mutual joy of discovery. Once, Penny placed a skateboard down on her driveway and suddenly a cub mounted it and began to ride it, without the slightest coaxing. Few days during the peak period of cub-raising went by without such discoveries. Play is a tremendously important factor in adapting the cubs to live in human society.

As the weeks moved into May, we awaited word from London on further financing. Some of the footage shot thus far had been sent over so that EMI executives could screen it and make a decision. The quiet from the Thames was ominous and upsetting. From the rushes we'd seen, footage of the big cats in action was spectacular. In our opinion, of course. We were confident that lions and tigers had never been photographed this way, and our "African" set looked authentic. We held our breath and kept working, mostly on credit.

Noel had run some Mack Sennett comedies while he was writing the script, and he took one idea from an old silent-film sequence in which an actor falls down, then a shelf above him collapses, dropping all manner of things on his head and knocking him out. Noel's version, with me as victim, climaxed with a jar of honey being knocked over, the sticky stuff dripping down over my face, in repose. A cat would then proceed to lick it off. When I first read the scene, I thought, I hope this works. If the cat decided to bite instead of lick, I could lose my face.

The day we started shooting the scene, the shelf in the kitchen of the African house was stocked with plastic movie prop bottles and jars—except the honey jar, which was made of glass. I got into position beneath the shelf and waited for the collapse. The lightweight props bounced off my head harmlessly—but not the honey jar. It was supposed just to tip over, oozing honey, but unfortunately the property man was inexperienced and the jar itself fell about four feet, raising a bump on my head. I was wildly angry at Noel as well as the prop man. Directors are supposed to check scenes of that sort to make certain all the props are rigged so that they can't cause injury.

I got my sense of humor back, and when we reshot the scene a few days later, everything worked. But I was still apprehensive about the "licking" scene. Five or six leopards and cougars were leaping around that room, bouncing off the walls; among them was a stocky black leopard, Pepper, with a personality that wasn't always good. Lightning fast as well, Pepper spotted me first. Eyes tightly closed, honey sliding down my cheek, I felt the claws of the curious cat on my right thigh, then the sandpaper tongue beginning to lick. Although we played it for laughs, I realize now that it was probably one of the most dangerous scenes in the picture. Handlers were about eight feet away, but they could not have prevented injury. I remember that the set was dead quiet that morning. I was holding my breath

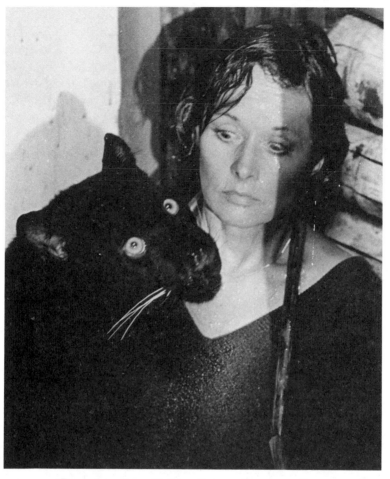

Pepper enjoys licking honey from my face.

most of the time. I stayed absolutely still until Noel said softly, "Cut!" Then I opened my eyes and there were the huge, cold hazel eyes of that ebony leopard not four inches away.

Timbo, our resident African elephant, was still waiting in the wings for his turn in front of the camera. Though we had acquired him five years previously, he had yet to do a day's work in exchange for his hay and alfalfa rations. Nor did we know just how he would react to being a thespian.

About a month after he arrived in the canyon I'd ridden Timbo up the riverbank for about two miles, thinking that he felt like moving asphalt beneath me. I was nervous. Steve Martin, new to handling elephants, didn't know much about him, and I knew even less. I remember the first time Timbo extended his trunk backward simply to investigate the thing that was on his back. Having his moist "nostrils" pressing against my face as we thumped along was a most unusual feeling. On later rides I found I preferred to sit back a ways on him, knees bent, doing the split, rather than up against his ears. I finally learned how to ride lying down on his back or standing up doing a balancing act. Timbo enjoyed human contact and was pampered by all of us, but his acting ability remained a question mark.

Unlike the Indian elephant, Africans are often high-strung and temperamental, having a reputation for being difficult to train. The Indians are smaller, with smaller ears and two prominent forehead

Timbo really prefers beer.

bumps, but they were always employed in the old jungle movies, with fake African ears glued to their lobes. Only experts could tell the difference. Just as circuses choose the Bengal tiger over the Siberian for performances, the Indian, or Asiatic, elephant is the choice for work in the rings.

The marvelous planning of nature was never better illustrated than in the size of Timbo's ears, which are loaded with blood vessels. By flapping them he cools the blood. The Indian elephant, living in the forest, not on the scorching savanna, has no need for the huge ears. Elephant's teeth are also adapted to their environment. They have six sets of teeth over a lifetime. With ridges in them, their molars are the size of small mayonnaise jars and are able to grind up brush. When the last set of teeth are worn off, the elephant knows it is time to die.

I also marvel at the "two-fingered" trunk of the African—the Indian has only one finger—so flexible and sensitive that it can pick up a single blade of grass. I've moistened a Tic Tac and placed it on the end of Timbo's tongue, then watched as his giant cheeks began to suck away on the tiny dab of candy. The trunk can also serve as a snorkel. An elephant can stay underwater for five or ten minutes.

Timbo's insatiable sweet tooth, as well as his liking for hops, was evident the first weeks we had him. And there were times, when he was irascible for one reason or another, that we controlled him solely with a case or two of beer. Since he can drink fifty gallons of water at a session, there was no cause for concern about drunkenness.

By spring of 1977, Timbo knew me almost as well as he knew Tim Cooney, though he refused to take orders from me, a matter of no surprise. Well aware that he thrived on companionship, I had made it a point to visit him often, even when I didn't ride him, bringing along carrots or apples or some other treat. There was a selfish motive in addition to one of friendship. I had to do a scene with him in which he would lift me bodily, and I very much wanted to have some control over events. Sometimes a scene has to be repeated a dozen times, eventually fraying the nerves of all concerned, and I did not want to stretch Timbo too far.

The normal lift to the elephant's back is via its knees. The elephant drops down, you step on the left front foreleg and then get a boost to the neck or swing up as you would with a horse. Simple maneuver; no bumps or bruises. But being picked up by an elephant, in the curve of its trunk, when you're standing with both feet on the ground is a different matter. Tim Cooney said, "Now, when he comes toward you, make sure you quickly get your right leg over your left one. Otherwise, his trunk will go between your legs and you'll end up hanging from the elephant in a very strange position."

I made a mental note of what I had to do and then said, "Okay, let's try it."

Timbo came toward me, lifted me, and though I attempted to cross the right leg over the left immediately, I ended up in that very strange position.

I began to yell at Timbo to let me down, and a half-dozen crewmen came running. When anyone yells in an animal compound, everyone else converges on the scene. They were all rewarded with the ridiculous sight of me hanging on to the elephant, his trunk exactly between my legs. So much for a first rehearsal.

Though Noel was credited for writing *Roar*, the best scenes continued to be scripted by the animals: creativity in its purest form. We just photographed whatever they did. Timbo inspired his biggest scene by systematically destroying a camper shell. Made of metal, it had been temporarily removed from a workman's vehicle and was sitting on the ground near the elephant barn when Timbo discovered it. He not only ripped the shell to pieces but then folded and flattened the remains.

Crewmen and Up-Front visitors were always warned not to park near his territory. Having a dislike for any vehicle, of any size, within his first two years in residence Timbo sat down on two hoods, totaling them. If a car was small enough, he would not hesitate to overturn it and then go about demolishing it. The VW was a favorite target. In Africa bull elephants have chased the "bug" through the bush. A practiced rock-thrower, Timbo has also shattered several windshields in the Up-Front area. Once he even took aim on the shining Rolls-Royce belonging to Robert Gottschalk, not a wise thing to do to an investor.

Even larger vehicles were targets. A Southern Pacific track runs close to the perimeter fence on the north side of the compounds, and several times a day a long, slow freight rumbles by. If Timbo was in his exercise area when the train passed, he would trumpet, then sometimes try to challenge it. Fortunately for the elephant the embankment was too steep to climb.

The African is not hesitant about taking on real or imagined opponents. One evening when John was walking Timbo home, subbing for Tim Cooney, they came face to face with a parked Caterpillar D-8 tractor, its scoop jawed out in front. In the twilight, the yellow earth-mover must have appeared challenging to Timbo. Trumpeting, he announced his intentions to charge. John coaxed him to a spot near his barn by giving him soda pop, but Timbo refused to enter it, still incensed by the presence of the tractor, which was on the other side of a fence, about twenty feet away. He kept on trumpeting and charging toward it.

Finally, someone got the idea to start the D-8, proving that it was a vehicle, not an animal. It was a bad idea. The roar of the diesel worsened the situation. The tigers in the compound next to the barn were now reacting to all the noise and excitement, roaring and pacing. Then Timbo went berserk for a few minutes, tearing down the chain-link fence guarding the tigers and a few lionesses. Except for Nikki, the cats scattered, wanting no part of a crazy bull elephant. It is in the genes of the tiger to fight the elephant, and Nikki truly resented the intrusion. He went for Timbo's head and trunk, the most vulnerable part of an elephant's body. Without it, the elephant can't eat, and Timbo tried frantically to stomp the big Siberian.

With almost superhuman strength, John grabbed Nikki by the tail, got him through the nearby production office door and slammed it shut, making his own quick exit through the window. For a few minutes, the enraged cat could be heard scattering papers and slamming furniture around.

Sylvie Loboda, coming back to the canyon from a date, went for several cases of beer, and the calming-down process began, until finally Timbo was led back to his barn and shackled for the night. Meanwhile, other handlers had rounded up the escaped cats, and workmen had mended the fence of the tiger compound. John then released a now docile Nikki from the production office and all was quiet once again in the compounds.

Not much had changed about my scene with Timbo since Noel sketched it out three years previously. Escaping from the cats, the family was supposed to climb into a rowboat, shove off and paddle into a cove, only to be confronted by an elephant. Timbo was then supposed to overturn the boat, dumping all of us, pick me out of the water and drop me back in, then destroy the boat. A large order for a large elephant.

In rehearsing, a very loose word for what was actually done, we discovered that Timbo had no desire to smash the wooden rowboat for the finale. Then we remembered he preferred metal over wood, probably due to the crunching sound. He had done a fine job on that camper shell. So we sent the property man to Palmdale to buy several

Timbo dumping the rowboat

metal boats. We aged them a bit and at last we were ready to shoot.

I had finally learned how to be properly picked up by an elephant, crossing my legs instantly, but Timbo, for unknown reasons, refused to drop me back into the water. He would run up on shore and I would fall off into the sand. Take after take, while I was screaming and flailing, doing my emoting job, I would hit the beach instead of the water. None of us stopped to think that *Timbo didn't understand that I was only acting.* But the giant animal was becoming more unnerved by the minute with all the silly movie histrionics. When you're working with wild animals each take increases the danger. And there were times when Noel would insist on shooting take after take even when I was convinced the scene had been sufficiently covered.

On the thirteenth take I didn't quite pull myself up onto Timbo's head and tried to adjust by holding on to his ears. In doing so, my arms were outstretched and my right leg went under his trunk to rest on the top of his right tusk. When he brought his trunk down, pinning my leg against the tusk, the pain was unbearable. An elephant can lift half his own weight with his trunk.

John tried to help me, then Noel. But Timbo was confused and didn't let go. It seemed an eternity as the crushing of my leg continued. Then, mercifully, I blacked out. Unconscious, I hung upside down in the air for a moment, swinging back and forth, still locked between trunk and tusk. Tim Cooney yelled, "Trunk up, trunk up," until finally Timbo released me. I don't remember hitting the sand.

In terrible pain, I was rushed to Palmdale Hospital, stretched out in a van. My leg felt as if it had been crushed, but all that showed was a pink area, between ankle and knee, where the tusk had pinned me. However, an X ray revealed a hairline fracture of the fibula. The doctors didn't really realize the force they were dealing with.

When I got back to the canyon in late afternoon, pain still surging, I was told that poor Cookie had just died. The cancer had been

Hanging upside down with my leg crushed between Timbo's tusk and trunk

relentless, and in one way I was relieved. Then Noel asked me, "Do you still want to go to the crew party tonight?" We had them twice a month in the crew dining room to keep morale up. Good times flowed.

Angry at everyone, including the elephant, I said fiercely, "Yes, I do." I needed some laughter to take my mind off Cookie as well as my leg.

The next day we filmed another sequence, though I could barely walk. Severely bruised, my leg had turned black and blue and was horribly swollen. Two days later I tried to do a kitchen scene on crutches with Boomer lion, but the pain was too much to handle. The following day we closed production once again, blaming it entirely on my livid purple leg. Actually, we were out of money.

—21—

THE CATS
ARE OUT

Late in May, when Noel was in town desperately trying to raise money to continue production, Jerry brought a new girlfriend, Mona Emigh, a pretty blonde, out to the canyon. Girls were still Jerry's first priority, and it was natural for him to show off a bit: go into a compound with a half-dozen big lions, have a roll in the sand with one, hug a couple. It was a macho thing to do and Mona would certainly be impressed. But Jerry forgot that he was wearing *tennis shoes*. He also forgot that Mike lion, who had spent much time at Knobhill, had a tennis-shoe fetish. Since cubhood he'd had a thing for tennies whether they were under the bed or attached to human feet. Mike "possessed" tennis shoes and went after Jerry's the moment the compound gate closed, attempting to remove them with his teeth. In doing so, he also got Jerry in the thigh, close to the groin. The wounds were deep and serious.

Leg propped up, I was at home when I heard that Jerry had been hurt. I hobbled out on crutches, wondering how much more we could take, as John rushed his brother off to the emergency room at Palmdale Hospital. Then Mona came up to me, asking, "Mrs. Marshall, would you like me to drive you to the hospital?" I'm sure she thought we were all crazy. Jerry had been badly bitten by a lion obsessed by tennies, and here was his stepmother on crutches, done in by an elephant. I accepted her invitation, but Mona was so stunned by what had happened that she hardly spoke to me all the way to Palmdale. She hardly even looked at me.

At Palmdale I asked the doctor on duty—he had recently sewn up both Noel and Jan de Bont—to check my leg, since it was still so painful and looked hideous. He examined it and said, "Tippi, you stay right here. You can't even go home for a toothbrush. You have gangrene."

Gangrene! Great! Just great!

I soon went off to Antelope Valley Hospital, in Lancaster, with Jerry, who needed more than emergency service.

If you are unlucky enough to have gangrene, it is preferable to be custodian of the black type rather than the green. Mine was black. I was put into a room directly across the hall from Jerry's, so we could visit back and forth. If my leg hadn't hurt so badly, it would have all been hilarious: Jerry bitten by a lion with a thing for tennies, me with black mortification. A plastic surgeon, Dr. Esfandiar Kadivar, worked on both our extremities. People who live around big cats do well to have plastic surgeons as their family doctors. Kadivar became ours.

Jerry left the hospital after a few days, but I stayed for two weeks because I needed a skin graft on my leg. And *Roar* was shut down for another three weeks after that, many members of the film crew going off to other jobs. When I returned to the canyon, I stayed away from the compounds, fearing that the big cats would see me hobbling around on crutches and remember it. Jerry also lay low.

Noel was in Tokyo searching for investors but having no success. Our Beverly Hills homes had for-sale signs on them, and there was little doubt that we would lose the undeveloped 650 acres we owned about fifteen miles to the west in Newhall. But I was absolutely determined that we weren't going to lose Soledad Canyon or the cats, film or no film.

Noel returned from Japan, talking defiantly, and we soon began filming, a day here, a day there, doing pickup work, trying to get by with one camera crew. Many independent films are shot inter-mittently, most for the same reason—lack of money. It is not the ideal way to make a movie, but sometimes it is the only way. I limped around for all of June and into July while we got five days of film into the can. Jerry was back at work on very tender feet. With about 70 percent of the film complete I was still convinced that we were simply at a low point with all these injuries and money troubles; that

196

something would break our way. I've always been an optimist. Someone, somewhere, would take a gamble on our totally unique film.

But then there was another blow, a sickening gut punch. EMI did not agree with our rosy assessment of the *Roar* footage they had screened and wanted their half million returned. At that moment, we didn't have ten thousand dollars, much less a half million. EMI had the right of immediate foreclosure and gave us less than a week to leave the Franklin Canyon home. The trauma of that demand was devastating. In the same week, Partner, my lovable ugly mutt of fourteen years, disappeared when I took him to Malibu while visiting Melanie. He simply vanished and I searched for him every day after work for more than a month.

I ended up feeling more defiant than ever. That applied to Noel as well. And as resourceful as ever, he started a new company, the Film Consortium, to make TV commercials, placing *Roar*'s production head, Chuck Sloan, in charge. Some kind of steady income was needed to feed the animals and meet the canyon payroll. The commercial business was booming and perhaps, later on, the Soledad facilities could be used for video and film work. The Film Consortium took up offices on Sunset Boulevard in Hollywood.

And, oddly enough, defiance, or *esprit de corps,* or pure pigheadedness, was never higher with the regulars of the cast, the film crew and the animal handlers that summer. They knew about the EMI rejection, knew that they might not get paid immediately; yet most of them stuck week in and week out. More than any loyalty to Noel or to me, or any below-scale money they might earn, I think it was the lure of the cats, and the challenge of completing the film, that kept them driving back down that rutted road every day. There was a definite family feeling among all of us. Everyone was welcome to see the rushes or dailies, the most recent work, which we screened in the commissary. Wednesday nights, complete with beer and popcorn, were movie nights, with Noel renting old films to run after the dailies were screened.

Some of the crew even lived in the canyon. A little village of used teardrop and other small trailers had sprung up in the center of the property, on the riverbank across from the kitchen and commissary. Named "Gumpsterville," after the Andy Gumps, the nearby portable toilets, the trailer village housed crew members who didn't want to drive back to town after a day's work. They were mostly sound and editing crew, many of whom worked late.

August and September are always the hottest months down in

the canyon, and we adjusted our work schedule accordingly. The cats went into the shade and slept during the hours from about ten to three, so we filmed early in the morning and again late in the afternoon. The animals could not be forced into action. During midday it was so quiet around the compounds that no one would know that lions and tigers were present.

It was also during this period of high heat that Noel wanted to do some retakes of the Timbo scene, the one in which I had injured my leg on his tusk. At first I said, "Okay," but I got to within thirty feet of that elephant and flatly refused to work. Though I loved him dearly, I was suddenly afraid of the power that his trunk represented, afraid to be lifted up by it. Almost a year passed, a year in which I had frequent contact with Timbo, before I found the confidence to do that scene.

There are other memories of that summer. At about five in the afternoon of August 19, after doing a scene with Jerry and John and approximately twenty-five young cats, Melanie reached down to scratch a cub and play with it. Not to be left out of the fun, Sheila lioness, the three-year-old daughter of Jenny and Togar, jumped Melanie from behind, rising up and placing both paws around her face as if to say, "Surprise, surprise!" The cat hung on and down they both went.

We rushed Melanie, final victim of the Marshall family acting ensemble, off to Antelope Valley, where Dr. Kadivar, who should have been on retainer, took over and began to repair the claw damage. I found it hard to breathe when I saw how close one claw had come to her right eye. While I hadn't used the slightest pressure to bring her back to *Roar*, I still felt guilty.

When we returned home, Melanie looked at me and said, "Mom, I'm not quitting. We'll finish this film no matter what."

Pale, blood still on her shirt, she was standing there with stitches in her face. I felt a surge of pride. Here was the girl who had been paraded through the gossip columns ever since her nymphet roles of a few years back, sometimes maliciously. Here was the daughter I had often found so difficult to understand. Now she was displaying great courage and responsibility. Melanie had grown up.

Another full crew quit that day, partially because of what had happened to Melanie, they claimed. It was an excuse, I believe, one they had probably been looking for for days. Soon, I thought, we would be down to students and Hollywood's chronically unemployed.

Still I could not blame them. I was always aware of the possibility

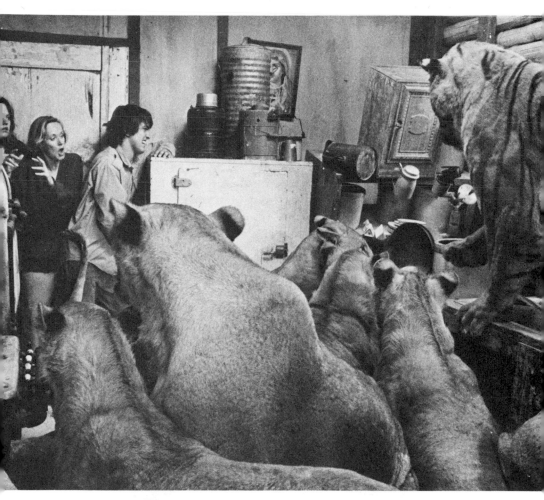

Trapped in the "African house" by wall-to-wall cats

of one or more of the crew being seriously injured or killed. Noel, on the other hand, ignored danger throughout. Once, shooting a scene on the lake in an amphibious car, he had electric cables running from shore through the water to power the lights and the camera. We could have been roasted. I shudder to think of those days. Only luck prevented tragedy. Ironically, that scene ended up on the cutting-room floor.

Summer finally over, one sunny, warm Saturday in October, when all of us should have been inside watching football, we were outside filming the scene that had first sent me to the hospital—lions

199

jumping over my back while I sprawled out on a log. I checked to make sure the handlers had Cherries safely locked up.

Just as I was now leery of riding Timbo, I was afraid of this scene. To be truthful, I was dreading it. The height factor, the same thing that Ozzie Bristow had warned about seven years previously, was again involved. When you are below a big cat's eye level, the cat believes it has total control. And most times, from my experience, it does have that control. The sound of Cherries' canines scraping my skull still lingered in my mind, and I'd never been as nervous in the compounds as I was that morning. I tried to hide it but couldn't.

Jan de Bont came over to me, put his arm around my shoulder and said, "It'll go well this time." Never once had he lost hope; never

Mother and daughter in a dispute with a big cat

once had he said a word about quitting, though he'd had offers.

I too hoped it would go well. But before the scene began I told the crew, "Pay attention to me. Watch these cats. If one decides to do something, don't just stand there."

As Jan predicted, it all went beautifully. The lions and tigers, twenty-six of them in a line, leaped gracefully along the log, their paws landing a few inches from my body, then bounded over. Not one stepped on me. Only one seemed the slightest bit interested. The dailies showed Gregory tiger reaching for me with a paw, hesitating, then jumping over.

When Noel yelled, "Cut," I felt a fear of months lift off. But there was one more angle to be shot, involving a single cat. At the very end of the run across the log, lioness Lynn was to come back and lie down on me, just for the fun of it, until Noel appeared to rescue me. A fiber-glass shell had been constructed to fit tightly over my body, providing protection. Unfortunately, it showed in Jan's lenses and was uncomfortable as well. So I said, "We'll do it without the shell."

Lynn, who weighed about 450 pounds, must have been on top of me for ten minutes before they got the shot. I thought I would be squashed. But not once did she make an aggressive move. I was well below her height, just as I'd been well below the whole parade of lions across the log. And it occurred to me as I lay under that hot quarter ton of lion flesh that Cherries' belligerent personality had caused the previous attack, not the height factor.

Further action of the scene, as scripted, had Noel pulling the cat off me. And I was so angry at him, as scripted, for allowing the whole family to be scared to death that I knocked him into the water. But what happened next was not scripted. Playful Lynn then pushed *me* off the bridge and into the lake. Jan de Bont's camera recorded it all.

It was a good and easy day of filming, one of the few we had, but we still seemed to pay, one way or another, for every success. That night—actually about three Sunday morning—Noel and I were awakened by a commotion. The wardrobe man, who lived in a little trailer near Jan's house, was pounding on Jan's front door. "The cats are out, the cats are out!" he was shouting.

We could hear bird screeches, their high-pitched and terrified sound cutting the dark night. We scrambled into clothing, grabbed flashlights and leads, guessing that the aviary was already under attack. Jan went with Noel to the bird area; I drove to Up-Front to arouse the maintenance men and Liberato, who lived in a trailer near the elephant barn. There were no strong lights around the aviary, so it was pitch black in that direction. But I'd never heard such a din in the canyon as the flamingos, ostriches and peacocks made in attempting to escape.

On the way back from awakening Liberato, I checked the compounds. Someone had deliberately opened the gates, releasing the cats. As far as I knew they were still within the strong perimeter fence, but a determined lion can dig out in a very short while. We had to round them up as quickly as possible. We could not wait until dawn.

I ran on toward the bird area, where there was still a lot of commotion and screeching going on. By that time, Jan and Noel had two lionesses in captivity and were taking them back to compounds on leads. I picked up Alexis tigress, who was saying "ff-fuff, ff-fuff," the friendly sound, between Jan's house and ours, securing her to a fence pole until she could be returned to the Up-Front area. Then I went to look for other cats.

Never before had we hunted multiple cats at night, and what made it so frightening for everyone was not knowing, *immediately*, which animal our flashlight beams were illuminating. Was it one of the gentle ones? Or was it Tongaru? There was no time to count noses and try to remember exactly which cat had been in what compound.

Excepting the cheetah, a cat's eyes are designed for night vision. Highly reflective tapetum lucidum lines the eyes' inner surface and intensifies any light that enters the pupils. All cats, even the domestics, have this gelatinlike substance, which can be seen as a green coppery glare in a flashlight glow. Why nature skipped the cheetah is not known.

As we spread out searching for the cats in the darkness, what we saw over an area of about twenty or thirty acres covered with brush and boulders were occasional glints of copperish green. But when we hit the cats directly with the light they could not see us.

"Keep walking, keep talking," Noel said. We hoped they would recognize our voices behind the strong circles of light.

One by one we found, coaxed and tricked all of them, and by first light, when we escorted Alexis tigress back to her compound, the ordeal was over. Four of Joel's ostriches were dead, but once again we couldn't blame the cats. Instinct had dictated their behavior.

Noel and I went back inside the house and sprawled out to get a few hours' sleep. We never talked about what happened that night. I think we were afraid to do that. Nor did we ever discover who had opened the gates or why. The thought of what might happen if someone did it again was too frightening to consider. But that morning we bought heavy padlocks for every gate and took personal custody of the keys.

As Christmas approached, I was determined to film a bit of action that Noel had adamantly rejected. In an early version of the script there was a destruction scene on the veranda of the African house in which the big cats demolish the luggage of the newly arrived family, literally ripping the bags to pieces and scattering clothing— all of which they would do naturally, no coaching needed. Among the family's possessions was a skateboard, and we knew that chances were good that an animal would mount it. But when we filmed the sequence, Noel declared that skateboards were out of style and the scene would be meaningless. I disagreed, and just before we closed production for the winter I asked Jan and the crew if they would come in to make the shot.

Skateboard champ

The next day, cameras were set up, luggage debris was scattered around the veranda, and in came the cats. As they milled around and sniffed and batted the already decimated luggage, we waited and waited—the real secret to filming animals. Finally, Lena cub examined the skateboard, put a paw on it and felt it move. We were in business! Fun and games with a skateboard, and the scene went into the picture, a moment of great charm.

At year's end, though it sometimes seemed that trouble and injury stalked us all through 1977, we had actually filmed on 145 days, enough time to make a *Star Wars*. And serious injury had occurred only four times. So perhaps it was the presence of tigers such as Singh Singh, the continual roaring of the lions, and the acknowledged threat of injury or death that had made the year seem much worse than it was.

—22—

FLOOD

Once again winter had stripped the cottonwood leaves, and those that remained were brown and withered. We couldn't match summer exterior scenes, so all filming in January had to be confined to the African-house interior scenes, of which three or four remained.

On the 29th of January, the first day of filming in the new year, Noel and Mativo were preparing to do a staircase scene that involved about a dozen of the big cats. With Mativo seated about four steps up, surrounded by lions, Noel was sitting on the second step of the entryway, a few cats sprawled around him. A homey scene, where the lions were concerned, the dialogue was about the impending arrival of the family.

Noel's wardrobe for that day was a shirt and shorts. Jan de Bont took one look at him and said, "Noel, you have to put some makeup on your legs. You're way too white for this."

Knowing that the smell of the makeup would probably attract some unwanted attention, Noel replied, "If I do I'll get it for sure."

A big cat's sense of smell is not acute, but if the cat is close enough he will usually investigate the odor, often with painful results. By the time the sniff registers in the cat's mind, jaws are only inches away, and, depending on the circumstances, the cat may bite, overwhelmed by curiosity. We always warned visitors to the compounds not to wear perfumes, colognes, shaving lotions or even scented creams.

Jan insisted. "If you don't use makeup," he told Noel, "we'll get a white glare. You won't be happy and we'll have a retake." Retakes were avoided if at all possible.

Noel surrendered, and the makeup man daubed his legs.

The cats had always been accustomed to seeing their head keeper in jeans. Now he was exposing a lot of flesh as well as coating that skin with an interesting smell. The combination was almost irresistible to animals that are first attracted by what they see. Nature compensated for the big cat's poor sense of smell by providing acute eyesight.

Noel had a tremendous amount on his mind during that scene. He had to watch twelve cats, particularly the ones bumping around Mativo, observe which cat was doing what, and remember his own dialogue. Mativo had not overcome his fear of the animals, so Noel tried very hard to protect the slim, tall Kenyan whenever they did a scene together.

It all began quietly enough, but in screening the footage later I could see marked annoyance on the faces of some of the cats. They clearly weren't in a very good mood that day. Suddenly there was a lot of movement in front of the steps, and young George lion, son of Togar, always rough and tough, came up to Noel, who was now standing. Cameras were running; dialogue was being recorded.

While Noel was trying to ignore the lion, hoping he would go away, big George was sniffing the made-up right leg. The look on George's face, in footage, seemed to say, "Okay, buddy, I have to find out what this brown stuff is all about." He then took a firm bite at the knee area, dragging Noel off the steps, canines embedded in his right leg. Noel was hopping on his left foot like a fire dancer as he was pulled into a corner, where handlers yanked the lion off.

The eight punctures in his leg were more than an inch deep, but Noel wanted to keep on working. No film had been shot for two months and this accident was just one more massive frustration. But wiser heads prevailed and off went the leader to Dr. Kadivar in Palmdale. But he refused to be hospitalized and was home within two hours.

I'd been at my mother's house in Palm Desert that day and didn't learn about what had happened until I returned to the canyon. By my count this was Noel's eleventh bite, but I had probably missed three or four nips. This one was the worst to date.

A friend asked, "If you're the king lion, why did George bite you?"

206

"The king wears jeans," Noel replied.

Severe puncture pain does not set in for ten to fifteen hours, but then it is excruciating. Noel was in a wheelchair, on pain pills, the next day when Banjiro Uemura brought a group of Japanese investors to the canyon. He talked to them through periodically gritted teeth.

The next day I checked him back into the Palmdale Hospital, and the doctors managed to keep him bedded down for a day or two. Then, restless and complaining, miserable to live with, he was home for a week. Finally he gave up, and I took him to Cedars of Sinai, in Beverly Hills, with severe blood poisoning. The punctures had refused to heal, his knee was like a mauve balloon, and Noel was warned he would lose his leg if he didn't behave. That scared him sufficiently. He was quickly hooked up to an IV tube for an antibiotic drip.

I really didn't think too much about the rain that was falling the day I took Noel to Cedars. It wasn't a heavy rain and the hills around the canyon were fairly dry, able to absorb a lot of water. But the steady downpour did not stop for five days, and soon the ground was saturated. Each day the timid little Santa Clara threading through the canyon grew a few inches; each day it looked a little more threatening.

On the far north side of our acres was a heavy twelve-foot wooden bulkhead, built to keep a dirt embankment in place, and on it was the high-water mark of the canyon flood of 1969. Little had been built below that level in our part of the riverbed since that time. The human-occupied houses, buildings and trailers were all three or four feet higher than the crest indication, but some of the animal compounds and den huts were below it.

What we didn't know was that over the past eight years Southern Pacific had built a number of berms along its railroad tracks, shunting water away from its roadbed in case of flood. Unfortunately, that water would travel in our direction. However, we expected no more than normal flooding from this lingering storm. The river might rise two feet, scare us a little and then retreat, as usual.

The other thing we didn't know was that the county had created a "dam situation" eight miles upstream at Aliso Canyon where an old unpaved road crossed the river, cars fording the trickle of stream. But in heavy rains that road always became impassable, so county crews had gone about building it up, placing big pipes underneath the roadbed for the passage of water. No one, apparently, thought too much about what might happen if those pipes became plugged up with debris.

The clear-water Santa Clara begins up in the San Gabriel Range and courses westward through Soledad Canyon over sandy bottom-land that is sometimes a half mile wide. In the summer there is often less than four inches of water in that river, which is usually several feet wide, except in occasional pools. Some very dry winters it rises to no more than a foot, though water spills down in countless little crevices and channels off the hills. Back East, the Santa Clara wouldn't qualify as a good "crick." There have always been definite signs of fury over miles of its riverbed—tree trunks and boulders that were washed down in times past. But during hot summer days, and the lovely crisp days of fall, you tend not to think of that peaceful white-sand flood plain with its ominous debris.

Rain was falling hard and steadily on the morning of February 9 and I had the radio tuned constantly to Weather Service. The forecast, I remember, was that the eye of the storm would pass over at about midnight. Clearing was expected the next day.

In late morning I put on high boots and walked around the whole place to see what was going on, and then stood out by the gray, swollen river for a few minutes. All of the lions were in their houses, only a few peering out. The tigers, not unexpectedly, were out and about, dripping, loving it. Timbo was cozily in his heated barn. So much for the animals.

Then I went back to the house, freshened up and changed clothes, intending to drive to town and see Noel at Cedars. I went about a mile west to where Little Africa had been and stopped the car to look at the river again. Water was flooding over some of the roadways in the trailer park, and I remembered the stories of Ralph Helfer's catastrophe. Wild animals loose, lions and tigers among them. Terrified animals swimming the current. I had a sinking feeling.

Returning home, I called Noel. "It's not good out here," I said. "I'm not going to come in." I didn't even want to go to Acton, ten miles away.

About one o'clock, Monique de Bont and I drove back to Little Africa to take another look. The river appeared uglier than ever. Then we went to a little country store not far up the road to buy some big green plastic trash bags. Some of the crewmen didn't have raincoats. With holes cut out for heads and arms, the bags would give them a little protection. The handlers and the maintenance men probably had a long afternoon and night ahead.

Then we began mobilizing, just in case. John, an excellent organizer, got on the phone to call in cattle cars and horse vans. I began calling our regulars, people who knew something about the cats and often came out to be around them. Gardner McKay, Chuck Sloan, Leo Lobsenz and about twelve others were contacted. I said I thought we might be in trouble and hoped they would be available to move cats. No one turned me down.

The twenty-foot cattle cars and the smaller horse trailers began to arrive in midafternoon, parking on the paved road above us near Up-Front. Our welder, Chris Gallucci, got his equipment out and began closing the openings along the sides of the cattle cars with chain-link fencing. Cows can't jump out of those two-foot spaces, but our cats could easily wriggle through. Sparks were flying through the rain at about 3:30 P.M. Each car could hold about ten carefully placed cats. But groups and certain individual cats could not be mixed. There would be bloody battle if Lena lioness and Chelsea were put into the same car, or if Togar and Casey or George were in the same space.

We made plans to construct a chain-link chute, by moving the portable fence panels, to funnel cats up toward the vehicles from down in the compounds. Some emergency cages, mainly used for transport, and some den boxes had already been hauled up to the higher ground. In fact, a few cats were already safely in this housing.

Since filming had been closed down indefinitely, relatively few of the movie-makers were on hand. Jan de Bont and Jerry were working on editing, as were three sound-crew members, residents of Gumpsterville, the teardrop-trailer village across the rising river. They'd been laboring on the sound track, but in midafternoon Jan decided to take every foot of sound tape to safety on high ground in John's house. He knew about flood waters.

Still-photographer Bill Dow had spent most of the day in his darkroom near the elephant barn, making prints, unaware of what was going on outside. Others around that day, men like assistant director Doron Kauper, had pitched in to help move the cats. Very athletic, Kauper, in his mid-twenties, had been working for us since the past October, becoming a big-cat devotee his first week in the canyon.

Thus far, we had invested more than four million in *Roar*, of other people's money plus our own, a sum that included the physical layout in the canyon—the "studio" and some of the filming equipment, the expensive Kem editing tables and sound transfer equipment, the dwellings, various work buildings and miles of fencing, trucks, tractor, backhoe and, most of all, the animals. The film, after two years of work, was 80 percent complete and we estimated that with any favorable change of luck we would finish by April. Editing and scoring would take another three months, and by July we would be looking for a worldwide distribution company. We were that close on this uneasy February 9, 1978.

But my main worry was never about the physical plant. I worried only about the cats that day. They are sensitive to a change in conditions, and, hearing the increasing roar of the river, some would be agitated, some would be fully panicked. They would have to be herded through the chute. Others could be safely walked on leads outside the chute to emergency housing; still others could be walked through the human fences, if that became necessary. But the Wild Bunch and the Tongarus, even mellowing Togar, could cause havoc, I knew. We had six experienced handlers and three or four less experienced volunteers to cope with about 130 animals; another six maintenance-crew "bodies" for use in human fences.

That afternoon there was a lot of confusion and sharp differences of opinion about how to handle the tough cats. Meanwhile, the clock was running out on us, though we didn't know it. Upstream at Aliso Canyon, a lake had been forming for more than forty-eight hours where the county had built up the roadbed. Brush and boulders had plugged the big pipes under the road, and the lake was now almost a mile long, six to ten feet deep in some places and almost a quarter mile wide. The clock *was* ticking and no one, official or otherwise, notified us.

I called the 49er Restaurant in Acton in late afternoon and asked if we could use their parking lot for cat-laden cattle cars and trailers, if that became necessary. The answer was yes. People in the high desert tend to be both rugged and helpful.

We were racing the night. There had never been need for area lighting except outside the office at Up-Front. Cats couldn't care less about illumination. Except at times like this, lighting their spaces was a waste of money. When darkness fell just after five o'clock that afternoon, flashlights by the dozen were needed. Volunteers scurried out after them. And soon Chris Gallucci was welding and the handlers were moving cats by torchlight. Chris quit welding only once from three o'clock to about eleven. He was temporarily living in a big unused freezer, and the handlers told him they needed it for leopard storage. After pulling all his possessions out, he went about welding four chain-link compartments inside the walk-in freezer, then returned to work on the cattle-car panels.

210

Flood waters swirling around the "African house"

Bill Dow emerged from his darkroom at about five-thirty into heavy, wind-blown rain and began helping the handlers and the fence crew. Plywood was being wired up against the compound fences to protect the cats. The cold was numbing, and all but the tigers had gone into their huts and den boxes. Soon, water was around Bill's ankles.

Alexandra Newman had been working alongside the crew all afternoon moving cats. She was as capable as any of the men and just as courageous. She had parked her camper-top truck up on the paved road and put two leopards inside it. The idea was to utilize any safe and dry space available. Scores of cats had already been moved, but at Up-Front I discovered that the troublemakers were still down in the compounds. I said to John, "Why haven't they been moved?" I felt that the handlers should have started with the tough

211

ones—the Singh Singhs and the Tongarus—during daylight, leaving the gentle cats until last. But everyone had been hoping there would be no need to move the bad actors at all. That hope was fading now and I suggested that the tranquilizer guns be loaded.

We seldom had to use the darts loaded with a mixture of tranquilizing agents, consisting mostly of phencyclidine and atropine. Fired with gas cartridges out of Luger-type pistols, they were always a last resort in controlling situations. Even then, we never allowed untrained personnel to use them. The cats must be hit in the shoulders or flanks, never in the belly. The tranquilizer takes five to ten minutes to become effective and it was possible that the guns might not be needed. But on the other hand I wanted them loaded and ready for instant use.

That evening the downpour increased, as the weatherman had predicted, and the person we all needed the most was Noel to say, "Do this, do that. . . ." Then it would be a matter of whether or not we had the guts to do it.

I sent people down to the river throughout the evening to shine a light on it and report back. There was no lack of help. Hot food and coffee went to Up-Front almost every hour for the handlers and maintenance people. The dryers in my house and Monique's were going steadily to keep pace with water-soaked clothing.

The unending downpour and now the darkness slowed down movement of the remaining cats to higher ground. John estimated that there were still forty in the danger areas near the river. Slowing down the procedure was the necessity to carefully choose the temporary spaces in which to place them. It was sometimes difficult to distinguish them in the flashlight beams. They were soaked, fur matted, and nervous. Some were being secured, temporarily, along the upper perimeter fence, about ten feet apart, until we could positively identify them, then take them to cover and safety. Timbo remained in his house, out of danger. The water was well away from the elephant barn and the office.

There were gaps in the chain-link corridor which stretched from down in the compounds about two hundred feet up to the high-ground areas where the trucks were parked. To fill the gaps human fences were already in use—Bill Dow, Chuck Sloan, Gardner McKay, Liberato Torres and then a half-dozen volunteers with little or no experience. Under most circumstances the living fences served adequately, but in this situation nothing but chain link was really safe. The cats couldn't be blamed for mayhem.

The scene was surreal. Driving rain. Stabs of light. Blue-red sparks from the welding torch. People shouting. Human fencing where there was no fencing. Cats moving uncertainly along the corridor, one at a time, grumbling, tails twitching. The experienced people saying to the inexperienced people, "Just stay steady. Don't move if a cat comes up to you."

One frightened lion broke through the human fence, shoving bodies aside, and got out of the corridor. John's voice cut through the rain and wind. "Everybody keep together. Stay in one group until we get him." Soon the cat was isolated down by the lake and brought uphill to safety.

Meanwhile, upstream at Aliso Canyon, water continued to collect behind the plugged-up pipes of the county roadbed.

—23—

"THE STORM HAS PASSED"

About midnight, Noel called to say, "There's no problem now. The storm has passed." He'd been watching the late-night news from his bed in the hospital. An operation was scheduled on his leg at ten in the morning.

"Well, I'm not so sure about that," I said, then told Noel the river was still rising. To me, that *was* a problem.

In fact, water was beginning to lap toward the house. With the help of one of the sound editors, I lifted the stereo off a low shelf in the living room and placed it and other things on top of tables in case water came in. Then I went to Up-Front to help move cats.

The worst was over, I thought, but Monique de Bont had been getting reports from the county road people, and about 1:45 A.M. Jan came up to me and said, "Tippi, if you need anything from your house, get it now. You've got fifteen minutes!" Monique had been told that the road "dam" at Aliso Canyon was about to burst.

I drove quickly back to the parking area outside Jan's house, then ran down to my house, a hundred feet away. Water had almost reached the front door. Mona Emigh, the same Mona of the Jerry–Mike tennis-shoe incident, now working in film editing, helped me pull out clothing. My closets were color-coordinated, and the stack of sweaters she grabbed was pink. For weeks I would wear nothing

214

but pink. I grabbed my jewel case, filled up my makeup case, took out some warm coats for Noel and myself, inexplicably picked up my small antique sewing machine and then dashed for the car.

Just as I was going back to the house a second time, a little after 2 A.M., I heard a noise coming from upstream. In the distance, it sounded like a huge rocket motor. Then I saw a wall of water eight or ten feet high, trees and boulders tumbling in front of it, coming down the canyon. I remember that a cold wind seemed to be blowing as it approached. Then it hit the house, cresting over. Lights went out instantly.

In seconds the wall went on downstream, smashing and sweeping away the commissary building and crew kitchen, then hitting the editing and sound buildings, carrying with it tables, chairs, refrigerators and my Great-Aunt Tillie's piano. Steel dollies and pieces of concrete were tumbling in it like soap chips.

In a state of shock, I was still standing in the middle of the road when the wave went on to hit the compound area, taking out fences. Cages began separating; the chute to safety for the cats collapsed. The teardrop trailers of Gumpsterville, overturned and strewn about as if a cyclone had hit the canyon, were now on an island in the center of the property, deep water rushing around both sides. Four of the sound crew, asleep when the crest hit, were now trapped out there.

Frank Tom, Mike Vollman and Alexandra Newman were with the last of the cats that had not been moved when the wall of water rolled down on the compounds. Tiger Ivan and lionesses Peaches, Cherries, Shirley, Mary and Melanie were in that group. Tongaru and Zuru were still down there, too, as were Sheba lioness and Joey lion. So were Togar and Jenny. Fortunately, Singh Singh and Panda Bear were in a compound closer to the elephant barn, up on higher ground. Almost instantly, Frank, Mike and Alex were swimming with nine or ten frightened big cats in the swirling water.

Chris Gallucci had finished welding and was helping with the animals, higher up, when he saw Alex in the water. "She had this chain on Condor cougar," he said later, "and it looked like they were both walking on water to get the hell out of there." And as soon as Alex touched firm ground with the cougar, she yelled, "Togar and Jenny are loose!"

"I saw that Togar and Jenny's door was open," Alex told us later, "and I was filled with complete panic. Togar had a sound that was different from any other cat. It was a low rumble and I thought,

Oh God, if I hear that . . ." Alex had been involved with Togar before and did not believe he had mellowed. Once, she'd had to shoot medicine into his eyes because of an infection, and apparently he'd vowed vengeance. He rumbled every time he saw her.

As the fences came apart, a total of twenty-eight cats were on the loose, panicky and disoriented in the frothing millrace. After Togar and Jenny broke out, the small family headed by Tongaru and Zuru leaped over downed fencing. Then Ivan's group of five lionesses joined the escapees in the darkness, cut now and then by flashlight beams. Other cats were seen scrambling for safety. None was interested in harming humans. All were busy trying to save their own lives, swimming for the high ground in the Up-Front area.

Two Latino hands working on fence maintenance, hired only a few days before, were about fifty feet from all this when the wall of water hit the compounds and the animals began struggling in the water. The men jumped into cougar cages that had been emptied earlier in the night and were still clinging to top bars at daylight.

As soon as the cats reached high ground, Tongaru took a liking to Togar's mate, Jenny, despite everything that was happening. Old Papa Togar, of course, took a dim view of this. A wild fight broke out between these heavyweights, and instantly other raging battles began on that patch of high ground about three hundred feet long and fifty or sixty wide, sloped upward toward the perimeter fence. Even in the worst scenario I could never have imagined anything more terrible: big cats on the loose surrounded by flood waters and fighting on a narrow strip of land which also contained half a dozen exhausted handlers.

It was time to use the dart guns. Togar, Tongaru and Jenny were hit immediately, and three or four of the other battling cats were also quickly sedated. Care had to be taken so they didn't drop into lapping water and drown.

To add to the confusion, about twelve members of the Los Angeles County Fire Department arrived in a truck to rescue the four members of the sound-editing crew who were still stranded on the island. Wearing yellow slickers and carrying ropes, picks and shovels, they marched down the Up-Front road in single file until Chris Gallucci yelled to the lead fireman, "Hey, we got lions and tigers loose down here." The firemen made a tight-circle about-face and marched back to the haven of their truck.

All of the cats except Mary, Melanie and a black leopard, Jana, reached high ground safely. Jana wisely went up a tall cottonwood that seemed to be firmly rooted, but Mary and Melanie, both about three years old and weighing around three hundred pounds each, had been swept far downstream before climbing out on the bank. Then they proceeded west toward the Cypress Park trailer camp. I'm convinced they had no intention of attacking anyone. Constant companions, they were always playing together in the compounds, never presenting any problems. Raised by us, they were extremely sweet and beautiful.

Throughout most of the night, the animals had given us a break. They were on unbelievably good behavior. Any problems had been created by confusion and fear, plus accidental mixing of the more volatile cats. But the sedative effects quickly set in on the animals that had been darted, and they were now lumps on the wet sand. Togar had keeled over, fortunately. He would be out for at least two hours. Tongaru was in the same shape. For another hour after they awakened they would be sluggish and drowsy, of no harm to anyone. To clear the area, handlers rolled the sedated cats onto a fence-gate litter and carried them up to the safety of the cattle cars.

Within an hour after the wall of water roared through the canyon, the situation was stabilized to the point where all the loose cats were contained within a single area. Little else could be done but wait for daylight. No one knew that Mary and Melanie were missing.

Many of the elderly residents of the Cypress Park trailer camp had stayed up throughout the night to be ready for evacuation if that became necessary. Now, at about 3:30 A.M., some of those who were peering out of windows over the rain-swept grounds could see the figures of two large animals prowling about. The trailer residents were well aware of their four-footed feline neighbors to the east, and some of them had discussed this very situation. The sheriff's department was quickly phoned.

Though the bewildered lost lionesses were not threatening any lives and wanted nothing more than to be led home to get out of all the wetness and mess, Mary and Melanie were shot to death within about thirty minutes. An officer from Animal Control, with a dart gun, was on his way, but the lionesses were dead by the time he arrived. I can't blame the park residents for their anxiety, nor do I blame the young deputies for pulling their triggers under the circumstances. But the deaths of the two fine animals was a tragic mistake.

About 4:30 A.M., Bill Dow got into his car and drove west along Soledad Canyon Road, which was partially washed out in places, until he found a phone that was working. He placed a call to Noel, telling him that the canyon was flooded, that some of the cats were loose and that things could not be worse. That wasn't altogether true. No human life had been lost.

At dawn, a little more than an hour later, Marty Dinnes, Steve Martin and Martin Downey, who owned a number of exotic animals, were on the scene voluntarily, hoping to be of help. They had staked out individual piles of meat to attract the last of fourteen cats that were still roaming around. The animals had converged on the meat, and the three men were preparing to tranquilize them, guns in hand, when a sheriff's helicopter came in low, its rotors beating the air, hovering. The cats scattered and the chopper lifted away, having ruined the chance to take the animals in a group. Now they had to be captured one by one.

Approximately another hour passed as individual cats were cornered and put on leads. Deputies were watching in the gray light as the handlers, somehow still functioning, took care of the last escaped cats. Two of the final few were Robbie lion and Gregory tiger. They were just outside the perimeter fence, and big Robbie, our star, was protecting his pal, Gregory, as usual. In tense moments, the lion sometimes became overly possessive of his tiger friend. Steve Miller was alongside Frank Tom, attempting to coax Robbie and Gregory

Melanie and Mary, who were swept downstream in the torrent, then shot to death by sheriff's deputies

Robbie, who was shot to death while trying to protect Gregory

back through the nearby opening in the fence, when suddenly Robbie charged.

Frank had seen the deputies with their rifles and immediately shouted, "Don't shoot!" He knew that Robbie would charge ten or fifteen feet, then go back. Neither Frank nor Steve was in any danger, though the deputies weren't aware of that. They weren't aware that Robbie had feinted repeatedly over the years. *It was his way.* He always rumbled and then retreated to protect his tiger friend.

One young deputy leveled his body in the sand, Swat Team style, and four shots rang out. Robbie staggered and moved toward some brush for cover as more shots were fired. Other deputies, hitting the sand combat style, joined in pulling triggers. A fusillade of twenty bullets hit that magnificent black-maned Rhodesian. And tragically that death too could have been avoided if the officers had listened to Frank Tom.

With tears in his eyes, Frank walked Gregory to safety.

Not long afterward, firemen threw a grapple rope across to the island, and the four stranded members of the sound crew, hooked to waistbands and bouncing like corks, came hand over hand to firm ground. Everyone was exhausted, but safe. All the animals had been contained. But as light widened, Gumpsterville and the whole canyon looked as if they had been hit by a tornado.

—24—

DEVASTATION

I didn't know of the cats' escape, nor of the deaths of Mary, Melanie and Robbie. After standing in the road watching our house being destroyed, then seeing the wall of water sweep on, knowing that all we had worked for was washing away, years of hope and dreams going down that river, I completely lost control. This was the disaster that we had courted. Our worst fears had become reality and I was helpless to do anything about it. I screamed hysterically until someone took me to John's house, well above the flooded area.

There, the first thing I remember was Monique pounding me on the back, yelling, "Breathe, you have to breathe, you have to breathe." She began walking me in a circle, through the kitchen, into the dining room, through the living room—around and around the candlelighted house for about twenty minutes. Then she guided me to John's bedroom and ordered me to get some sleep.

I remember nothing else until Monique awakened me at about six-thirty. "Tippi," she said, "you have to get up. Noel is here."

Bill Dow's call to the hospital was quite enough to make Noel leave his bed, though he was still due for an operation at 10 A.M. His leg was still badly swollen, purplish in color around the knee joint. And the nurses at Cedars of Sinai flatly ordered their patient back to bed after he requested a wheelchair. But he had already dressed himself and was out in the hallway, cane in hand. A friend, aroused in the predawn by Noel, was waiting in a car down by the hospital entrance. Noel's vocabulary was, on occasion, the color of his leg, and I'm sure he used most of it on the nurses before hobbling off.

After Monique awakened me, it took me a moment to realize where I was. I had been dreaming. The driving rain, the rising river, that wall of water rushing down the canyon destroying everything in its path—it had all been a terrible dream. But as I left John's house and looked down the road below, I saw that the destruction was real. The back wall of the master bedroom of our house had been broken through and the house was off its foundations. Water several feet deep was still rushing through and around it.

Looking west, it appeared that the kitchen and the commissary were gone; the buildings next to where the commissary had been were tilted over. I could not see the African house from where I was but doubted that it had survived. The flood waters had receded a bit, but the river was still a quarter mile wide through the property, stretching over to the railroad tracks. It wasn't possible to walk up there. Rapids three or four feet high were still tumbling down the river. Trees and debris from upstream were littered everywhere. Devastation was everywhere.

I got into my car, which was still parked where I'd left it the night before, to drive to Up-Front to find Noel.

Out on the paved road there was a barrier, and a deputy said, "Lady, you're not going any further."

"Yes, I am," I said. "I own that property down there." Or what was left of it.

About fifteen minutes earlier, when Noel had arrived, the cats had greeted him with "aa-oohs," and several of the lionesses chained along the perimeter fence pushed up against him. Their ordeal was over. The head lion, their protector, was back. Their human lion had returned and all would be well.

Noel looked awful. Around his eyes he looked like a man who'd been beaten unmercifully, yet there wasn't a mark on him. It was all inside. Because the road had been washed out to the west, he'd had to hobble about a quarter mile, pain lancing up his leg with each step. His face was ashen behind the stringy beard. The first thing he said to me was, "Some deputies killed Robbie." I didn't learn about Melanie and Mary until later.

There was no use our saying to each other, "We're wiped out.

We're through—no movie, no house." Words were unnecessary.

We walked to the African house. White-streaked brown rapids were still eddying around it. It was tilted down on one end and a huge tree had rammed it, sticking out as if someone had driven a giant leafy stake into it. A dressing-room building was lodged against it on one side, and there were also a car and a tree embedded in what had been the dining room. Yet the building had miraculously survived, thanks to the depth of the telephone-pole foundation.

The handlers, plus Chris Gallucci, all bleary-eyed and past exhaustion, were still moving animals into the cattle cars and the horse trailers for transport to the 49er parking lot in Acton, and Noel promptly went to work, grabbing cats, to help. But the second cat he touched, eager to get away from the perimeter fence where she'd been restrained for several hours, swerved unexpectedly and the 5.0 lead chain with its inch-long links wrapped around Noel's injured leg and he was dragged over the sand for about two hundred feet. The chain squeezed his swollen infected knee, forcing pus out. Noel said later that he hadn't even felt the pain.

I remember looking around at all the tired faces and thinking how incredible it was that they were still there, still on their feet. How easy it would have been for them to say, "What am I doing here in a flood, with lions and tigers running loose?" Not one of them left. The animal crews, the film crew, the volunteers, all performed acts of heroism without a thought of the danger involved. I marveled at the courage and loyalty they displayed that night.

Their rescue operations were not yet over. Several inches of water flooded the compound housing Singh Singh and Panda Bear, though the fencing had held. Panda Bear was deep inside her den house, but Singh Singh, splashing around in the water, was making angry noises. Doron Kauper aimed a dart gun at him, trying for his flank, but the cat moved and the dart hit his right front paw. Another one was on target in the hip. Ten minutes later Singh Singh was in no shape to argue and Frank Tom led him to a squeeze cage for transport to safety. Chris Gallucci quickly boarded up Panda Bear's den house, and a forklift took her out of the compound.

Jana leopard was coaxed down from her tree in midmorning, and by noon every surviving cat was in Acton or safely housed in trucks parked at Up-Front. However, the aoudads were gone, we soon realized. The North African sheep were sighted weeks later, alive, near Little Rock Dam, about thirty miles away.

By noon, the editing crew began picking up more than 100,000

Tim Cooney rescues the flamingos.

feet of film which was in tangles all over the ground. Later, neighbors reported seeing film hanging on low-lying tree branches five miles away along the river. The negative, of course, was in the lab in Hollywood and the sound transfers were in John's house.

I found it difficult to look around. The lake was gone, flood waters having deposited ten feet of sand, so there was nothing to define it. Almost all of the cottonwoods had been uprooted and washed away. Debris was everywhere. I felt completely helpless. And when I drove to Acton to call my parents, my sister Patty and Melanie, to tell them what had happened, there was virtual silence on the other end of the lines. They didn't know what to say.

I now realize I was a zombie all that day as I walked aimlessly

223

Noel and I inspect the ruins of the "African house."

around, picking up everything from a frying pan half buried in the sand to a crewman's torn T-shirt from Hussong's bar in Ensenada. At one point I remember taking off now worthless lion and tiger posters from the exposed interior walls of the wrecked editing building. The walls had been flattened against a hill. I also remember worrying about the black-and-yellow-striped king snake that had lived under our house. Had it survived?

Jan and Monique went into town, so Noel and I stayed in their house on that bone-tired, red-eyed night. We could still hear the gurgle of water as it slowly receded and I remember Noel saying, finally, "We don't have any choice but to finish it, do we?" He'd gone back to the hospital and checked out. The operation on his knee was no longer needed. The lioness had performed the surgery.

"No," I said, "we don't."

Obsession, once again. But eight years of work and planning and punishment could not be abandoned because of one wet and terrible night. It was more than a matter of money, which we didn't have, anyway. Anger, pride and plain bullheadedness were all involved.

Next day, Saturday, we removed sopping furniture and clothing

224

Film was scattered for miles by the raging waters.

from our house, wading in and out of sloshy sand up to our hips. Renting a moving van, we parked it nearby for storage.

Sunday morning's *Los Angeles Times* told of the devastation of Soledad Canyon and the plight of the homeless lions and tigers. Dozens of people, most of them complete strangers, responded with offers to help. Truckers offered vans. People brought in portable fencing. We even got a call from Omaha: the Southern Pacific, offering to send railway cars to house the cats.

Almost every friend we had joined us to begin shoveling sand out of our house, and I think it was on that Sunday that our big office safe was found five miles downstream. Supposedly waterproof, weighing seven hundred pounds, it bore the marks of a wild ride. Even the door had been torn off. Such was the power of the Soledad Canyon flood, and it had lasted no more than twenty minutes.

A day or two later, the insurance company representative visited to take a look at our house and promptly said, "It's totaled. Get a new one." We'd lost fine houses in Sherman Oaks and Beverly Hills, and the replacement was a mobile home. Yet, then and now, the latter was the most important.

To replace the house, all that sand had to be removed simply to

Dejection

truck the parts up the hill. But as soon as we were dug out, it was discovered that the frame wasn't even bent. The house had moved five feet west and another five north, a tree was now in the middle of the door, but Levitt evidently built them rugged. Why not dry it out, juggle it back onto the foundation and leave it there? After all, it had survived, joining the rest of us. I suddenly had an emotional attachment to it.

Oddly enough, the only material possession that I'd lost that meant anything to me was a reel of black-and-white film that was in the editing room. On it were commercials I'd done in the 1950s, including the one Hitchcock saw on the *Today* show that led directly to *The Birds*. The reel was part of personal history and couldn't be replaced. Lost also were family photos, slides of our first African trip and Food for the Hungry photos. Important pieces of my life had gone down that river. But there was one small ray of hope. By week's end, President Carter declared parts of Los Angeles County a disaster area. Soledad was included and we presumed we would be eligible for a low-interest loan.

There are degrees of broke-ness, and we were first degree in the aftermath of the flood. The most important man in our lives was

Herb Dorfman, owner of Mission Meat, in the San Fernando Valley. He agreed to carry us so that the animals could be fed every afternoon. The only people we kept on salary were a half dozen of the regulars— handlers and maintenance men. They hauled food to the cats in the Acton restaurant parking lot each afternoon. One of the crew members had to be up there twenty-four hours a day.

We knew it would take months to restore the compounds, weeks before our house would be livable again, so Jan and Monique rented an apartment in Los Angeles and Noel and I moved into their mobile home, staying close to the entire operation as rebuilding began.

One night, after a day when he had few kind words for anybody, Noel said to me, "I don't know why I'm so angry with you. You didn't cause the flood."

"No, dammit, I didn't," I replied.

The stresses and strains on both of us were enormous.

Our first job was to refence the compounds and get the cats out of the trucks and on familiar ground again. Locked up, they weren't happy. The first cat to return home was pregnant Lilian, and she gave birth to Robbie, Jr., on Valentine's Day, four days after the flood. The cub looked a lot like his late father.

By the middle of the week, we had shifted all of the cats out of the Acton parking lot back to the canyon, but they were still living in the cattle cars, one supersized moving van and nine horse trailers. We had only two compounds in operation by then, which meant that all cats would have to use these two fenced areas for exercise. Setting up hour-and-a-half shifts, we cycled them out of the holding spaces to the compounds and then returned them to the vans. Maneuvering unhappy cats jammed into small spaces was nightmarish. Lions like Tongaru came out of the van snarling.

Incredibly enough, two weeks later, at just about the time we were beginning to see an approximation of normal life returning to the newly fenced compounds, another flood came rolling down the Santa Clara, undoing much of the work. We evacuated Jan's house and got all the animals to high ground again. We were weary of it all, and so were they.

Trouble draws press attention; the more trouble, the more press attention. Soon after the flood, story after story about us began to appear, all of them making Noel sound extremely interesting—and quite a lot insane. On March 5 the *Los Angeles Times*'s Wayne Warga wrote:

Noel Marshall, with his ferocious intensity, his thick, wavy hair, his long unkempt beard, and his watchful eyes, actually looks something like a lion. It is as if he is some rogue human being who has come to try to dominate the animals that surround him, and instead they have metamorphosed him.

He is a man passionately obsessed to complete the film called *Roar*, one of the most improbable productions in an industry long ago given to the unlikely.

A few weeks later William Arnold's story appeared in the *Seattle Post-Intelligencer*:

With a kind of Ahab-like singlemindedness, a Hollywood producer named Noel Marshall has been sinking millions of dollars and herculean effort into making a unique and deeply personal kind of wild animal picture . . . many Hollywood insiders are betting it will be the grandest unfinished movie since *I, Claudius*. . . .

Big cats, temporarily housed in a moving van, glad to be back home

Arnold went on to describe Noel as a man with a "Rasputin beard," certainly a picturesque comparison, and then quoted a *Daily Variety* editor as saying, "People in this industry simply do not understand a man who'll gamble everything on a personal vision. They don't know if he's a gutsy genius or a colossal madman. He's already broken every rule of big-budget moviemaking and in a town that always plays it safe that alone is enough to be considered a lunatic."

In another story Noel was likened to the animal-loving protagonist in Romain Gary's *The Roots of Heaven*, another man who might be judged somewhere between eccentric and insane. If one read all the stories and believed them, we were indeed a bunch of crazies led by a legendary lunatic. The floods, crews quitting, the injuries— everything was included. And the stories were not untruthful so much as they were flavored toward making us sound as if we were voyaging in a ship of fools.

That kind of publicity we could do without. So we screened what there was of *Roar* for Wayne Warga and he admitted, in print, ". . . what has been completed contains some of the most remarkable— and frightening—photography of animals and people that has ever been produced."

Fair enough! But we hadn't yet completed the film, and what few money people we had left dropped us as fast as phones could be dialed, with the exception of Jack Rattner and Banjiro Uemura. "You're in too much trouble," they said. And to a degree, they were absolutely right. However, two longtime friends, a married couple, wrote us out a check for $50,000. It was a gift. Moments like that lifted our spirits.

Once again, it was Noel's job to go out and get the money we now needed more desperately than ever. We had earth-movers but no cash to pay anyone steadily to man them. So we started with a crew of three or four wielding shovels, then ten, then twenty. I was making lunches every day for all of them until the work force reached thirty. Then I said, "Help, I'm out of my league," and hired a cook. I was learning how to do a lot of things that modeling and acting never taught me: run a backhoe, fill a dump truck, run the other heavy vehicles that Timbo hated. I went to bed at night aching and exhausted but feeling good about myself.

It took eight months to rebuild everything, and, because it all had to look exactly the same to match previously shot film of the "African" location, every day we were reminded of the devastation. Joel supervised that job while his father was out raising money. He started with the landscaping by removing thousands of tons of sand, then resodding. He brought in six or seven hundred fully grown trees to replace the ones we'd lost. Then he began scooping out the area where the lake had been and damming it, directing the river back to its channel to feed the lake. A viaduct was built to make the Santa Clara stay away from our door. Then Joel restored the African house. Little by little, day by day, the phoenix was rising.

Whenever Noel brought in money, we would surge ahead, and I don't remember once discussing the possibility that we would fail. We *had* to rebuild. We *had* to finish the film. And during this period I learned how much you can do without, that you don't really need an awful lot besides food and shelter, that possessions are often meaningless. I tried to keep my sense of humor, but there were times of silent despair. Even Noel, with his sleepless, oxen stamina was slowed down by the enormity of the problems we faced.

A marriage can be solidified by that kind of adversity, but ours was beginning to dissolve slowly in the backwash of all that had happened. Our commitment to the animals and to the film seemed to outweigh our commitment to each other. I think we both recognized that trouble was ahead, but we didn't talk about it. As optimistic as ever, perhaps we both thought we could solve that problem too in the end.

In India, the elephant is often considered a good-luck token, and when Circus Vargas offered us Kura, another pachyderm who detested life under the big top, we said okay. When all the other Vargas elephants went to the right, we were told, the African lady usually went to the left. When the others went forward, she had the tendency to go backward. Disliking ring performances, she made life miserable for her trainer. We certainly needed some good luck, and after six lonely years Timbo needed some companionship. So, accepting Kura as she was, we retired her from further entertaining. Timbo was ecstatic, trumpeting loudly when the seven-thousand-pound former circus lady sauntered down the ramp of the truck. He ran his trunk all over her, and they intertwined trunks, making happy belly rumbles. Another mouth to be fed, a big one; another hundred thousand pounds of hay and alfalfa a year, but who was to worry about such things?

Many people consider film-making a flimflam art. How could anything so insane, absurd, immoral and downright stupid be called a business? But Noel chose to label it strictly business in applying to

Timbo and Kura getting acquainted

the Small Business Administration for a loan. Having no insurance, we looked to the great givers in Washington for help, and SBA appraisers, scratching their heads, visited the compounds in late May. Accustomed to lending money for flooded shoestores or burned-out laundries, the appraisers were taken aback by the big cats. A roaring session began just after they arrived, and one asked me nervously, "You sure these fences are strong?"

The only way to legitimize us in Washington was to enlist help, and on June 22 we screened *Roar* for Representative William Ketchum, a Californian. After the Congressman looked at the still pictures of the flood damage and listened to our tale of woe, he promised to help in every way that he could. Two days later, he dropped dead of a heart attack.

Kura's Indian luck did not seem to be working very well down in our canyon, after all. Eventually Senator Samuel Hayakawa did much better in persuading the SBA that we merited a disaster loan.

231

—25—

NOELLE

While reconstruction and landscaping of the African-set area proceeded slowly during the summer of 1978, we began to prepare for filming in the fall, hoping to finish that final ten minutes of *Roar* by year's end. Noel had managed to line up commitments for just under a million and prospects seemed favorable again, but each day for me, mentally, began with crossed fingers.

The main film work yet to be done was the action scene in which one of the lions would attack a pair of "bad guys" and maul them. The attack, of course, had to be carefully orchestrated, carried out with much noise and bared canines on Rick Glassey and Steve Miller. We hoped the lion would perform on signal; we hoped he would look very ferocious while being semigentle.

Robbie had been scheduled for this scene, with Togar as his double. But now Robbie was dead and Togar was more a pussycat than ever. Estimated to be at least eighteen years old, the black-magic lion had become so tame that you could sit beside him and chuck under his chin and he would barely blink. So we had to substitute tough Tongaru for old Togar, and Zuru for Robbie, spraying their manes black with nontoxic off-the-shelf Streaks & Tips.

Doubles are used in almost every animal picture. On any given day, the star animal, be it Lassie or a lion, may decide not to work.

Pleading and calm reasoning may persuade a human actor to return to the camera, but there is no way to persuade a stubborn beast to perform.

Lions and tigers used in circus or nightclub acts are seldom, or never, trained to attack or even simulate attack. Obviously, it is too dangerous, because the animals are prone to get carried away and do real, not simulated, bodily damage. Once triggered, big cats are always difficult to stop. While they will bat forepaws, snarl and feint charges for circus audiences, aggressive contact with the lion tamer is not made. We should have known that in trying to stage a realistic attack we were asking for trouble.

During the late afternoon of July 6, when Steve Miller and Darryl Sides were working with Tongaru and Zuru, preparing them for the fight scene, assistant director Doron Kauper approached the compound and asked if he could enter. He wanted to talk to Steve. The handsome twenty-seven-year-old Kauper had been raising cubs for us and was deeply interested in big-cat behavior. He enjoyed being around them daily and had made friends with a number of the animals. But, in retrospect, I think that that day Doron was almost too sure of himself, always a perilous attitude for those who enter lion or tiger compounds. Tongaru was friend to no man, except Frank Tom, and even Frank never turned his back to the lion.

Steve and Darryl, who was filling in that day for Rick Glassey, had been training Zuru and Tongaru to mock-attack when the "bad guys" bent from the waist. They probably should have warned Doron of that trigger. Under the circumstances, Steve should have suggested that Doron remain outside the steel barrier.

When the high gate swung open, Tongaru was in peaceful repose in the sand, stretched out on his stomach, forepaws extended, apparently relaxed. Doron approached him, said hello, and bent down to scratch the 475-pound lion under the chin, certainly a friendly gesture, one that most cats like. Doron was well aware that Tongaru could be savage; he'd seen Tongaru attack other animals; he'd seen him threaten humans. Talking to Steve, Doron then arose, *bending at the waist*, and Tongaru, in a delayed reaction, sprang out, ramming him in the left side of the head, breaking three teeth. Doron went down with the cat on top of him, canines entering his throat less than an inch from his jugular vein. His left ear was almost severed as the teeth went down the side of his head and into his throat.

Describing his reaction to the attack, Doron later said it seemed that he wasn't involved with the cat. For a flash, he saw himself looking down as Tongaru had him by the throat, as if he had separated from his own body. "I felt like I was watching someone else being attacked. It was eerie."

Steve and Darryl grabbed the lion by its black-dyed mane, pulling him off, and Doron began crawling back toward the gate. Just as he reached it, the determined Tongaru broke loose and got Doron again, in the butt. Doron was finally dragged outside the compound by a maintenance man.

Rushed to Palmdale, where nearly five hours of surgery was performed by Dr. Kadivar, Doron was hospitalized for three weeks. He had truly come within an inch of death. Had the lion even slightly moved his head, the jugular would have been severed. Thank God Doron was the last casualty of *Roar*. By early September he was back at work again, closely involved with the big cats. He wanted to go back into Tongaru's space to see if it was possible to become friends. I ordered him never to go near that cat again.

Meanwhile, Steve, Darryl and Rick continued to train Tongaru and Zuru for their upcoming fight scene with humans. For reasons I cannot fully explain, people will do incredible things, take stupid risks, when a camera lens is focused on them. They do it for more than money. I should know.

By early October, when the leaves were turning brown on the newly planted cottonwoods, we were ready to begin filming again. Comparing the set with still photos of the preflood period, we found it difficult to tell that there'd been any damage at all, much less a catastrophe in the canyon. Joel had done a masterful job, and the regular maintenance crew, all with some talents as carpenters or plumbers or electricians, had matched his efforts in the rebuilding. Several miles of fencing had been replaced. Animal security was better than ever and their quarters were larger. All the buildings had been repaired, including our home, and the African house looked just as peculiar as before.

Summer gone, only motion picture people would have appreciated the sight of Joel up on ladders spraying all the cottonwood leaves an apple green so that we could match the footage shot the previous July. Grass, whenever it came into the merciless stare of the lenses, also got the green treatment. Joel ended up as green as the trees.

Cameras rolled on Friday, October 13—why did we always have to keep flirting with omen dates? But the scene went smoothly and no one suffered so much as a scratch from the dozen lions involved.

Staging a mock attack

They behaved, the weather was fine, and I remember telling Noel that night, "Our luck has changed." But we had yet to film that mock attack.

For more than a week, Rick Glassey had been going back and forth outside Tongaru's space wearing bandages on his head. He could see the lion eyeing him. If he got close to the fence, Tongaru would close on him, eyes locked on the head bandages. "Tongaru really wanted to get at me," Rick said later. And that too was in preparation for the attack scene.

Next morning, Rick and Steve donned swimmer's wet suits under their clothing—little protection against claws and teeth. Those who have not been knocked down by a lion or a tiger, scratched or bitten by a big cat of any kind, cannot begin to imagine what it is like to feel the crushing power of the animal, look at the fangs inches away, and smell the foul breath. I have never been able to adequately describe it. But Rick and Steve were willing to risk it.

The "set" for the mock attack, an open area, had been fenced off, the chain link camouflaged with brush, camera positions well hidden. In costume, bandaged up again, Rick said to the handlers, who were wearing green and were hidden inside the fencing, "As soon as I yell, 'Get him off me!'—move! I don't want him chewing on me." The same applied to Steve, who was similarly bandaged. Just whom Tongaru would attack first was anybody's guess.

"Roll film," said Noel, and the two men began walking along, holding rifles.

"Tongaru in," said Noel, and the handlers opened the gate.

The lion with the store-dyed mane rambled into the set, took one look at Rick and charged, man and animal going down in a pile after a short struggle upright. "Get him off," Rick yelled, "get him off!" and five handlers raced in to grab Tongaru. On the next take, Steve was the target. The fight went on for another day, filmed from various angles, and miraculously neither Steve nor Rick suffered anything more serious than a few bruises and scratches. But then we closed down filming for the usual reason—no more money.

Exceptionally heavy rains in the California winter always leave a time bomb. The wetness of the winter past raised a brush crop double the usual, and the summer heat turned it brown and crisp. Brushfires were threatening much of the Antelope Valley by late October, some of them not too far from Soledad. On one day, we made tentative plans to evacuate the animals and stayed close to home, nervously listening to the radio reports. But county crews battled the fire and won.

Two more days of uneventful filming were accomplished in November. Slowly but surely. But for the first time I was beginning to wonder why we even bothered. In October and November we had screened what was completed of *Roar* for every studio in town, as well as such independents as Francis Ford Coppola, maker of *The Godfather*, with no success. Studio heads wanted sex and blood, not furry quadrupeds. They all admitted *Roar* contained the best animal footage they'd ever seen, but they definitely weren't interested in family entertainment, and that's all we had to sell. They claimed pictures like *Born Free* and *Daktari* and *Roar* wouldn't make back negative costs. They said even Disney had given up on animal flicks. Even though only one out of ten Hollywood films ever turns a profit, and the studio heads have generally been proven more wrong than right as to public tastes, there was little use in arguing with them. The future of *Roar* seemed bleak.

Christmas that year also seemed bleak. Noel and I decided not to exchange presents, thinking that being able to move back into the house was Yule gift enough. Yet we were given an unwrapped surprise that cold, rainy Christmas morning.

About 8 A.M., Brad Darrington, one of the handlers, knocked on the door, clad in a glistening yellow slicker. He was holding a tiny, very special package. One with stripes. As far as we knew, none of the cats was pregnant, yet here was a cub weighing one pound, ten ounces. It looked like a thoroughbred tiger. Its base coat was orange, stripes predominant.

"I found her hidden behind the den box in Nikki's compound," Brad said. "She was screaming."

I was puzzled. "Who's the mother?"

"Debbie, I think. I looked around for other cubs but didn't find any." Debbie, an orphan from Los Angeles Animal Control that we'd had since 1974, was a lioness.

Six-hundred-pound Nikita tiger was the father, without doubt. Nikki ruled his nine lionesses benevolently, and what Nikki and Debbie had given us this Christmas season was, of all things, a rare "tigon." The offspring of a tiger and a lioness is called a tigon, while the cub of a lion and a tigress is a "liger." This one, on closer look, was definitely a tigon, and premature at that.

I hadn't noticed any difference in Debbie's appearance lately, hadn't seen any swelling in her abdominal area or in her nipples. Even Liberato, usually infallible on cub arrivals, hadn't spotted the coming of this one. Yet Debbie wasn't the first cat to give birth surreptitiously to cubs.

"I don't think she wants this one," Brad said. "She didn't even look at me when I took it."

The orphan tigon, a female, was wet and cold, shivering. Placing her in a thick towel, I rubbed her vigorously to increase circulation, then held her in my arms wrapped in a heating pad for three or four hours.

Only in the Gir Forest, in India, are both lions and tigers found naturally in the wild. Even there, both species are so rare that they would not normally come in contact with each other. And if they happen to cross paths in the jungle, it is unlikely they would breed. The lion, always social, stays with its own kind, and the tiger, a loner, stays away from the lion. So a crossbreed is extremely rare and has happened only in captivity. So far as I knew, there were only three other tigons in the United States.

Noelle—half tiger, half lion—with her father, her mother and me

In honor of the Yule season, and with a nod toward Noel, we named our orphan Noelle. Her little face had the look of a lion cub, complete with mottled markings on top of her head and around her throat. But everywhere else she was crisscrossed with stripes. I had a hunch that Debbie had refused to feed this infant, so I hunted up Billy's wicker basket and the baby bottles and preemie nipples. Quite often it is easier to teach a cub to nurse from a bottle if it hasn't nursed from its mother first, but by now I was an old hand at this, and within a couple of hours Noelle was nursing happily from a bottle, swallowing warm distilled water. Formula followed in the evening.

During the first week I never placed her on the floor. All of us coming in and out from the compounds were potential carriers of germs from the adult cats. Noelle went into an ordinary baby's play-pen in which I'd placed several layers of bath towels. Keeping her warm and sterile was a good part of the battle for the preemie's survival. Without her mother's colostrum, she was at a disadvantage.

From the beginning, Noelle was unique. There was a different quality about her that set her apart from any other cub I'd known.

238

Nursing Noelle

Her sounds were unique. She spoke the language of both the lion and the tiger. When she was five days old, she began making those delightful nasal puffing "ff-fuff" sounds of the tiger. But she also made the cries of the little lion, the happy "aa-oow." Unlike the tiger cub, which does not want to be held under any circumstances, Noelle displayed the traits of the lion cub. She loved to be cuddled and quickly displayed the normal affection of a little lion. Yet her nose was definitely a tiger nose, which is never as blunt as that of the lion. Her eyes opened on the tenth day and were intense blue, a condition shared by both tiger and lion cubs.

A few days later I noticed that Noelle was limping and assumed she'd strained something. Off she went to veterinarian John Bernstein, former partner of Marty Dinnes. Marty was now jetting all over the world to take care of wild animals, and Dr. Bernstein stayed close to home in Inglewood, a section of Los Angeles. He quickly diagnosed her problem as septic arthritis. I was astonished. Arthritis in a cub? Again I was reminded of the fragility and susceptibility of the baby cats. No wonder the casualty rate is so high.

One of our most reliable cub-raisers, Pat Breshears, happened to live about five minutes from Dr. "B's" hospital, and she temporarily took charge of the tigon. Noel and I planned to go to Africa within a few weeks to film authentic exteriors for the opening of *Roar*, and it made sense for Pat to play foster mother while we were gone.

Though I've always loved to travel and will go scooting off around the world at the ring of a phone, I can usually count on some horrendous thing happening days or even hours before departure. For some reason there is certain to be a crisis of some kind as soon as I buy my ticket and pack my bags.

In the early morning of December 27, one of the handlers came

Noelle makes phoning difficult.

running up to the house to say, "Kura's down. She's been hurt."

Crisis!

Noel and I dressed hurriedly, then went out to the elephant barn to find Tim Cooney on his hands and knees beside Kura. She lay in a pool of blood. Near her, big Timbo, obviously guilty of something, was swinging his trunk nervously.

"It happened sometime during the night," Tim said. "Timbo worked her over."

"Why?" I asked, staring at the bull.

Tim shook his head. I had never seen him so distressed. His love for both of these elephants was genuine. And as far as we knew, they had lived together peacefully and happily since March. After living alone for six years, Timbo had never been so content as with Kura, we thought. It made no sense.

Kura's head was bloody. "You can't see it, but half her ear has been torn," Tim said. "She's got a hole here in her face, and he gouged her in the right front leg."

I kept looking at Timbo, wondering why he had attacked Kura so viciously. But his small, secretive eyes never really told you what he was thinking, and he seemed to be getting more and more distraught as more people gathered around the injured female.

With Marty Dinnes still halfway around the world, the only "elephant doctor" available at the time in southern California was Donald Dooley, at Lion Country Safari in Orange County, about 120 miles away. I ran to the phone to call him. I described Kura's condition and Dr. Dooley said, "You must get her up as soon as possible. If fluids collect in her lungs she'll go within hours." An elephant can't stay on one side for more than four hours. Dooley said he would be on his way immediately.

Tim had already tried to make Kura stand up, but she had refused, and you can't coax a seven-thousand-pound elephant to its feet unless it wants to rise. "We'll have to lift her," he said.

"How?" Noel asked.

"The only way I know how is a block and tackle."

I knew they were pulleys of some sort, and soon the maintenance crew brought two of them into the barn, then began rigging support timbers, tying them to the overhead beams. The whole barn might collapse, I thought. Meanwhile, Timbo began to act up, trumpeting, and Tim led the bull outside, chaining him to a thick tree. Trumpeting for the next two hours, pulling at the restraints, Timbo wanted to rejoin his mate.

Tim Cooney (right) comforts Kura after she was attacked by Timbo.

Fire hoses were split to make covers for the chain slings so that they wouldn't cut into Kura's hide. The slings were placed just behind her forelegs and just in front of her hind legs. Then the lifting began, with about forty men on each of the block-and-tackle rigs. As she was inched upward, hay bales were pushed under her belly for support. Once, the ropes broke and Kura squealed in pain. Time was the all-important factor. Tim had tears in his eyes as he tugged at the ropes. By the time Dr. Dooley arrived, Kura was on her feet, hay bales carrying all of her weight.

By midafternoon, Dr. Dooley had completed surgery and I asked, "Any idea why Timbo did this?"

"I'll give you a guess," he answered. "Love affair. He wanted to, and she didn't."

Tim moved his cot, TV set and coffeepot into the elephant barn to stay with Kura until she recovered. She had to remain propped up on the hay bales and in the sling until she indicated she was ready to stand on her feet. That finally occurred one night when she pulled the covers off Tim and turned over his cot.

—26—
FIRE

Two days after Timbo's attack, Noel flew off to Kenya with Jan de Bont, and I followed them on January 8, 1979. Returning to Africa convinced me that something changes inside most people once they see the wild animals en masse in their own natural domain. During the annual migration at Masai Mara, west and south of Nairobi, as many as 100,000 can be observed, slowly moving congregations of zebras, gazelles, antelopes, rhinos, giraffes, hippos, jackals, lions and other animals. Although we did not see the full migration, I was spellbound and had a momentary desire to release all of our animals, jetting them over in a modern Noah's Ark, saying tearful goodbyes and wishing them good luck in a new life. Thinking of those steel-wire compounds back in Soledad Canyon, I said to myself, "Oh, what if . . . ?" A ridiculous idea, of course. But watching great herds move freely across the plains reminded me of the reason we were making our film.

The grassy land beyond Nairobi toward Masai Mara, a northern extension of the Serengeti plain, seems to roll on forever, dotted now and then with scrub acacias. Made to order for photography, the East African sky often serves as a backdrop by providing lazy piles of white clouds. The opening scenes of any movie, sometimes combined with the title treatment, should say something of what the film is about, giving a feeling of locale as well, and that's why we were on the plains, Jan de Bont's cameras tied down in several Land Cruisers.

Within *Roar* there were already a half-dozen gift shots, unrehearsed scenes provided by the animals; spontaneous bits of action we would never have thought of. In all probability, they wouldn't have worked had we dreamed them up. But we had learned from the animals always to anticipate surprises, and to be ready to start cameras instantly.

On the first day of photography, near the Mara River, which empties into Lake Victoria, a huge giraffe gave us one of those precious gifts. Noel was on a motorbike, going right to left across the screen, when the bull giraffe, splitting off from a herd, decided to race the two wheeler. Galloping joyously at thirty-five miles an hour, he kept up with the bike for almost a quarter mile, head eighteen or nineteen feet up in the air, providing us with opening footage that would have been impossible to stage. We filmed two more days around Masai Manyaka and Lake Bogoria, in northern Kenya, then flew home pleased with what had been captured, saying a prayer at 36,000 feet that the cameras hadn't malfunctioned.

In late January, I received a birthday gift from Noel, a pair of breeding cheetahs, and I went out to Lion Country Safari to pick them up. I'd had a wonderful relationship with Pharaoh and with Kenya, Gardner McKay's easygoing cheetah, and assumed they were all alike, mostly friendly, gentle animals. Five minutes after I'd entered the cheetah compound at the Orange County preserve I realized how wrong I'd been.

None of these fifteen or so cats had been hand-raised. They stalked around us, occasionally snarling or striking out with a karate chop. They lowered their heads and arched their shoulders, annoyed at our invasion. Plainly, these cheetahs were antisocial. Nonetheless, I picked out a good-looking pair, about two years old, and we headed for Soledad Canyon. They sat in the back, cold-eyed and glowering, but I was determined to make friends with them.

So that they would have constant human contact, could see us entering and leaving, and hear our voices, we had built a compound for them in front of the house. The chain-link fence was about twelve feet high, and there were den boxes about four feet high, for shelter, placed about two feet from the fencing. About two hours after settling them in, well after dark, I looked outside and saw the female, which

New arrivals, Rhett Butler and Scarlett O'Hara

we were soon to name Scarlett O'Hara, but there was no sign of the male, whose name was to be Rhett Butler. I entered the compound to check in his den box. No Rhett! First night at home and he'd already escaped, obviously leaping from the top of his house over the twelve-foot fence.

Noel was in town that wintry evening, so Joel and I got flashlights out and began a search inside the perimeter fencing. Joel finally located the cheetah and put a lead on his neck, walking him back to his mate. It wasn't a very good start for the latest additions to our family of big cats.

The cold weather continued and one day I shifted the cheetahs to an area on the other side of the house, which would allow them entry into the guest bedroom at night. Then I went into the room just to talk to them, determined to win them over. For a moment I was hopeful, especially when Rhett put his nose up against me. I was scratching between his ears, talking very softly to him, when he sank his teeth into my right thigh, without warning. Yet, perhaps I hadn't heeded his warning—*he wasn't purring*. He hadn't said, "It's

245

okay to scratch me." Several days later Scarlett gave me a painful chop when I went out to fill her food bowl. I was very disheartened about the way they were behaving, their refusal to be friendly, yet I had hopes they would produce a cub I could hand-raise, an animal as lovable as Pharaoh. The close and successful human relationship with big cats, if it is to be achieved at all, should start at cubhood. With these cheetahs the age of two was too late.

The African location filming had exhausted all our money once again, except what was needed to feed the animals and maintain the compounds. So the rest of the late winter and early spring were uneventful for me, with the exception of Noelle's return. The tigon was now four months old, in robust health and weighing about forty pounds. The preemie had not only survived but thrived. Immediately, she took charge of four little Siberian tiger cubs, eight weeks old, offspring of Singh Singh and Panda Bear. We had shifted the cheetahs to another compound, and the little Siberians were living outside our bedroom wall. Knowing the ferocity of their sire, we felt that human contact was doubly important. Noelle went about teaching them how to play, but if they played too rough she cuffed them in exactly the same manner a tigress will cuff misbehaving cubs. That Noelle was doing this parenting at four months was rather surprising. By now, her brilliant tiger stripes were beginning to diminish, turning a soft brown. The lion blood in her was starting to assert itself.

Suffering numerous scratches and bruises in the raising of young-ster cats, I had learned from the late Needra not to teach a cub to jump into my arms. Grown-up Needra weighed almost four hundred pounds and still thought it was great fun to come flying through the air at me. My only defense, when I saw her preparing to make that leap, was to sprawl out flat on the ground. Out of pure affection, no intent to harm, she had vaulted at me many times until the virus took her in 1975. But I was resolved to train little Noelle, who was showing early signs of becoming another high-flying Needra, not to jump on fragile human beings. Mother cats, of course, hold their cubs down with a paw and remonstrate with them in severe cat language. I began doing the same with Noelle, using the tried-and-true sharp *"No!"* on her, firmly holding her down at her shoulders. It worked.

Of all the cubs I had personally raised thus far, twenty or so, Noelle seemed to be the most intelligent, the most cunning, the most lovable and, to me, the most beautiful. Whether or not those attributes were the result of mixing lion and tiger blood I'll leave to the scientists.

Noelle, our tigon, up in the trees

In observing her daily I noticed many of Needra's infant habits: the careful plotting to obtain something that was surely off limits—a pillow on a couch, a candlestick on the dining-room table. Yet she wasn't as destructive as most cubs I had nurtured.

Another trait of Noelle's was exceptional agility. Instead of dodging around animals, in the usual way of most tigers and lions, Noelle would often leap over them, rather like a gazelle. Very early, she was leaping into trees and crawling out gracefully on low limbs to peer down on whichever human was around. From her first weeks on earth, the tigon was very different. She remains so today. She's a striking example of a human-oriented big cat.

In late June I flew to Singapore for Food for the Hungry. Our relief vessel, the S.S. *Akuna*, a converted naval patrol ship, was roaming Asian waters to aid the boat people, refugees from Communist domination in Vietnam. Boarding it in Singapore harbor, I spent the next two weeks on the South China Sea helping to search for and aid these tragic, heroic people. Such a mission always made problems at home seem minor. Overcrowding of the boats, little or no food and no fresh water were often compounded by the attacks of Thai fishermen who inflicted brutal beatings, rape and theft on the refugees. Holding a starving baby in your arms does wonders in erasing self-pity. Coming upon the wreckage of a boat, seeing a child's sandal floating in the water, wondering if a small body has been ripped to bits by fish, jolts one to harsh reality. *We were too late!* At moments like those, Hollywood film-making seems a silly endeavor.

Yet there was some good news from home. The suit against Bill Blatty for Noel's share of *Exorcist* profits was finally settled out of court while I was gone, and Warner Brothers would now make payments direct. As soon as all the legal papers were tidied up we would begin to collect. At last it appeared we would finally have the money to complete our film.

Meanwhile, Noel had rounded up enough in mid-August to film for four torrid days and then estimated that we needed only one more week's work to finish *Roar*. It did not seem possible. I'd begun to think I would be a senior citizen before we called it a wrap.

The day that we shut down production, Boomer, always one of my favorite lions, and usually gentle, was in a very playful mood. Now about eleven years old and about 480 solid pounds, he'd been residing on our deck, and first thing in the morning Noel would open our door so that Boomer could come into the house. Like the rest of the cats, he loved to snoop around to see how we lived, endlessly curious, and then relax, sprawling out on the living-room floor. His tail was a menace whenever he was in the house. It swept dressers and coffee tables clean. On this particular morning I hurried to close the bedroom door, because he loved to jump up on the bed with me in it and had broken it once. The frame was no match for his weight. He saw me hurrying down the hall, ran after me and tripped me, turning me over. Then he began tossing me around as if I were a rag doll. Outside, in the sand, it was okay, but in that tight hallway my head was bouncing off the walls in this happy early-morning romp. Then he took my shoulder into his mouth.

Noel heard me yelling for Boomer to get off and came into the hallway. "Try and move over," he said, "and I'll have him get on top of me."

Boomer thought this was just the greatest of fun, two humans playing with him inside a house just past dawn. I could almost hear him laughing. But Noel's ploy didn't work, so he opened the hall door that led outside, and Boomer bounded through it. On my hands and knees, nightgown smudged, I watched him. He hit the sand, rolled over, and the four Siberian cubs who were living with Noelle pounced on him. Within seconds, he was bouncing the cubs around as if they were volleyballs.

I am not one who usually believes in hauntings, stray demons or Egyptian curses, though it had occurred to me from time to time that *Roar* had had an extremely unusual and prolonged run of troubles. And with our track record of inviting disaster into the canyon, it seemed to me the only one we hadn't suffered so far was fire. We'd taken note of the previous year's fire scares; even the ones dating back to 1971, fires that had come within a few miles of our part of the canyon. And fire, not flood, was the main concern of most people in the area. We had talked to ranchers who had experienced the nightmare of trying to handle horses while the hills were ablaze. Remembering the night of the wall of water, we could well imagine what it might be like to handle lions and tigers when walls of flames approached.

So we had a careful contingency plan that required forty horse trailers and cattle cars to evacuate the animals in a big hurry if that was necessary. We had also gathered fire-fighting tools and pumps and high-pressure hoses. There was a list of volunteers who could be contacted to help. Plainly, we did not intend to go up in flames as the aftermath of the flood. All year long we had watered and irrigated to keep fire resistance at a maximum. Liberato and others of the maintenance crew spent hours chopping at dried-up weeds and low brush that might become tinder if flames swept down off the mountains.

September, we knew, was the time of greatest danger, and early that month the U.S. Forest Service began its familiar and ominous warnings. Temperatures were topping 100 degrees in many areas from the Mexican border north, and the National Weather Service predicted hot, dry and smoggy days for the middle of the month.

Then in midmorning, Thursday, September 13, as Noel was preparing to shoot the final sequences of *Roar*, a fire, quickly named "Sage" by the Forest Service, broke out near Kennedy Springs, on the Angeles Crest Highway. Another, "Monte," started late that evening, also in Angeles Forest. That night we could see ominous glows in the sky to westward. We got up several times during the night to listen to the radio and check the progress of the fire fighters. More than a thousand were already involved.

On Friday morning, when a column of smoke about five miles long and thousands of feet high spread across the sky, I asked Noel if it was wise for me to go off on retreat. There was a weekend board meeting of Food for the Hungry in Dana Point, south of Los Angeles, and I didn't want to miss it. Antifamine representatives from throughout the world were attending.

"Go ahead," Noel said with characteristic optimism. "We'll be all right."

The filming crew would be on hand that day and the next, so there would be plenty of help if we had to clear the compounds. John, Jerry and Joel were all in the canyon, as were members of the maintenance crew. Upward of sixty people were available to move cats. So I drove to Dana Point, 130 miles away, listening to radio reports of the fires. I remember that one announcer said that nine were burning and that the Sage fire had already consumed twelve thousand acres. Gray ash kept floating down and bouncing off my windshield. The smell of burnt brush was heavy in the high heat.

I talked to Noel that night and he said that filming had gone well and that there was no sign of fire near Acton, though the Sage and Monte blazes were still raging. The dreaded Santa Ana winds, hot and dry off the desert floor, were blowing up to 25 miles per hour and the prediction was that they would increase over the weekend. Said one Forest Service official, "It seems like the whole damn county is on fire."

I listened to broadcasts again Saturday morning, September 15, while getting dressed for a breakfast meeting, and heard another Forest Service official say, "This is a perfect day for fire." I remember his precise words and I also remember saying to myself, "Oh, Lord, not again."

In late morning I called the office at the canyon, asking bookkeeper Nancy Landry, "How close are the fires?"

"Nothing to worry about," she said.

Wind was always the determining factor in the path a brushfire takes. I asked about that.

"There's a breeze but no heavy wind," Nancy said. "Everything's fine. Noel is filming."

Relieved, I went off to lunch and then to a meeting in early afternoon. There was an agreement among the board members, mostly church people, that no calls would be accepted. Yet an emergency call for me came through at about 2 P.M. "Tippi," an excited Nancy Landry said, "we're completely surrounded by fire. Noel is evacuating the cats."

"I'll get there as soon as I can," I said.

Board members Don and Fritzi Simonson had flown in from Santa Barbara in their twin-engine Cessna and volunteered to take me to Agua Dulce Airport, a small field near Acton. Just before I left the meeting room, Larry Ward, president of FFH, said, "We'll have a prayer session for you."

"Yes, please," I said. "Thank you." They weren't idle words. I believe in the power of prayer.

We were airborne within twenty minutes.

The Acton, or "Crown Valley," fire, as it was code named, had begun about twelve-thirty that day, probably the work of an arsonist, and Steve Martin's place up on the hill was threatened, as well as ours. Several ranches in the canyon were also in the path of the flames. By midafternoon a total of twelve fires were burning over an area 250 miles long. As we flew on toward Acton, the sky was yellow-brown and leaden in places; we could see splotches of flame for miles, half-moons and jagged lines of it cutting through the smoke. On the approach to Agua Dulce, billowing black smoke on either side, I could see our preserve in the canyon and prayed fervently for the animals. I had prayed on the night of the flood so the endeavor was nothing new.

Nancy met me at the airport, tears in her eyes. "They won't let you go through," she said.

"Who won't?"

"The sheriffs."

About five minutes later we pulled up at a roadblock manned by deputies. The one in charge said, "Lady, you can't go up there."

In a replay of the morning of the flood, I said, "I'm going. My animals are there. My husband is there." Quickly I explained, and they let me through.

As we rolled across the bridge over the Santa Clara and onto our property, I could see fire on both sides of us, but it seemed to be dying down. Aerial tankers were bombing it, and county fire crews were hacking at brush.

"I don't believe this," Nancy said. "When I left here the fires were all around us." The smoke had been so black she could barely see to drive out of the canyon.

251

Tugging a lion into a horse trailer as the brushfire approaches

But sparks were still dropping, and smoke rolled across the half-emptied compounds. I could see places where fires had started from windblown sparks. Some were near the compounds. Several hundred feet away, at Up-Front, Noel was directing traffic for the evacuation vehicles. I ran up to him. Blood had dried on his right cheek.

"I'm okay," he said. "Scarlett O'Hara got carried away." Leave it to the cheetah! The cheek gash was not serious. He had also been clawed in the chest, but that was not serious either. His face and clothing were smoke-stained, his eyes bloodshot. I'd seen him looking better.

About half the animals had already been moved, driven west to park overnight at several of the trailer camps upriver. Our neighbors were always accommodating. Tim Cooney had led Kura and Timbo westward, escorted by a sheriff's car.

Typical of that afternoon, and of Noel, I saw him calming down a group of cats. He said to Patricia jaguar, who was hissing, head cocked to one side, canines bared, ready to kill, "Everything's going to be okay, baby." With all the commotion, the whirring of the choppers, the crackle of flames, the drifting acrid smoke, the big cats were understandably nervous. As many as five strong men were needed to persuade just one adult lion into a horse trailer.

I joined the work of loading and calming the animals, thinking that the prayers of the FFH people at Dana Point *had* been answered. The fires on both sides of us had miraculously stopped just in time. By five o'clock, every animal and bird had been sent to safety. There was only one casualty—a marabou stork dead of smoke inhalation.

Though someone later said, "Well, you finally got lucky," I firmly believe that the power of prayer, that beseeching of minds, had more to do with it than any sudden bestowal of luck. The wind had changed and dropped in velocity; the flames had not jumped into the cotton-woods.

Even before the flood, Noel, as well as several members of the crew, had talked seriously about the "curse of *The Exorcist.*" Well publicized during the filming of that picture, there was a fire, gutting a locked set, that could not be explained, actor Jack MacGowran died suddenly, light stands toppled over, and there were numerous injuries to cast and crew. "Strange accidents," said the *Hollywood Reporter.*

Tim Cooney taking the elephants to safety during the fire

Now, after the fire was over, Noel said to a local newspaperman, "Yes, bad luck seems to have plagued me ever since that movie." *Something* had plagued us.

Noel's gains from *The Exorcist* were financing the completion of *Roar* and paying back some loans. So the films were at least connected that way. And there are some ventures, in the way of making movies, that seem cursed from the start. Just as I didn't believe in good luck, I didn't really believe in bad luck either. But blaming the devil for our problems was convenient as well as expurgating.

On Tuesday, October 16, 1979, just one month after the fire that could have been the ultimate disaster, I wrote in my date book, "Finished filming *Roar*." The principal photography was completed. A few pickup shots remained, but for all purposes we'd done it. That same day, one of Noel's brothers was killed in an auto accident. It remained uncanny that each victory was so quickly followed by a defeat.

Yet our greatest victory was the film itself. And at year's end, I decided to nose-count our animals: seventy-one lions, twenty-six tigers, ten cougars, nine black panthers, four leopards, two jaguars, one tigon, two elephants, six black swans, four Canadian geese, seven flamingos, four cranes, two peacocks and the surviving marabou stork. An impressive cast for any film.

—27—

UNHAPPY
ENDINGS

The big-cat female is probably the worst sexual tease in existence. Where romance is concerned there's a definite mean streak in her, and I've often felt sorry for the male. One day I was looking out my dining-room window into the adjacent compound, where Gregory tiger was peacefully asleep, as were lionesses Debbie and Wendy. Then I noticed that Debbie was stirring from her afternoon siesta, and soon she came over to awaken Gregory by nuzzling him. Once he was wide awake she began to flirt by rolling over on her back and pawing the air. Within a few minutes she had him aroused and wriggled into position for intercourse. At that moment, she bashed him in the mouth and gleefully ran off into a corner. Gregory pursued her for about ten minutes, then finally gave up after several more rejections and went back to sleep, nursing a bruised mouth and a shattered ego. Having had her fun, Debbie flopped down and also went to sleep.

Apart from episodes like that, we'd had such success with ti-gers—always the loners of the cat world—living amiably with our lionesses that we thought we might also solve the problem of Garbo-inclined tigresses by matching them with suitable lions. For instance, tigresses Natasha, Alexis and Anna had demanded to live alone, forcing us to provide small, individual quarters for them. They had carried the I-want-to-be-alone thing too far for their own good. If they would agree to living with a lion—and if the lion also agreed—we could give them space of several acres with streams running through, companionship would be provided, and the quality of life would definitely improve. This matching of different breeds had certainly worked well in the compounds occupied by tiger Ivan and his lioness harem, by Nikki and his ladies, and by Gregory and his tawny companions, despite Debbie's cruel teasing. But it remained to be seen whether one or more tigresses could live happily together with a lion.

For our initial experiment we picked Siberian Natasha, the pretty lady who liked to watch Westerns and ice-skating on our living-room TV. Definitely a mellow cat. For the male lion we chose my old love Billy, now nine, living at Up-Front with Casey, Berries, Trans and other lions. Billy and Natasha had played together as cubs on Knobhill but had not been kept in the same compound for many years. For all I knew they'd completely forgotten about each other. In any case, they would have to be reintroduced very carefully, with great patience.

First we placed Billy in an adjoining compound where he could watch Natasha from dawn to dark. He was definitely interested. I often checked the situation and on several occasions caught him eyeing her closely, his nose against the chain link.

Then we put the two of them together in an exclusive hideaway midst the cottonwoods, and Billy, at close quarters, immediately found the tigress attractive. But Natasha hissed and snarled at him, threatening him with a forepaw. From the fence, I told her that Billy was a wonderful cat. It was no use. Natasha let him have it with every swear word in her vocabulary, head cocked to one side, ears flat, an indication that she meant it.

Discouraged, Billy promptly went into a far corner and sat down, head low. It seemed incredible that Billy, who could be as tough as any cat in the compound on occasion and could hold his own even with Tongaru, was terrified of this tigress. I berated him for being chicken but then started to think of other pairings that might be more successful toward the beginning of lion-and-tigress harems.

A day or so later, with relations between Billy and Natasha still strained, I had an appointment in town and made the mistake of entering another compound wearing a musk-based perfume. I wanted to check on the healing of a lioness bite wound and forgot that I had daubed on the scent. Immediately, I was surrounded by seven fully grown tigers, two lionesses and Noelle. They were all sniffing and I got out in a hurry, having no desire to be jumped by twelve-foot Siberians. But on the drive into Los Angeles I thought, Maybe it would work for Billy and Natasha. Using the perfume was worth the try, I thought.

Next day I poured a little of my Estée Lauder Youth Dew, which had seemed especially intriguing to the tigers, into a small spray bottle and sought out Billy. I aimed several puffs at his mane and he became annoyed, curling his lips and making throat noises. Even at me! Then I retreated to a tree outside the compound and watched.

Within about five minutes, as the perfume wafted on the breeze, Natasha looked over at Billy with interest. Then she walked up to him, wrinkling her nose in a grimace, opening her mouth to take in more of the Youth Dew. Clearly, she had changed her mind about this lion. She was now gazing at him with what could be interpreted as "You are absolutely gorgeous. Where have you been all my life?"

Billy was puzzled for a moment, still leery of her, I think. But, like any other red-blooded male, he was more than willing to take advantage of a proposal. Natasha walked over to him, nuzzled him, "ff-fuffed" to him and began luxuriously rolling on her back. The flirting continued throughout the day, the Estée Lauder scent still lingering on Billy's mane. And thereafter, even without the perfume, the two cats got along famously.

However, we quickly discovered that the male lion is much more possessive of his females than the tiger. Billy became totally unmanageable over beautiful Natasha, and we soon abandoned the entire project.

I was still hoping for cheetah romance and a resulting cub, but so far Scarlett, like her fictional namesake, had displayed little interest in Rhett. Perhaps, I thought, a little perfume would work with her too. So I sprayed Rhett with Youth Dew and waited to see what would happen. Scarlett sniffed Rhett, seemed to be pondering for a moment or two, then walked away from him. They did a lot of nuzzling and grooming, but weren't interested in romance. The breeding habits of cheetahs are a little bit unusual, anyway. The female has to watch an encounter between two males before she is aroused. A good fight usually brings the female to heat and the winner then possesses her. I had no intention of bringing in another male and staging a fight simply to turn on Scarlett. But, in retrospect, I realized I had named them perfectly. Scarlett was going to "think about it tomorrow," and Rhett simply "didn't give a damn." They

Rhett and Scarlett—just good friends

were the most frustrating cats in the canyon. Finally we gave up, and Penny and I flew them to Winston, Oregon, there to live with another cheetah at the Wildlife Safari Park. The first thing Rhett did on arrival was to deliver a karate chop to the jaw of administrator Frank Hart.

Though *Roar*'s principal photography had been completed in the fall of 1979, there were those inevitable pickup shots to be made, and Jan de Bont's cameras had rolled several times since in an effort to plug up obvious holes in the story. It is a frequent occurrence with any film. The work of editing, building the sound-effects track and readying the film for music scoring in London would go on for the next several months.

Meanwhile, our animal actors had been retired, and comparative quiet had settled over the acres I now called Shambala, "meeting place of peace and harmony for all beings, animal and human." But at times, as I walked the compounds, it seemed that the cats longed for all the activity of the old days. They appeared to be bored after the excitement of the past four years, the chance to play crazy human games. I wished there was some way to tell them how truly magnificent they would be up on the sixty-foot screens.

We hired Terrence Minogue, a young composer, to do the score for *Roar*, and Terry moved to the canyon, installing a piano in one of the reconstructed office buildings, almost directly across from the compounds. He wanted to be near the big cats for a while, watch them, hear them roar. Also in residence for a while was Robert Hawk, another young talent, who would write the songs for some of Minogue's music. *Roar* was scored by the National Philharmonic in London as one of the final steps of production.

Looking for a distributor, Noel began to run the film, at last a finished product, with music and all effects, and my date book for September 20, 1980, noted: "Screening *Roar* everywhere. Charlie Bludhorn (Paramount/Gulf & Western) saw it last night. . . ."

The following month I noted: "Paramount wants *Roar*; ABC wants *Roar*."

Noel and I were a mile high and wildly optimistic about the film's chances. Looking back, we weren't wearing rose-colored glasses; ours were smoke-colored. We could not see beyond our own hopes and egos.

Two months later, another notation, notably less optimistic: "Screened *Roar* for Warners."

Again a favorable reaction to the film, but all the American majors were offering deals that hogged any possible share of profits. "Look, you've got an animal show here," they said. They remained unable and unwilling to comprehend family films. It was, of course, easier to sell sex and violence.

Three months later, on February 22, 1981, John flew off to London with a print of *Roar* to screen at Pinewood Studios for possible Swiss and Hong Kong buyers. We were looking all over the world for distribution heads to say, "It's sensational—a blockbuster. Let's make a deal." And we did make deals in England, Japan, Germany, Italy, Australia and other countries. But not in the United States.

The slowly gathering truth was devastating to Noel and me, and to those close around us. We had not made an international blockbuster, after all. We had captured wild animals in an astonishing and absolutely unique way. But the human story, always secondary in *Roar*, was lacking, we now recognized. The people had been excuses for the actions, reactions and interactions of the big cats. And that was not enough.

We had gambled everything, risked our lives and those of loved ones as well as crew members, to make the picture. Our personal financial stake was enormous, and we were also deeply in debt to others. But it was our pride that was hurt the most. We had defied the odds at every turn and had lost.

Togar, who had fathered so many of our fine young lions, who had been such a good but fierce papa, died at the age of nineteen or twenty on April 30 of that year. Old age, not fighting, finally took him. Outcast of the San Francisco Zoo, before that the pet of the mysterious black-magic man, Togar had lived a good life in the canyon, I think; with much more space and freedom than in his previous home. I saw him every day during his last weeks on earth. He was

Sitting with Togar near the end of his days

just very tired and wanted to die. Though I was afraid of Togar for much of his life, and rightfully so, I still felt a deep loss when he left us.

I found myself drawing closer to the animals that summer, a natural reaction in times of stress. I spent hours walking around the compounds and swam in the lake with Timbo and Kura. Talking to the animals, going in and sitting by those that were friendly, touching them, was a great reliever of pain and pressure.

It was a very troubled time for me. My marriage to Noel had collapsed and there was talk of divorce. The strains had been too many and had lasted for too long. With the goal of *Roar* in common our union had survived, out of necessity, through hospital emergency visits, flood, fire and financial debacle. But now that the goal had been achieved, turning out to be a hollow victory, there were bitter arguments and recriminations. After all we'd been through together, I could only meet this last disappointment with sadness and tiredness.

In late October, we all put on a good front and flew off to the world premiere of *Roar* in Australia. Melanie, John, Mativo and Robert Hawk joined us in Sydney for the rounds of parties and press interviews. We were all so enthusiastic that I found myself thinking that previous negative reactions by the Hollywood majors might have been totally wrong; that *Roar* would emerge from Down Under and become an international hit after all.

The day after the premiere, *Daily Variety*'s representative cabled his trade review to Hollywood:

> The noble intentions of director-writer-producer Noel Marshall and his actress-wife Tippi Hedren shine through the faults and shortcomings of *Roar*—touted as the most disaster-plagued pic in Hollywood history.
>
> Given the enormous difficulties during production—devastating flood, several fires, an epidemic that decimated the feline cast and numerous injuries to actors and crew, it is a miracle that the pic was ever completed.
>
> Here is a passionate plea for the preservation of African wildlife, meshed with an adventure-horror tale which aims to be a kind of *Jaws* of the jungle. If it seems at times like a *Born Free* gone berserk, such are the risks of planting the cast in the bush surrounded by 150 untrained lions, leopards, tigers, cheetah and other big cats, not to mention several large, ill-tempered elephants.
>
> Pic is flawed by lapses in continuity and silly dialogue.

Hedren and her daughter, Melanie Griffith, have proved their dramatic ability elsewhere; here they and their co-stars are required to do little more than look petrified.

The film's strongest selling points are the spectacles of wild animals and humans filmed at such close quarters, something akin to the perverse fascination of going to the circus and watching agog as the lion tamer puts his head into the beast's mouth. That, plus the Marshall family's laudable desire to focus attention on the slaughter of many animal species.

Other trade reviews were somewhat the same. When the film opened in England, David Robinson, in the London *Times*, wrote:

It is better to forget and forgive the story. The animals, though, are superb, and shamelessly skillful in all techniques of upstaging; and there is an irresistible thrill in seeing an understanding between humans and animals that overturns centuries of preconceptions about relationships in nature.

Noel had had a vision and together we had accomplished it, no matter the cost, in both money and human terms. Oddly enough, the financial aspects did not matter. Story aside, we—Noel and I, the children, everybody who had anything to do with making *Roar*—could all be proud of capturing the big cats on film in a way that had not been done before and probably will never be done again. And, scratched and bitten, but certainly wiser in the ways of big cats than we had ever dreamed was possible, we had all survived.

My marriage to Noel did not survive. We were divorced on January 19, 1982. We had rented a cottage on the John Barrymore estate in Beverly Hills the summer before, and Noel moved there, continuing his work with the Film Consortium, his TV commercial business. I remained in the house in the canyon, by the animals. I much preferred it to Beverly Hills.

After the final months and moments of the marriage came to an end, after the anger and the hurt, after it was all over, I felt such relief and peace. I believed in myself again, positive that I was once more in charge of my own life. Seventeen years of living with Noel had gone by, seventeen years of climbing mountains that no sane person should climb, seventeen years of pursuing sometimes ridiculous dreams. I did not regret those years. There had been enough excitement, enough surprises and challenges, to fill several lifetimes. Now it was time to move on to other things.

A solitary walk with Billy

—28—

THE TI-TIGON

Noelle, the tigon, was a celebrity of sorts in the cat world, photos of her appearing in far-off places from Moscow to Bombay to Manila. At the age of four she was a little larger in size than the average tigress, longer-legged and taller. The vibrant stripes were now a subtle brown instead of the usual coal black. The base color over her entire upper body was orange; her belly was tiger's white. The only colorations left from cubhood were the mottled spots on the top of her head. In appearance, as well as in other ways, Noelle was quite unique. Her roar was very feminine, almost shy, but she spoke both languages, though more lioness than tigress. She had the best qualities of both, loving and social like the lion, persevering and playful like the tiger. Unlike the average lion, she liked to swim and loll in water.

Of all the animals in the canyon, Noelle soon qualified as the champion jumper. The gently sloping roof of my house is more than ten feet off the ground, yet she could leap to it in one fluid vault. The first time I became aware of that prowess she was no more than three years old. Awakened by a thudding on the roof, I thought some prowler had lost his mind and was trying to enter the compounds by crawling over the roof. I ran outside, and there was Noelle peering down at me in the thin light. It has happened a half-dozen times

Noelle's favorite spot on the roof of my house

since, usually just after dawn, and I have to summon Liberato or Penny Bishonden or Jesus Torres to help entice her back to the ground. Sometimes she plays games with us up there, knowing she has caused a bit of excitement and that what she is doing is different and adventuresome.

Insofar as relations with humans are concerned, she was usually playful, even as an adult, enjoying tackling, especially strangers, or the lion's trick of tripping with a paw. Yet, as early as two years old, she became one of the most possessive cats in the compounds and once kept Noel at bay for almost three hours over a gunnysack of leaves. He had taken her for a walk along the river and, spotting a burlap bag, she immediately seized it. Noel did the smart thing and patiently waited her out. Then or now, she does not like to be backed down and seldom refuses a challenge. Standing on her hind legs, she measures thirteen feet, tip of tail to nose, and only a foolish person would attempt to test her.

At the age of four, she quietly dominated the females with whom she lived—tigresses Veruska, Lily and Lieka, and lionesses Nancy and Sarah—though she bowed to the authority of Anton, the usually serene five-year-old Siberian. Anton controlled his harem with looks and a few choice sounds. His family was the epitome of Shambala's harmony, most of the time. Occasionally, there were spats between the females—normal, I suppose, for any harem.

All of the ladies in all of the compounds had been on birth control since *Roar* opened in Australia. Visiting the Royal Melbourne Zoological Gardens, I had talked to the head veterinarian, Dr. Ray Butler, about the population problem in the compounds, and he had recommended twice-weekly doses of megestrol acetate. Not a cub had been born in the Melbourne Zoo in two years though mating had gone on nonstop. That's for us, I decided, and called Penny that night to forthwith put every tigress and lioness on the pill. Penny discussed the side effects with Dr. Bernstein, and then all big-cat females in Shambala, excepting the tigon, went on the pill. Noelle was supposedly sterile and was always available to Anton when she was in heat.

But in the spring of 1982 I noticed that she was mating frequently with Anton and soon afterward appeared to be gaining weight. Convinced that she was sterile, I said to Penny, "Let's put her on a diet. She's getting to be huge." Soon her nipples seemed to be swelling and, mystified, I called Dr. Dinnes, who was home from his globe-girdling. He came over and examined Noelle's teats and squeezed her stomach—not many vets can do that to big cats that have not been sedated.

"No way," he said. "She's not pregnant."

"Well, look at her nipples," I said.

"I see them, but she's not pregnant."

Noelle's symptoms soon went away. Maybe it was a false pregnancy? Whatever, she soon appeared to slim down and I forgot all about it. Yet I would look at her from time to time and wonder: Can you or can't you?

That summer and fall were rather placid seasons in the canyon, though Timbo knocked one wall out of the barn. I busied myself with various chores, and the year closed out with a heavy snowfall in the canyon, the tigers loving it, as usual, the lions loathing it, as usual. I took Noelle for a long walk in it. The cottonwoods were beautiful, mantled in white, and the African house looked strangely handsome with its coat of snow.

During the cold weather, we always had heat lamps in the quarters of the geriatric cats, and no lion appreciated his more than Monte, who was now between twenty and twenty-five. We always put the older cats into special quarters so that the young ones wouldn't pester them. Monte was in with Boomer and Scarface and Linnie, who was adorable and going through her second childhood. As they age, the big cats have many of the same problems as humans, and Monte had been bothered with arthritis for almost a year. He had other ailments as well, but Dr. Dinnes said he didn't want to put him through the stress of making tests. The age factor couldn't be reversed, so providing Monte some calm months, in with a friendly group of his own kind, was the best we could do for him.

During the fall of 1982 Monte would sometimes almost run out of his house in the mornings, stamping his legs to get Linnie to play for a bit, but as the weeks went by it became apparent that his whole body had fused. His legs weren't working well and he went to the warm spots immediately and sprawled out with a long sigh. As the day warmed he always seemed better. But we generally knew when a cat was going to go, and all of us went to his compound to spend some time with him. Frank Tom, Penny, Mike Vollman, Chris Gallucci—we took turns sitting and talking to Monte, rubbing him gently. Finally, on January 27, 1983, old Monte, of the Wild Bunch, sprawled out in the warmth one last time. The next day, wrapped in a ground cloth, he was buried.

Though death is to be expected now and then in the compounds and twenty years is actually a good and full life for big cats, I always find it difficult to handle. The size and beauty of the animals seem to enlarge the grief. The death of a cat you've known for a long time is shattering. I tell myself each time that I'll be stronger on the next occasion and not let it get me down. However, I'm still my same weeping, sad self when it does occur, and I doubt that will ever change.

On Saturday, March 19, Noel and I took a slow walk all around the compounds to talk about the future. The big cats were part of our lives, and Noel had previously volunteered to take care of them, financially, as long as they lived. We had assembled them for a purpose, and though that purpose had been fulfilled we still had a responsibility for their lives. Noel loved them as much as I did, but committing himself to feed them and maintain Shambala was more than a decent thing to do. Among my plans was one to establish the Roar Foundation, a nonprofit organization to assist in the care of the animals and continue further in-depth study of the great cat in captivity.

Spring and summer passed in the compounds with no more than the usual pleasures and problems. Then on September 16, Penny, who was getting ready to head for town and pick up cat medicine, had her hand on the door to her van when she heard thin crying that sounded as if it might be coming from the compound that contained the old African bus, which the cats use as lookout, rain shelter and napping place. For a moment, Penny thought one of the house cats had gotten out. We never allow them to roam beyond a fenced enclosure at the front of the house. They taunt the big cats from safe positions outside the compounds, literally driving the lions and tigers into a state of rage. One cat, Miaow, deliberately paraded in the house windows just to taunt the big felines. A six-pound cat bedeviling a five-hundred-pound tiger may sound hilarious, but it is quite dangerous.

Penny circled the perimeter of the compound and then noticed that all the inhabitants were assembled near the old bus. She quickly determined that the crying sound was coming from beneath it and entered the compound to discover that "sterile" Noelle was protecting a cub that was no more than an hour old. Mother and baby were about four feet from the front wheels, lodged under the chassis in the sand. Also present were the usual family members: the three tigresses, the two lionesses and Anton—the father, without question. They were assembled around the bus, observing the new arrival.

Knowing that any of them might decide to kill the baby, Penny yelled for help, then began herding some of the big cats into a holding area, one usually used for feeding purposes. But suddenly tigress Lily decided she wanted the cub and darted in under the bus to steal it from Noelle. Penny dove under, too, punching Lily on the nose and forcing her to drop the quivering infant. While Penny scooped it up—Lily's teeth had punctured the cub's shoulder—Mike Vollman maneuvered Lieka, who also seemed to have kidnapping ideas, into the holding area, along with Lily.

All the while, Noelle paced around the bus, making deep-bellied growls. Carrying the cub, Penny quickly led Noelle to another holding area in the corner of the compound, but the new mother was still nervous. It was obvious she wanted to get her baby away from her companions.

268

Penny ran to the house and decided to use my office as a nursery. She cleaned things out from beneath a high table, an old movie prop from an Egyptian film, that I used as a desk. Under it she placed a sheet over the carpeting. Cabinets flanked the desk, so a three-sided space was formed to offer some privacy for mother and cub.

Nursery prepared, Penny went back to the compound and with the aid of Mike Vollman brought Noelle and her newborn across the river and into the house. The inhabitants of the compound, led by Anton, lined the fence as the little procession went out. Any unusual activity is apt to bring residents of a compound to the fences. Whether he knew it or not, Anton had sired a male.

Penny put the cub down under the desk, and Noelle flopped down beside him, going to sleep, contented and safe, within a matter of minutes.

I was in Villa Park, in Orange County, that morning when the phone rang. "Are you sitting down?" Penny asked.

That question was always scary. *A cat was out! A fire had started! Someone had been hurt!* Apprehensively, I asked, "What's wrong?"

"Noelle just had a cub."

I was on my way to Shambala within minutes.

Noelle and her ti-tigon cub, Nathaniel, at the age of ten days

Anton, Nathaniel's father

Noelle had been raised in that house by the river and had spent much time in the office, some of it beneath that same old Egyptian table, so she was quite comfortable with her cub in human surroundings. I soon named him Nathaniel, deriving it from my own baptismal name of Nathalie. Tippi is a nickname, given to me by my late father.

I was so fascinated by the little cub that it did not sink in, right away, that we had an extremely rare "ti-tigon," perhaps one of the few in the world. Tigons are rare enough; this second-generation animal, apparently in good health, might be, according to the zoologists I consulted, the only specimen alive at the time.

Nathaniel had clearly defined stripes at birth, even to facial markings, and a coat that was thick and long for a cub. He resembled a tiger much more than a lion, which made sense. His mother was half tiger, half lion, his father a full tiger. From the first, Noelle always spoke "tiger" to her new little cub.

My office has a door to the outside, opening to a sand-floored space about twenty by twenty where older cubs had stayed occasionally, and even larger cats for a brief time. We left that door open so that Noelle could be fed outside and claw the large tree there. She settled in quickly, a sign of a happy mother. She was extremely clean and covered her excrement, which the big cat seldom does; she also covered any leftover food. Neither act was so much for cleanliness as it was for protection. In the wild, the mother big cat takes all sorts of precautions to prevent discovery of her whereabouts and the whereabouts of her cubs. I think Noelle knew perfectly well that the other cats couldn't harm her baby, but instinct dictated caution.

During the next six weeks her behavior was totally instinctual, and of the wild. At first, different pieces of furniture—chairs, a wastebasket, the typing table—seemed to annoy her, and we removed them. She then began to clear my desk with swipes of her paw, so I removed those objectionable things. Next were pictures on the wall. Down they came! Some high shelves with books and art objects on them were her next targets. Down they came! Reaching them was no problem for Noelle. She could rise to full height and touch the ceiling. Soon we had removed almost everything in the office except two big filing cabinets, which we felt unnecessary to take out because they were too heavy. But Noelle finally turned one over, partially blocking her access to Nathaniel. Frantic, she bit and clawed them, leaving punctures in the steel about the size of .45-caliber bullets. We had no idea why she wanted that room cleared out until other events, linked together, indicated that she was planning to raise that cub as a "wild animal," not one under human auspices. It had never happened before in the canyon.

Within a week, Noelle, who already had the marked tendency to be possessive, showed the first signs of jealousy over Nathaniel. That was understandable, were it cat or human mother. She allowed us to go quite close to the cub but watched us carefully and tensely, three or four feet away, her beautiful head hovering, mouth slightly open. Frequently, either Penny or I would lie down close to the desk and talk to Nathaniel very softly, our fingers a few inches from his body. We were trying to begin that absolutely necessary human relationship.

On about the tenth day, Penny was on the floor beside Nathaniel, talking to him, touching him, when Noelle rose and came up behind her. Penny's head was about a foot away from the cub, and Noelle took Penny's neck into her mouth, both rows of teeth closed around it. Thank God Penny knew this cat. She didn't resist. The teeth were firmly on her neck but were not puncturing the skin. "I understand Noelle," Penny said quickly. And with that, the tigon let go of her neck but then used her paws to move Penny to the center of the room. The lack of resistance and Penny's clear understanding of what Noelle was saying most likely averted serious consequences.

I enjoyed having Nathaniel and Noelle in the house, watching the mother–cub relationship and her unusual efforts to convert the cub to the wild. But by the end of six weeks we realized we had left them together much too long. Usually, cubs in captivity are separated from their mothers in about two weeks. Longer periods result in imprints that make weaning difficult. The longer the period, the more difficult for both mother and cub. Equally important, the human imprint on the cub must begin at a very early age to avoid serious problems in behavior later on.

To wean cubs away from big-cat mothers, it must be done swiftly and without compassion. You call the mother outside at feeding time and shut the door. That simple. *Done! Over!* An uncomfortable and unpleasant but necessary procedure. So at feeding time we walked Noelle back to Anton and her family in the red-bus compound and that was that. Nathaniel screamed for three days and wouldn't let us come near him. We went in constantly to comfort him. Claws out, he glared at us. He wouldn't eat. It was traumatic. Hearing him yelling two rooms away, I couldn't sleep. I would look out into the compound and see Noelle pacing, pacing, pacing. She could hear him, too.

After being on his mother's nipples so long, Nathaniel refused the bottle. Finally, Penny and I decided on the tried and true. We whipped up some Zu/Preem in a blender, added some water to it, and I dipped a finger in. I also spread some on his paws, knowing a cub's desire for cleanliness. He would lick them, of course. Half starved by now, he got the idea. And soon he was eating out of a bowl.

Noelle teaching manners to Nathaniel

Not only did he survive, but Nathaniel soon began to take on the proportions of a linebacker in the National Football League. Huge for his age, and strong, he played with the abandon of a young bull. When he was several months old, I tried to teach him the meaning of "No." The word meant nothing to him. He knocked me off my feet at the age of six months but finally began responding to "Leave it," the phrase that works on some of the older cats.

When he was ten months old, I took him out to see his mother. Noelle turned her back on him, apparently not wanting to be involved with a battering ram. Then I took him over to the geriatric compound, where Boomer and Scarface were sprawled out in the shade. Immediately Nathaniel began to play rough with these dignifed old lions. Boomer, who was consistently one of the best cub-sitters in the canyon, belted him halfway across the compound, with an accompanying roar. Nathaniel squealed in surprise and fear. The learning process had begun.

Later Noelle finally accepted her rare offspring and began giving him lessons in manners, even in how to treat humans, it appeared. She freely boxed his ears and literally sat on him when he became too rambunctious. Calmly gazing about, she held the screaming cub to the ground. But she also played with him. And slowly Nathaniel the ti-tigon began to turn from the impossible to the angelic.

273

Saying good morning to Zazu

—29—

SHAMBALA

Night down in the canyon is usually quiet, except for the frogs chirping by the lakeside. A few cars speed along the road above us, headlights making a sweeping white wand in the darkness, and I hear an occasional aircraft whine overhead. The exotic birds, the peacocks, macaws, cranes and flamingos, the night walkers, chatter and move around. Sometimes Steve Martin's wolves, up on the hill, decide to serenade. During the early evening, depending on the direction of the wind, I may hear soft Latino music from the mobile homes of crew members. Sometimes their voices carry above the gurgle of the river.

The big cats may break the silence several times during the night, probably when one bumps into another in the darkness. A few animal words are then spoken, say in Anton's group, and they are echoed far up the preserve by a lion in Casey's group. Sometimes Steve Martin's Simba will answer back. The conversations vary in length and occasionally result in a genuine, full-blown roaring session. Quite a few of the big cats don't even bother to acknowledge this nocturnal gabbing. Some raise their heads and then flop them back. Others apparently sleep through all the noise.

Bright moonlight or blackness, there is always a feeling of stealth in the compounds after sundown. The cats approach humans, and perhaps each other, differently from the way they do during daylight hours. I find it difficult to describe that difference, but I know it is there, in their eyes and in their movements along the fences.

Either moon-bright or moon-dark, one senses the aliveness of the place. Most of the coots have gone into the thick reeds by the lake, but a few motor around on the water, making splashing sounds, quibbling raucously. Up by the bird sanctuary and pond there are muted sounds and frequently the spectacle of all the flamingos standing up on shore in a little cluster, asleep for the night. A possum or a raccoon or a skunk can interrupt the peace of the aviary, but we set "kindness" traps, ones that cannot injure the animal, stocked with food and water, hoping to make only short-time prisoners of them, then take them several miles upstream next day and release them. The small invaders wisely stay away from the cat compounds, of course, but have no fear of the birds.

I seldom walk the compounds on moonless nights, not because I'm afraid of the residents, but simply because I can see very little of them. Those awake may come to the fences and I'll place the back of my hand up against the wire to be licked. We talk and walk side by side to the compound's end. But if I walk very softly and don't shine the beam of a flashlight around to announce my presence, I can hear the lions and tigers snoring. As for the elephants, they can be heard a hundred feet away. They are awesome on the intake.

The hours of darkness within the preserve have a texture that is both compelling and suspenseful. But I believe that dawn, when the horizon flushes pink and yellow over the low chaparral mountains to the east, is the favorite time of day for the cats. The air is usually still and sometimes a faint mist lingers, the river and lake sending up thin, damp wisps as the animals begin to move around and survey the new day. The first sound is often the roosters that reside up at Steve Martin's place, then the coots and mallards and red-winged blackbirds join the awakening. It is then that roaring begins in earnest, and I've always felt that it is joyous talk, particularly within the lion families. I can never really vouch for what the mysterious tigers are thinking about.

The talk of the lions is sometimes preceded by activity in the bird sanctuary and the pond, the stately flamingos beginning to stride around, the pugnacious black swans crying plaintively in the widening light, fluttering in spurts across the small pond. Whichever group starts the day, feathered or furred, dawn is an enchanting time in Shambala.

Now and then I'll awaken to Penny talking to her teenage lions, Melbourne and Sydney, in the compound next to my bedroom. Almost three years old, weighing about 375 pounds each, they have their own tables, or platforms, for eating. And since they are still growing animals, Penny feeds them twice a day. I hear her saying, "What do good boys do?" and I pull open the drapes to watch. These good boys take their seats on the four-inch-high platforms, so that the meat doesn't go into the sand, and await their breakfast. If they get off their seats, Penny reprimands sharply, "What do good boys do? Seat! Seat!"

At that moment, I wish the whole world could see what is going on just outside my window. Two big lions minding their manners. It is a breathtaking way to start the day.

Unless there is some special occasion—a trip to the vet's or an exchange of living space with another group—the day of the big cats usually consists of head rubbing, some grooming, perhaps sharpening of claws, some play, perhaps a little lovemaking. And contented sleep. Always plenty of sleep. And, of course, that afternoon highlight—food in white buckets.

Play seems to be important, and it makes sense that the two peak periods for play are in the early morning and again just before twilight, after the meal has been digested. The playtime of the adult is a subdued extension of the cub antics of wrestling, chasing, stalking and pawing. At times, I've caught a great-maned lion stretching his dignity, actually looking around in hope that no one has seen the silly thing he's just done. They can be very funny animals during these play sessions, which may last no more than five minutes.

I've been treated to sessions at 7 A.M., one lioness chasing another in Ivan's group or Buster leopard scrambling through a tree after a friend. A wrestling match may or may not follow. Or Peter and Jeremy may decide to swat at each other with their forepaws, either sitting or standing up. Occasionally, they'll rise on their hind legs to play this lion's version of patty-cake. Though they vocalize during these sessions with moans or growls or grunts, they are affectionate sounds. No fighting! In fact, the lions have definite play faces.

Either before or after the play sessions, there may be a period of head rubbing all over the compounds. Nothing is really scheduled, but there do seem to be patterns of activity. There are also definite styles of rubbing, absolutely sensual, even with males who have learned to live together. The lion that decides to initiate contact may

277

first rub the face of the other lion, eyes closed, and then go gently along the entire body, softly humming or moaning. The contact may be repeated, and then there is reciprocation. Cubs do it by instinct and the rubbing lasts the life long.

The head and the neck of the big cat are the only places that cannot be groomed by the animal itself, and maybe a half hour after the rubbing some sprucing-up will take place, one animal doing the favor for another. The animal being groomed will often keep its eyes closed, turning its head to expose slowly the parts needing attention. Such grooming is commonplace in pairs of domestic cats, of course, but I'm always struck by the gentleness and the affection displayed when these huge animals set about to beautify each other.

Perhaps a little claw-sharpening is in order later in the morning, with tiger Gregory squatting down before the big logs we've dragged into his space. His lionesses may or may not join him in the honing. However, I've seen as many as five or six cats simultaneously scratching away, muzzles raised, eyes often closed.

As the morning wears on, rest and sleep become important in the compounds, but I've noticed that almost any human activity near the fences will capture the attention of those animals awake. Liberato will be carefully watched as he comes by with his wheelbarrow. He is visually tracked as a matter of interest. If his work brings him near a fence, one or more of the cats will come close to take a better look at what he is doing. Alphonso, the gardener, digging holes to place black dirt and elephant dung in them, prior to planting zinnias or calendulas or gladiolas, is certain to have an audience by the fences. There are many flowers in Shambala, flourishing along with the big cats, nodding outside their spaces.

If the weather is hot, or even warm, the noon hours are sensibly devoted to sleep. Visitors to the compounds are lucky to have the response of a raised head. Even calling the cats by name often brings no more than a bored sigh in recognition of human presence. Why should they make a fuss over the odd-looking, odd-smelling two-footed intruders?

The trainers have various chores during the day involving one or more animals. Penny may have to take Stevie lion to Dr. Dinnes for an eye problem. Chris may make his weekly check of the elephants' feet, to clean or pare them. Frank Tom and Mike Vollman may have a shift of space scheduled for Charlie's group or Johnny's group, an exchange that could involve up to thirty minutes of concentrated attention, though the traveling distance of the cats may be less than two hundred yards.

In any exchange of living quarters, the cats must first be placed in holding areas while the spaces are emptied and den houses cleaned and checked. Then the cats are moved, one by one, or in groups, to their new homes. Care must be taken in the routing. Moving a group of lionessess past compounds occupied by lions, particularly the aggressive ones, can start battles behind the fences. So we avoid such routing. The compounds of Shambala are intertwined with lion runs and chain-link corridors for safe passage of the animals and ease of handling. After they have been moved through these corridors, finally the gates to their new homes are opened. Even though they may have lived in the same space several weeks previously, they go about inspecting it and marking it with urine as if they had never seen it before, seemingly delighted with their new accommodations.

During summer, the trainers put Pet-Guard, an insect repellent, on the ears and noses of all the cats, two places that the tail brush cannot flick. This is a morning chore, the flies becoming aggressive as the day warms. Though it sounds routine, dabbing the cream on the suspicious animals is not all that simple. Some don't mind; others

Buster taking his noontime nap

want no part of it. I've watched Mike play games with the cougars in order to administer the sticky, smelly salve.

About noontime the chopping up of around a thousand pounds of meat, thawed the previous day, begins. As far as the cats are concerned, this is the most important chore undertaken by the humans. Those animals in the Up-Front compounds, near the chopping table, seem to be well aware of this activity. They forget sleep and begin to pace. For some of the cats the anticipation turns to tension, and that dinner-hour electricity that I mentioned earlier crackles around the compounds. There is vocal machine-gunning as the white buckets approach, and the pacing may quicken to short, angry dashes along the fences.

In the winter, the cats dine early, usually around two o'clock, and then often romp for a while before dark. The winter chill in the canyon seems to get their juices flowing. During the summer, they feed at about four or four-thirty, and then they usually flop down, surrendering to the heat that lingers on the flats until eight or nine o'clock.

The lions usually go to bed early in the winter, entering their huts at twilight, while the tigers stay up and around much later. If it happens to be a cold, rainy night, the tigers that have lioness harems are apt to come in soaking wet, much to the displeasure of the warm and comfortable females that will have to suffer in wet straw the rest of the night. I've seen tigers soak in the river at night and then come sopping into their houses. They are not at all considerate. But in the lion compounds not a slumbering muscle is moved. Lions are sensible creatures where comforts are concerned.

As for my day, administering a private wildlife preserve is hardly glamorous, though seldom dull. There are the routine matters of seeing that the payrolls are met, the food bills paid, and trying to find the best price for meat. Next to that priority item is security, the constant checking of the fences. Then there is inspection of the living spaces. In walking around, I might see that one of the little offshoot streams that wind through the compounds is sluggish or plugged up. Or the problem can be much larger, what to do with the monthly mountain of elephant dung. Then there are the matters not so routine, as when Timbo kicked a propane tank and started a $40,000 fire. In some ways, every day is a challenge but one that I feel privileged to face.

The rewards are many. Every day I can step over eleven big rocks across our little river and take another twenty steps to the red-bus compound, greet the cats in that space and then turn around to the compound where Noelle and Nathaniel now reside. He is a constant source of wonderment to me. Will he roar like a lion? Will he grow a mane? Will he become solitary like a tiger? How large will he be? I can't keep my eyes off him.

Turning around again, I see Chelsea and Lena. I suppose time can heal most things, and it has apparently sorted out the relationship between those two brawling lionesses. They've made peace, apparently no longer interested in dominance or clawing each other to death. They now sprawl out together on the roof of the bus.

Farther on, I can walk past Lion's Run and enter the compound where Boomer and Scarface reside. I usually give Scarface a big hug and sit on the sand beside him, scratching under his chin or into his mane, talking to him. Then I go over to Boomer and do the same thing. I know these two old men will not be around too much longer, but I also know they have lived a good and peaceful life in the canyon. They're loved and I think they know it.

At that point, I can cross the tree bridge over the east end of the lake, near the waterfall, past the African house, and go on by the hill compound, where six cats live, and then by Ivan and his lionesses, stopping at each place, and finally to the elephant barn before completing the circuit of the preserve.

There is a human story as well as an animal story in that barn. Chris Gallucci, the tough ex-biker, ex-welder, ex-drifter, has turned his life around with the elephants. When I first met Chris, I didn't think he had any particular purpose in his life. I thought he'd soon move on from work-about for us in the canyon to something similar somewhere else. Then suddenly the elephants were without a handler and Chris said he would like to try it. I had seen him on the night of the flood, his welding sparks flying through the heavy rain; I don't think he stopped work for fifteen hours. That was dedication enough. But it takes something special to handle animals, elephants in particular. I had a suspicion that Chris had that "something special."

About three months after Chris became guardian to Timbo and Kura, I went to the barn one evening at feeding time and saw that Chris had prepared a great semicircle of good oat hay for each animal. On top of the hay was a large mound of grain with molasses mixed in. Inside all that were hidden four apples, three oranges, six bananas and a half-dozen carrots. And near Chris's feet I saw the dessert—four fresh coconuts.

"Do you do this every night?" I asked.

He grinned. "No, not every night."

One night a few months later, I came home late and noticed a

Chris Gallucci eye to eye with Timbo

light at Up-Front that was not usually visible. When I investigated, I saw that the barn door had been smashed to pieces, surely the work of Timbo. I phoned Chris, saying, "I hate to bother you at one o'clock in the morning, but Timbo is off his back chain and has broken the door down. Kura is fine."

Until Chris arrived, I waited with the elephants, talking to them. What else does one do with a pair of pachyderms to pass a wintry night?

Timbo obviously knew he had committed a crime, because he began rumbling the moment Chris's car drove up. As soon as his handler got close, he wrapped his trunk around Chris's head, holding it gently. Next he placed the top of his trunk on Chris's head, then rubbed his cheek and finally brought his head toward his mouth, almost enclosing it. They were all signs of affection, all signs of apology. The last thing he did was lift one foot and hold it above the ground. During this whole time Chris had not said a word to Timbo, but there was little doubt that man and animal had established communication. I suppose it is because of the sheer size of the animals that he has conquered Timbo and Kura with affection, not with the human dominance so common to the usual elephant training.

From the elephant barn off toward the river and the railroad tracks is the compound inhabited by Tongaru and Zuru, a place where only Frank Tom can move about freely—another example of a unique human-and-animal relationship. And then there is the compound that houses Casey's group. Billy, of course, lives there, and he is still possessive of me—still another human-and-animal relationship. When I am alone, I always linger awhile to talk to him.

Summer and winter, I take walks. Winter comes on both slowly and overnight. By September, the summer heat has begun to yellow the leaves, but they usually stay on the trees. Then around the second week in December a strong wind climbs up off the desert, and the papery leaves go flying. One day it is fall, the next winter. Spring comes slowly into the canyon, heralded by the frogs.

No matter what the season, or the time of day, I find great pleasure in my leisurely strolls through the preserve. How many people have been graced with the rare good luck to know such animals intimately, to watch them grow, to learn their behaviors and to make and keep friendships with them? Even indoors, I am constantly reminded of where I am, and it is more than the vocalizing of the cats. From most windows of the house, I can see some of the residents of Shambala. A half-dozen are always just a few feet from the house and make their presence known in many ways. To some people all big cats may look alike. But to me, each one is as unique and as immediately recognizable as my human friends. During the periods when Noelle's group resides in the compound directly by my kitchen window, I can always tell when she passes even though I can't see her. The window level is about four feet off the ground. Yet, if three tails come flagging by, I know instantly which one belongs to Noelle. Her movements are distinct and she unquestion-

After a walk in the high desert, Zuru and I survey our domain.

ably has the most flexible tail in the canyon. That glimpse tells me where I am and how lucky I am.

And I think our animals are lucky, too. They are allowed to be lions and tigers, allowed to live together if they choose, allowed to live alone if they choose. They are not asked to do ridiculous things. No tricks. They more or less do what they want to do, with little interference from humans. We take great pride in their health and their appearance. They are a source of beauty, to be observed like a fine painting. I'm now convinced that, raised in captivity, they are capable of much deeper human relationships than previously thought possible. We, not the big cats, are the predators. And those that survive in the wild must be protected and preserved from human destruction.

My life began to change when I met Dandylion on the Zimbabwe border, and I've never regretted letting my film career slide. I don't look back. The big cats are so refreshingly honest, so uncomplicated. Their every sound and movement says, Take me for what I am. I can't envision a life without them.

Afterword

If the animal cast of *Roar* enjoys peaceful retirement, its human cast is busier than ever. Noel is working as an independent filmmaker and continues with his support of the ranch. Jerry is producing TV commercials and documentaries in New York, while John is production manager and assistant director for several companies that turn out commercials seen daily on TV. Joel, still at Shambala, oversees his bird sanctuary in addition to working as property manager for the making of commercials.

Melanie continues starring roles in her film career, the latest being *Body Double,* and after study with Stella Adler she is heading for the stage. Married to actor Steven Bauer—*Scarface, Balm in Gilead, Thief of Hearts*—she shuttles between Hollywood and New York. We get together as often as possible and sometimes talk about arranging a *Roar* reunion at Shambala. All a little bit older and wiser now—including the cats—we would certainly have a lot of memories to share.

The years of making *Roar* provided unique learning experiences for many people, paving the way, in some cases, for careers in the motion picture industry, and in others for careers in animal training. Mativo is finishing graduate school at UCLA and will soon achieve his doctorate in African studies. Meanwhile, his latest acting credit is *Baby*, for Disney Productions.

Roar was Jan de Bont's first American film as cinematographer. His credits now include *Clan of the Cave Bear, Flesh and Blood, All the Right Moves* and *I'm Dancing as Fast as I Can.* Monique commutes to Holland and Germany to star in European films.

Rick Glassey, invaluable during the action scenes in *Roar,* especially in handling the tigers, is trainer for magician Doug Henning, putting big cats through their paces during stage and TV illusions. Also with Henning is Alex Newman, working a spider monkey and a black leopard as well as the tigers. Still-photographer Bill Dow parlayed his *Roar* experience into steady work at 20th Century–Fox, Universal Pictures, Aaron Spelling Productions and others. Former elephant trainer Tim Cooney, based in Hollywood, is now a sound supervisor for feature films. Assistant director Doron Kauper is now producing TV commercials and designing computer software for the TV industry.

Out in the canyon, Ron Oxley remains "down the river" from Shambala, running his Action Animals business. Wonderful old Neil lion passed away but lives in the Humane Society's Patsy Award Hall of Fame and in our memories. Steve Martin is still on the hill above me with his felines and primates of Working Wildlife. At Shambala, the main cat crew—Penny Bishonden, Frank Tom, Mike Vollman and Chris Gallucci—are to be found daily within the compounds, pampering the animals sinfully. They have other interests as well. Penny is a fine artist, specializing in big cats, Frank instructs judo several nights a week, and Mike plays in a rock band most weekends and is a serious student of classical music. Liberato and Jesus Torres are also to be seen moving about the acres throughout the day, especially at feeding time. And Ben Sanchez and his fence crew still mind the security, keeping the cats from humans and vice versa.

Continuing to provide superb medical care for Shambala's residents. Dr. Jon Bernstein remains on call twenty-four hours a day and has yet to grumble when summoned on a weekend or at night. And Dr. Marty Dinnes is also available for vet services or consultation when he's in town.

There are so many, many people to thank for Shambala as it exists today: Richard Rush, Claude Roberts, Pat Breshears, Eve Rattner, Leo Lobsenz, Chuck Sloan, Yvonne Garner, Marina Malchin, Betty Rose, Danil Torpe and Merrie Post, all of whom raised cubs; and Sue Barton, Carol Eckhardt, Gardner McKay, Steve Martin, Martin

Downey and Dr. Marty Dinnes, who helped out during the flood. Hubie and Lillian Boscowitz literally saved us after the flood with their support. And Herb Dorfman, of Mission Meat, often came to our rescue by granting credit month after month so that the animals could be fed.

I also want to thank Gary Dartnell, who engineered the EMI funding of *Roar*, and Robbie and Ellen Little, who set up the European and Far East releases of the film. Upward of four hundred people worked on *Roar*, and it is impossible to thank each one by name, but I do want to single out Rita Riggs, Virginia D'Arcy and Robert Dawn, all of whom helped me personally. Also deserving of thanks are Maureen Nolan and Ken Jones. And Elaine Newman, who gave impetus to the birth of the Roar Foundation.

I am also grateful to author and film critic Donald Spoto, who was the first to encourage me to write about what happened at Shambala, Leo Lobsenz, who was instrumental in helping me attempt a first draft, and Dr. Marty Dinnes, who read the rough manuscript and added his expertise to technical matters. Thanks, too, to Simon and Schuster editor Fred Hills, who guided the project after meeting the big cats and listening to stories of life around the compounds, to his able associate Burton Beals, who enhanced the manuscript with his editing, and of course to Ted Taylor, my co-author who has become my good friend. Ted succumbed to the magic of the animals the moment he saw them.

Last, but very special, is Luis Barrenechea, who gave me his support and love and patience as the pages and chapters mounted up.